Ready-to-Use
CONFLICT RESOLUTION ACTIVITIES *for* SECONDARY STUDENTS

RUTH PERLSTEIN
GLORIA THRALL

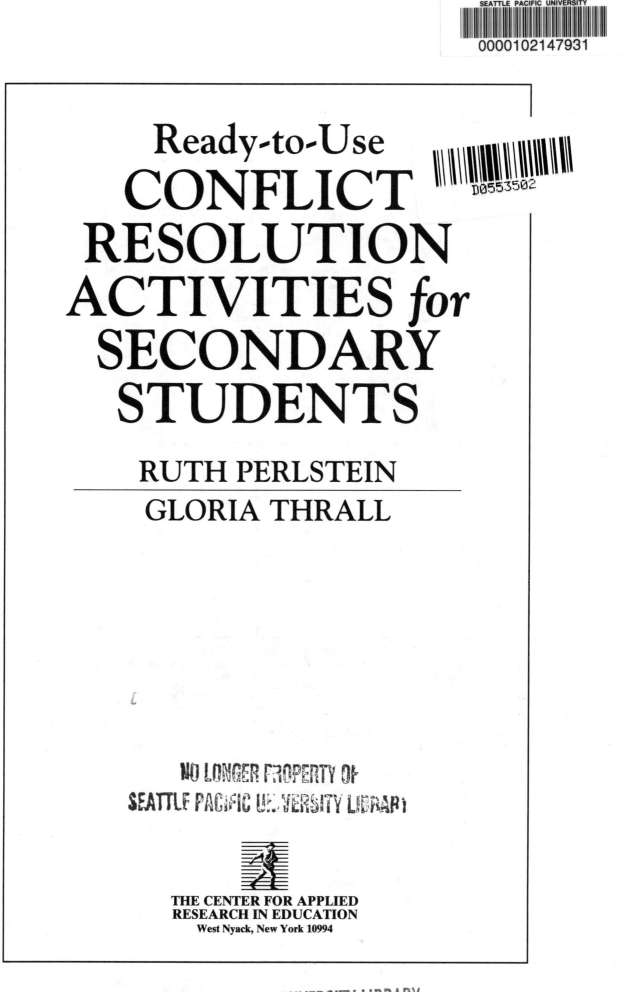

**THE CENTER FOR APPLIED
RESEARCH IN EDUCATION**
West Nyack, New York 10994

Library of Congress Cataloging-in-Publication Data

Perlstein, Ruth (Ruth L.)
 Ready-to-use conflict resolution activities for secondary students:
strategies for dealing with conflict in real-life situations, plus
guidelines for creating a peer mediation program / Ruth Perlstein,
Gloria Thrall.
  p. cm.
 Includes bibliographical references.
 ISBN 0-87628-195-1
 1. Conflict management—Study and teaching (Secondary)—United
States. 2. Mediation—Study and teaching (Secondary)—United
States. 3. Peer counseling of students—Study and teaching
(Secondary)—United States. 4. Interpersonal conflict in
adolescence—United States—Prevention. I. Thrall, Gloria.
II. Title.
HM136.P5438 1996   95-23617
303.6′9′0712—dc20   CIP

Printed in the United States of America

10 9 8 7 6 5 4

Production Editor: Zsuzsa Neff
Interior Design: Dee Coroneos

ISBN 0-87628-195-1

**THE CENTER FOR APPLIED RESEARCH
IN EDUCATION**
West Nyack, NY 10994
A Simon & Schuster Company

On the World Wide Web at http://www.phdirect.com

Prentice-Hall International (UK) Limited, *London*
Prentice-Hall of Australia Pty. Limited, *Sydney*
Prentice-Hall Canada Inc., *Toronto*
Prentice-Hall Hispanoamericana, S.A., *Mexico*
Prentice-Hall of India Private Limited, *New Delhi*
Prentice-Hall of Japan, Inc., *Tokyo*
Simon & Schuster Asia Pte. Ltd., *Singapore*
Editora Prentice-Hall do Brasil, Ltda., *Rio de Janeiro*

DEDICATION

To David Perlstein and Lloyd Thrall for their patience and support.

ACKNOWLEDGMENTS

The impetus for establishing a peer mediation program at West Potomac High School came from a visionary administrator, William Harper, now a principal at South Lakes High School in Fairfax County, Virginia.

Linda Hale, from the Institute for Conflict Management in Fairfax, Virginia, and Marsha Blakeway, from Children's Creative Response to Conflict in Arlington, Virginia, provided inspiration and excellent background information about conflict resolution. In addition, Dr. Kathy Heer helped train peer mediators and collaborated in creating an excellent program at West Potomac High School.

Many of the lessons in Part I are based on the Peer Helper/Mediation program curriculum guide developed by the Fairfax County Public Schools Department of Student Services, under the direction of Nadine Maxwell, who has been instrumental in encouraging the development of sound curriculum materials to help students resolve conflict.

The concept of conflict based on unmet needs was presented to us by Linda Hale and is based on the work of Dr. John Burton, who has written and lectured widely on this subject. Dr. Burton wrote *Resolving Deep-Rooted Conflict: A Handbook* (1987), and edited *Conflict: Human Needs Theory* (1990), which provided interesting theoretical background.

We would particularly like to thank Jane Dreyfuss, Elaine Simmerman, and Steven Perlstein for their insights, expertise, and wisdom. Officer Carl Taylor of the Fairfax County Police Department provided insight into mediating with conflicting groups, and Janet Rust created the illustrations.

We would also like to thank Connie Kallback of Simon & Schuster for her advice, encouragement, and support.

ABOUT THE AUTHORS

Ruth Perlstein has been a counselor at West Potomac High School in Fairfax County, Virginia, for over 20 years. She trains peer mediators, organizes leadership retreats, and regularly presents workshops on peer mediation and the college admissions process. She is a past president of the Virginia Association of Specialists in Group Work and edited their newsletter for several years. Ms. Perlstein is a teacher consultant for the Northern Virginia Writing Project and has written articles for *Groups for Secondary Schools* (Charles Thomas, 1989), *Leadership*, and *Mathematics Teacher* magazines. Ms. Perlstein has developed curriculum materials for peer mediation and leadership classes for Fairfax Country Public Schools. In 1994 she was selected the Virginia Association of School Counselor's "Secondary School Counselor of the Year."

Gloria Thrall has taught in Fairfax County for 15 years. She has sponsored student government; coached cheerleaders; worked with at-risk students for a National Institutes of Health research program; sponsored a mentoring program; presented at in-service conferences for math, science, and English teachers in Fairfax County; and planned interdisciplinary curricula at McLean High School in Fairfax County. She is currently a counselor at West Potomac High School.

Ms. Perlstein and Ms. Thrall have designed the curriculum for a leadership class, which they taught at West Potomac High School in Fairfax County.

ABOUT THIS RESOURCE

High school teachers and counselors see conflict on a daily basis. We see students arguing in classrooms. When rumors spread, when students call each other names, when they accidentally bump into each other in the hallways, and when they suspect their hats, pencils, and Walkmans have been stolen, we hear students threatening to beat each other up. After informally polling ninth graders, we found fighting and potential violence their number one concern. National headlines, conversation in teachers' lounges, and informal comments in the hallways of high schools remind us that high school students need to learn how to deal with conflict intelligently. When philanthropist Walter Annenberg offered his unprecedented $500 million gift to reform public education, he focused on youthful violence. Much of this funding is earmarked for curriculum improvement to help prevent violence.

This book is a practical resource on conflict management for you, the teacher, counselor, or anyone who works with teenagers from coaches to youth group leaders. You will find the ideas, activities, and reproducible handouts in this book useful in helping high school students learn about peaceful alternatives to dealing with conflict. These concepts will be helpful in the classroom, on the athletic practice field, and at club meetings . . . wherever teenagers congregate.

❏ **Part One** covers the basic concepts of conflict resolution, including an explanation of each concept with concrete illustrations typically found in adolescent groups. Each section contains specific activities and reproducible handouts that teachers, counselors, and youth leaders can use to teach each of the concepts. Counselors can use them for classroom guidance lessons and teacher advisors can use them for guidance activities on a regular basis. This group of lessons provides the training material for a peer mediation program, and the reproducibles, placed in a three-ring binder, can become an excellent training packet or review material.

❏ **Part Two** describes ways for counselors, teachers, and club sponsors to apply the concepts in Part One to reduce conflict as it naturally appears in the classroom, the counselor's office, and in extra curricular activities. The sections contain specific conflict scenarios and suggestions for various ways to resolve the conflicts they describe. In addition, we have included relevant sample lesson plans that teachers can use to teach conflict resolution through academic classes across the curriculum.

❏ **Part Three** focuses on peer mediation programs. One section explains how to set up a schoolwide peer mediation program and includes a sample peer mediation training agenda. It also suggests how to include activities in a peer counseling class and in counseling groups. Another section addresses ways to publicize and sell peer mediation as a useful tool for solving problems. The section includes a script for a videotape.

This book contains many scenarios and role plays which present typical conflicts that appear in the secondary school. Students can use the scenarios and role plays written in the third person as backdrops for improvisational role plays. Others, written in dialogue, provide actual beginnings for role playing scripts. The role plays and scenarios throughout this book can be used in ongoing mediation training, club meetings, counseling groups, and staff development training.

The plans in this resource have been tested in the high school environment. We have found them effective. Our students have commented, "We really learned how to solve problems . . . we're beginning to listen to each other instead of battling with our egos . . . I didn't think this stuff would work at first, but it really does . . . I find myself walking up to people in the library and helping prevent fights . . . .I'm learning to talk things out and not fight now."

These ideas have worked well for us. We sincerely hope that this resource will help you and your students both in school and out of school as well.

Ruth Perlstein
Gloria Thrall

CONTENTS

PART ONE—1

SECTION ONE:
DEFINING CONFLICT—3
(Background Information)

SECTION TWO:
DIFFERENT KINDS OF CONFLICT—13
(Background Information)

SECTION THREE:
DEALING WITH CONFLICT—29
(Background Information)

SECTION FIVE:
COMMUNICATING—75
(*Background Information*)

SECTION SIX:
COLLABORATIVE PROBLEM SOLVING—115
(Background Information)

PART TWO—187

SECTION EIGHT:
CONFLICT IN THE COUNSELOR'S OFFICE—189
(Background Information)

SECTION TEN:
CONFLICT RESOLUTION IN THE CLASSROOM—251
(Background Information)

SECTION ELEVEN:
EXTRACURRICULAR ACTIVITIES—283
(*Background Information*)

PART THREE—307

SECTION TWELVE:
SETTING UP A PEER MEDIATION PROGRAM—309
(Background Information)

SECTION THIRTEEN:
PUBLICIZING PEER MEDIATION—329
(Background Information)

APPENDIX—339

Part One

THE BASIC CONCEPTS OF CONFLICT RESOLUTION

Section One

DEFINING CONFLICT
(Background Information)

  PROBLEM CHARACTERISTICS

  CONFLICT AND UNDERLYING NEEDS

  IDENTIFYING THE PROBLEM: AGAINST THE WALL

DEFINING CONFLICT
(Background Information)

What is conflict? In a word, conflict is a "clash," a disagreement between two or more parties. Although conflict often fosters insight and growth, it is frequently perceived as a problem, something that persistently signals trouble. Someone involved in a troublesome conflict usually feels angry and the clash between the disputants can escalate and explode.

A troublesome conflict can be visualized as a type of problem based on a problem. In a way, conflict is surrounded by a problem.

$$PROBLEM$$
$$\downarrow \quad \downarrow$$
$$CONFLICT$$
$$\uparrow \quad \uparrow$$
$$PROBLEM$$

Consider the teenager dealing with the loss of a grandparent, difficulty in algebra, and a painful argument with a former "best friend." This teenager has several problems, only one of which is really a conflict, the conflict with the best friend. Characteristic of this conflict is an underlying problem. Why have the friends had a painful argument? What does each want? What does each need? What might be the real underlying problem?

Problem Is the Key

When defining conflict, the word *problem* is the key. One must always ask, *What is the problem?* Although the conflict with a friend is a kind of problem, it is also based on a problem. Perhaps another friend offered some inaccurate information about the former "best friend." Perhaps the conflict has a history, and the real problem is the rivalry between the teenagers in a different setting a year ago. Was there incomplete or inaccurate communication between them? Had one of them heard an inaccurate rumor? Was at least one of them experiencing stress overload? Did they argue because they really had different viewpoints or values? Did limited resources make it difficult for them to share something they wanted? Or even more basically, what were the unmet psychological needs underlying their conflict?

Conflict Is Based on Unmet Needs

Inevitably, conflict is based on one or a combination of unmet psychological needs. These basic needs are

- [ ] identity
- [ ] security
- [ ] control
- [ ] recognition
- [ ] fairness

5

Identity

Identity is who you are, your individuality, your association with a group to which you might belong. You may be Swiss, male, and a member of the drum and bugle corps. Girls fighting over "best friends" are really expressing a need for identity. Each is saying, "I am the best friend of so and so . . . that is who I am and how I wish to be labeled."

Security

These bickering young teenagers may also need **security** or safety and think, "I don't want my position as 'best friend' threatened."

Control

Control or power is also an important need. After all, these girls probably think, "My position as a 'best friend' makes me important or powerful." The need for power or control is usually more difficult to handle than the need for security or recognition.

Recognition

The need for **recognition** frequently underlies conflict. Singers fighting over which dressing room to use before a choral production might complain, "The soloists always use the red room." Club members arguing about who will sponsor a powder puff football game are often expressing a need for recognition.

Fairness

Disputants sometimes want their stolen property returned because of their need for **fairness** rather than a desire for the property itself. ("I really didn't want the old sweater anyway, but it wasn't fair for him to take it!") When disputants have strong, opposing feelings about what they consider to be fair, the resulting conflicts are often difficult to resolve because it is difficult to negotiate values. People understandably have strong feelings about what is fair or right.

All these basic needs are powerful and lie beneath conflicts everywhere. Neighborhood battles, family arguments, and inner office politics revolve around the issues of identity, security, recognition, and control. Fairness is also a related issue, particularly when people argue about procedures. To understand a conflict, it is important to focus on the problem beneath the conflict.

The Most Important Question: What Is the Problem?

When defining a problem, one must continue to ask, "What is the problem?" Jumping to conclusions too quickly can prevent good conflict resolution by completely bypassing the real issues. For example, the student wishing to drop a class might say, "My problem is that I need to get out of that class," when the real problem might be fear of failure (need for recognition and control) or dislike of other students in the class (need for security). The statement, "I need to get out of my class" is really a solution, not a definition of a problem. Similarly, the student who asks a teacher to remove another student from a laboratory or class project group is offering a solution and not presenting a problem. The teacher might be wise to listen to the subtext before jumping in to solve the problem.

The lesson plans in this chapter help students sharpen their observation skills and define problems. In addition to being useful to classroom teachers, they can provide club sponsors and youth group leaders with activities to help teenagers understand conflict.

PROBLEM CHARACTERISTICS

To the Teacher: All good lesson plans begin with a "hook." Often the best way to capture a student's attention is to ask the student to look at his or her own experience. This lesson causes students to become aware of the characteristics of their own problems and understand that these factors accompany most conflicts.

Objectives: Students will understand that conflict is based on problems.

Students will become aware of the characteristics of problems that lie beneath conflicts.

Activities:

1. Ask students to think about a conflict they have experienced or observed. (Students may jot notes.)

2. Distribute the reproducible "Conflict Problem Characteristics" (1-1) and ask students to check the items on the handout in relation to the conflict they thought about.

3. Review the checklist and ask students to indicate by a show of hands which items they checked.

4. Explain that a conflict is a disagreement between two or more parties. To analyze a conflict, one must ask, "What is the problem?"

5. Subdivide the class into small groups of four or five students.

6. Ask volunteers in each group to share conflicts and their understanding of the underlying problems in their conflicts.

7. Ask spokespersons to report to the class.

8. Discuss the importance of defining problems before beginning to solve them.

CONFLICT PROBLEM CHARACTERISTICS

Directions: Check the characteristics that apply to your conflict.

INCOMPLETE COMMUNICATION
(I/he/she didn't hear the whole story.)   _____

INACCURATE INFORMATION
(At least one of us/them had the wrong information.)   _____

STRESS OVERLOAD
(At least one of us/them was confused, overloaded,
and stressed.)   _____

DIFFERENT VIEWPOINTS
(We/they see things differently. They have different beliefs
or values.)   _____

LIMITED RESOURCES
(We/they can't have it all because there is not
enough to go around.)   _____

UNMET PSYCHOLOGICAL NEEDS
(My/his/her need for identity, security, recognition,
control, or fairness is threatened.)   _____

2   CONFLICT AND UNDERLYING NEEDS

To the Teacher: Since conflicts are really based on unmet psychological needs, it is worth taking the time to have students understand this connection.

The scenarios in this lesson supply a good basis for the discussion of the relationship between conflict and underlying needs. The scenarios illustrate these needs as follows:

> *"The New Cheerleader" (2-1)*
> Lynette: Security, recognition, and control
> Beth: Security, recognition, and control
> Squad members: Identity, fairness

> *"Homework from the New Student" (2-1)*
> George: Control
> Mike: Security and identity

Objective: Students will understand that conflict is frequently based on unmet psychological needs.

Activities:
1. List the following basic psychological needs on the chalkboard: *identity, security, control, recognition,* and *fairness.*

2. Ask students to recall a conflict they have experienced or observed during the previous week and jot notes in their notebooks.

3. Ask volunteers to offer examples of conflicts and the unmet needs that underlie them.

4. Distribute the handout "Conflict Scenarios" (2-1) and ask students to identify the unmet needs in the conflicts.

5. Ask students to share responses in pairs.

6. Discuss responses with the class.

7. Ask students to write a journal entry describing a conflict they experienced or observed and show how the conflict is based on unmet needs of identity, security, control, recognition, fairness, or any combination of these needs.

CONFLICT SCENARIOS

Please identify the unmet psychological needs of the disputants in the following scenarios:

— THE NEW CHEERLEADER —

Beth, the squad co-captain, is furious at Lynette, a new cheerleader from Texas. She is talking to the other co-captain, Joey.

"And you know what that Lynette can do with her list of cheers and chants that she brought from *TEXAS?*" snapped Beth. "A bossy little peroxided witch is what she is. Did you see her telling Jane how she could improve her jumps? The nerve!"

Joey understands that Lynette did come on rather strong, but once Beth got something in her head, it was impossible to change her mind. The friction between Beth and Lynette was bad enough, but half of the squad sided with Lynette and the other half with Beth.

Lynette's needs _____

Beth's needs_____

Possible needs of squad members _____

— HOMEWORK FROM THE NEW STUDENT —

Mike is a shy, conscientious student who is new at Hallmark High. George is a popular student who eats at the "jock table" at lunch. George has invited Mike to join him for lunch and includes him in plans to hang out at the mall that weekend.

Mike sits behind George in math class. When George realizes that the teacher will check homework, he whispers to Mike, "I never got this stuff. Do me a favor . . . slip me your answers before she gets here." Mike is upset, but slips George the answers.

Mike's needs _____

George's needs_____

IDENTIFYING THE PROBLEM: AGAINST THE WALL

To the Teacher: In the following lesson plan, students take turns identifying the problems beneath the conflicts they hear. Be aware that students who act out their conflicts sometimes do not like hearing someone else define their problems. If students express resentment about someone else defining their problem, it is worth discussing the value of having disputants develop insight into their problems as opposed to having an outsider offer analysis. Although a skillful definition of a problem can facilitate considerable insight, telling someone what their problem is can be risky. This concept is important in mediation.

Objectives: Students will increase their skill in defining problems on which conflicts are based.

Students will begin to understand the importance of ownership in problem definition.

Activities: 1. Subdivide the class into groups of four and ask groups to congregate near a section of the classroom wall.

2. Ask one student in each group to stand facing the wall.

3. Ask two students in each group to role play students arguing. They may choose a role play from the handout, "Against the Wall Role Plays" (3-1).

4. Ask the fourth student in each group to be an observer.

5. Instruct students facing the wall to turn around and explain what the problem really is when they think they understand it.

6. Ask disputants to respond: Is the student against the wall's statement of the problem correct? How did you feel about hearing the statement?

7. Ask the observers to report their observations to the class.

8. Discuss the value of problem definition in conflict resolution and the difference between having someone else point out your problem and figuring it out for yourself.

ROLE PLAYS:
AGAINST THE WALL (3-1)

— THE BROTHERS' CAR —

Sam and Ram are twin brothers who share a car. Sam is a "neat freak," and Ram is a complete slob. It is Sam's turn to have the car this weekend, and he's looking forward to taking Sarah to the party at Marie's house on Friday. Since Sam has a busy work and homework schedule, he has no time to clean up the car that Ram has trashed. Resentment has built up between the brothers, and they can hardly stand to look at each other.

— THE SCHOOL CALENDAR —

Miranda and Mike are sophomore and junior class presidents, respectively. Both want their bake and craft sales scheduled in the fall, when the sales traditionally make the most money. Each class desperately needs money for the prom, and the class presidents are anxious to start the year with a successful fund raiser. The sophomore class has particularly serious budgetary problems, and Mike based his whole election campaign on his ability to raise funds. Miranda insists juniors should get to choose before sophomores. They are both being difficult and have become really angry at each other.

— THE BAND —

Jayne and Monica are supposed to choose the band for the prom. Both have strong opinions about what kind of music is appropriate at the prom and insist that if "their kind of band" doesn't get the contract, all of their friends will boycott the prom. They are both stubborn and are ready to cause trouble.

Section Two

DIFFERENT KINDS OF CONFLICT
(Background Information)

DIFFERENT KINDS OF CONFLICT
(Background Information)

There are different kinds of conflict:

- ❐ conflict within self (intrapersonal)
- ❐ conflict between two or more parties (interpersonal)
- ❐ conflict between two or more parties within a group (intragroup)
- ❐ conflict between groups (intergroup)

Interpersonal Conflicts Can Become Intragroup Conflicts

The conflicts between new and established students in groups like cheerleading squads, siblings, and class officers are examples of conflicts that threaten to involve others and become conflicts within groups. As such, they are largely dependent upon the dynamics of the groups in which the conflicts occur. For example, the conflict between two cheerleaders becomes more severe when the squad members start taking sides. When the cheerleading conflict becomes an intragroup conflict, the captain's security is more threatened because it is more difficult to save face when there is an audience. Furthermore, if factions with their own identity emerge and become rival factions (e.g., the junior cheerleaders and the senior cheerleaders), the rivalry may create new and more serious conflicts than the original ones. Similarly, the brothers who share a car are members of a family unit whose dynamics potentially might cause a family feud with all family members fueling the fight.

Intragroup Conflicts Are Often Power Plays

Conflicts within a group are, of course, frequently power plays and are difficult to handle because they quickly become "no-win" situations when the parties continue to argue. Since the family unit, the classroom, and the athletic team comprise typical groups, parents, teachers, coaches, and club sponsors frequently become enmeshed in power plays. These power plays escalate and cause much grief to all parties. A teacher really loses by engaging in a conflict with a difficult student when the class happens to side with that student.

Interpersonal Conflicts Can Escalate Into Intergroup Conflicts

Sometimes groups take on lives of their own. When groups conflict, particularly when group members have a strong sense of identity with the group, the potential for violence tends to increase. "French Fries All over the Place" (6-1), one of the scenarios in this section, is a typical example of a potentially violent intergroup conflict that began as an interpersonal conflict.

Disputes Often Combine Different Conflicts

Many disputes are combinations of different kinds of conflicts. Conflicts are like snowballs. They pick up momentum and volume when group members attach themselves.

The following lesson plan and the accompanying scenario, "Athletes and Parties" (4-1), can help students understand the different kinds of conflict.

4 KINDS OF CONFLICT

To the Teacher: Brad's intrapersonal conflict involves whether or not he will report Andy to the coach. Brad and Andy conflict with each other, with the group taking sides. When the golf team gets involved, the school has a full-blown intergroup conflict on its hands.

Objectives: Students will understand the difference between conflicts within self, conflicts between others within a group, and conflicts between groups.

Students will become more aware of the impact that groups have upon conflicts.

Activities:
1. Distribute the scenario "Athletes and Parties" (4-1).

2. Discuss Brad and Andy's conflict. What is it?

3. Define the different kinds of conflict:
   ❑ conflict within self (intrapersonal)
   ❑ conflict between individuals (interpersonal)
   ❑ conflict between members within a group (intragroup conflict)
   ❑ conflict between groups (intergroup conflict)

4. Use the scenario to illustrate the different kinds of conflict with the scenario.

5. Ask students to jot notes about examples of each type of conflict from an experience or observation.

6. Ask volunteers to share examples of conflicts.

7. Assign students journal writings on different kinds of conflicts observed in current affairs or literature. In the journal they should summarize the conflict, explain who the disputants are, identify the kind of conflict (intrapersonal, interpersonal, intragroup, intergroup, or a combination), and explain what effect the group has on the original conflict.
   Examples: A neighborhood dispute in the local paper; Moby Dick and Ahab.

8. Plan to have students prepare presentations on their findings.

SCENARIO:
ATHLETES AND PARTIES (4-1)

Andy was steaming. Brad, the team captain, was accusing him of violating the team rules.

Andy lashed out, "What'd ya mean you heard from some reliable sources? I haven't had a beer or anything else to drink since football season began. Where do you get off telling me I'm benched?"

"Andy," Brad answered in as calm a voice as he could muster, "as captain of the team, I have to call the shots. When reliable sources say someone on the team's been breakin' rules, I have to report it to the coach. And you know as well as I do that if there's drinking or anything else like that goin' on, the whole team could have to forfeit playing at all. Now."

"BUT I WASN'T DRINKING. DOES THAT MATTER?" yelled Andy.

Brad looked at Andy and wondered. How he hated the coach and the system for putting him in this bind. Andy looked sincere, but he'd been known to stretch the truth. Brad looked beyond Andy and saw the other players. They were already almost physically dividing themselves between sides, Andy's or Brad's. The problem was growing.

When the golf team got wind of the problem, some of the golf players muttered, "Oh, those gorillas couldn't play football without being drunk." Then some of the football players overheard the golfers and shouted, "You guys are so snooty, you're above it all. You're all show. You just drink behind closed doors." At lunch the guys on the football team and the golf team sat at adjacent tables. They had been exchanging insults and glaring at each other. Someone was bound to start punching.

IDENTIFYING A CONFLICT WITHIN A CLASS

To the Teacher: Conflicts that occur during the classroom activities haunt teachers. Although we have devoted a chapter to teacher management of conflict, we place this lesson plan here to illustrate how teachers can use the classroom group to define a conflict. The experienced teacher may choose to substitute scenarios that resemble a real conflict and use the format of this lesson plan to address it. When using a real conflict, the teacher should focus on the situation or behaviors, not the people involved. The teacher should also take the time to set clear limits, reinforce the concern students have for their relationships with each other, and provide the disputants in the real conflict with an opportunity to save face.

Objective: Students will practice defining conflicts and improve their conflict observation skills.

Activities:
1. Distribute the handout "Get Out of My Space" (5-1) and the handout "Conflict Observation Sheet" (5-2).

2. Have students volunteer to briefly act out the scenario.

3. Ask students to fill in the conflict observation sheets.

4. Ask volunteers to form a panel to discuss their observations.

5. Ask the panel why they think someone would behave like Waynette? How do they think Luke should have dealt with Waynette? What should the teacher do?

6. Ask students who have role played the scenario to critique the panel's presentation.

7. Ask students to write journals explaining what they have learned and observed about conflict and how the larger group affects it.

ROLE PLAY:
GET OUT OF MY SPACE (5-1)

Actually it had been a rather calm English class that day. "Too calm," Waynette thought, as she scanned the room and saw too many students reading their assignments.

"Seating charts," Waynette snorted under her breath. How she hated being told where to sit. She looked at Luke, the guy who sat next to her.

"Luke," she called out to him in a whisper. He acknowledged her with a questioning look on his face.

"Luke," said Waynette, "sharpen this pencil for me."

Luke looked at Waynette, shrugged, and got back to his reading.

"Luke!" Waynette called in her loudest whisper.

Disgustedly, Waynette got up and passed Luke to get to the pencil sharpener.

On her way back to her seat, she caught Luke in a huge stretch. His long athletic arms stretched way out and accidentally blocked Waynette's journey back to her seat.

"GET OUT OF MY SPACE!" Waynette yelled as she pushed Luke aside.

"Why don't you just sit down and shut up?" Marla shouted. "I'm sick of your mouth always yapping in this class."

"What's your problem, Marla? You got a problem with Waynette, you got a problem with me," Tina yelled at Marla.

The class started dividing into different camps—those who favored Waynette, those who sided with Marla, and another group who grumbled that the teacher should get control of the class.

The reading assignment was over.

CONFLICT OBSERVATION SHEET

Describe the conflict.

	Disputant A	*Disputant B*
What happened?		
What is the problem?		
How did the disputants feel?		
What did the disputants want?		
What do the disputants need?		
How did the disputants respond?		
How did the conflict end?		
What could have been done differently?		

ANALYZING AN INTERGROUP CONFLICT: FRENCH FRIES ALL OVER THE PLACE

To the Teacher: Dealing with multicultural issues requires considerable sensitivity. It is important to point out that people often generalize and stereotype. The comments in the reproducible reflect some perceptions that do stereotype. For example, one student's statement, "Anglos pick on Hispanics," stereotypes students and is not based on fact.

Objectives: Students will understand that defining a problem can be complex and they will begin to practice unmasking layers of causes.

Students will understand that different people perceive and define conflicts differently.

Activities: 1. Distribute the scenario "French Fries All over the Place" (6-1) and ask students to read the description of what happened in the cafeteria at a different school last week.

2. Ask students, "What is the problem?" and record their responses on the chalkboard.

3. Distribute the handout "French Fry Perceptions" (6-2) and ask students to compare their responses with the student responses from the other school. Discuss their reactions to the similarities and differences.

4. Ask students to examine the student responses listed on the handout, jotting notes about possible causes underlying each statement.

5. Subdivide the class into small groups and ask them to discuss their observations.

6. Have spokespersons from each group report their conclusions.

7. Discuss who can best decide what the real problem is.

SCENARIO:
FRENCH FRIES ALL OVER THE PLACE (6-1)

Maria sat at the cafeteria table, enjoying the free time she had with her friends. Occasionally, she noticed a group of guys out of the corner of her eye. They seemed to keep looking over at her and her table.

One of her friends asked her what she was looking at. Maria replied, "Those guys. They keep staring over here."

"Looks like they could say the same for you!" commented Alisha with a laugh.

"Not me!" replied Maria as she flung her hair behind her shoulders and started chatting and sharing French fries with Pedro.

At the other table, the guys talked and laughed as they continued to look at the table where Maria sat. "Nah, she doesn't look a thing like Gloria Estephan. You better get your eyes checked, man. Gloria is a dog compared with that chick," said one of them.

His friend suggested, "You just need to see her up close. C'mon, get your tray and check her out up close."

The two guys grabbed their trays, and sauntered over to the trash bin located near Maria's table. This time there was no doubt about it. They were *really* staring at Maria.

Pedro noticed the guys staring too, and as Maria sat there munching a fry, Pedro endured their stares as long as he could. He threw a French fry at them.

The food fight had begun.

FRENCH FRY PERCEPTIONS

To the Student: After a food fight at a neighboring school, students responded to the question, "What is the problem?" with the following statements. Please think about each statement and jot notes under each one. (Why do you suppose someone offered this suggestion? What do you think the problem really is?)

After completing your responses to the individual statements, turn this sheet of paper over and describe what you think the problem really is.

— STATEMENTS —

According to the Hispanic value of honor, boys are expected to protect girls.

_____

Anglos pick on Hispanics.

_____

Hispanics are unified and fight back as a response to being picked on.

_____

Anglos blamed Hispanics because of misinformation.

_____

Hispanics have difficulty explaining themselves verbally, particularly when under stress.

_____

Anglos think that the scene of a group of Hispanic girls being upset is amusing.

_____

All boys think that girls are silly to get upset about food fights.

_____

Students were upset when adults did not come to their rescue.

_____

Adults thought that students had the situation under control.

_____

Boys and girls perceive food fights differently.

_____

SIFTING THROUGH A COMPLEX CONFLICT: "THE PROM PARTY FROM HELL"

To the Teacher: The scenario on which this lesson plan is based is frightening because it results in violence. Like many complex, volatile conflicts, it is difficult to define. When one tries to figure out what happened, the observer feels as if he or she is attempting to separate slippery strands of spaghetti.

Objectives: Students will increase their skill in identifying problems.

Students will understand that breaking a problem into parts can help them define problems.

Students will understand that there are different ways of dealing with conflict.

Activities:

1. Distribute the scenario script "The Prom Party from Hell" (7-1) to two students and ask them to read the script aloud.

2. Instruct students to listen carefully, take notes, and try to define the problem.

3. Distribute copies of the script to students so that they can clarify what has been said.

4. Ask students to draw diagrams to clarify what happened at the party. As an additional option, distribute "Prom Party Analysis" (7-3) and ask students to complete it.

5. Distribute copies of the "Prom Party Web" (7-2) so that students can clarify what happened.

6. Ask students to generate lists of problem definitions.

7. Subdivide the class into groups and have the groups arrive at a consensus about what the problems are.

8. Ask spokespersons to share the lists of problems and develop a list on the chalkboard.

9. Discuss different ways the characters dealt with conflict.

10. Distribute the "Conflict Observation Sheet" (5-2) and ask students to choose two disputants from the Prom scenario and complete it.

11. Discuss ideas in "Implications of the Prom Party" (7-4).

SCENARIO:
THE PROM PARTY FROM HELL (7-1)

Teressa: Dave hit John because he couldn't hit Dalia and now Brent is in the hospital. It's all Dalia's fault.

Ms. T.: What happened to Brent?

Teressa: John hit him.

Ms. T.: Why?

Teressa: Dalia invited John and his buddies, Dave and Brent, to my party room after the prom.

Ms. T.: Who was Dalia's date?

Teressa: John, but she wanted to break up with him, so she invited her new boyfriend Steve to the party too. You see, when John gets mad, then Dave gets mad and wants to stick up for him. So when Dalia started mouthing off, John got mad, and Dave got mad, and John got madder. Dalia knew she was pushing him and I warned her, but she still told John to "get lost." That's when John wanted to hit her, but he sort of hit Dave instead. Then it was utter chaos.

Ms. T.: What happened?

Teressa: Brent tried to get the two guys to stop fighting; he tried to calm them down. Big mistake. Brent got hit so hard that he had to go to the hospital. We all got thrown out by hotel security. I've heard Brent is in the hospital with broken ribs and teeth.

Ms. T.: What's going on now?

Teressa: Mary, Regan, and I are angry at Dalia because she ruined our party by crashing it. Regan is afraid that John will kill Steve, Dalia's new boyfriend. Mary thinks Dalia didn't handle breaking up with John very well and that she didn't anticipate Dave's temper. We think Dalia is always setting someone up.
(long pause)
Dave, John, and Brent all look up to Pete.

Ms. T.: Who's Pete?

Teressa: He's the guy who taught them to always aim for the face when they fight. Regan wants to fight Dalia for revenge; she'll feel better if she breaks her ankles. I want to punch Dalia for ruining my postprom party.

Ms. T.: Are you planning something?

Teressa: I don't know. We are afraid of our own tempers.

PROM PARTY WEB (7-2)

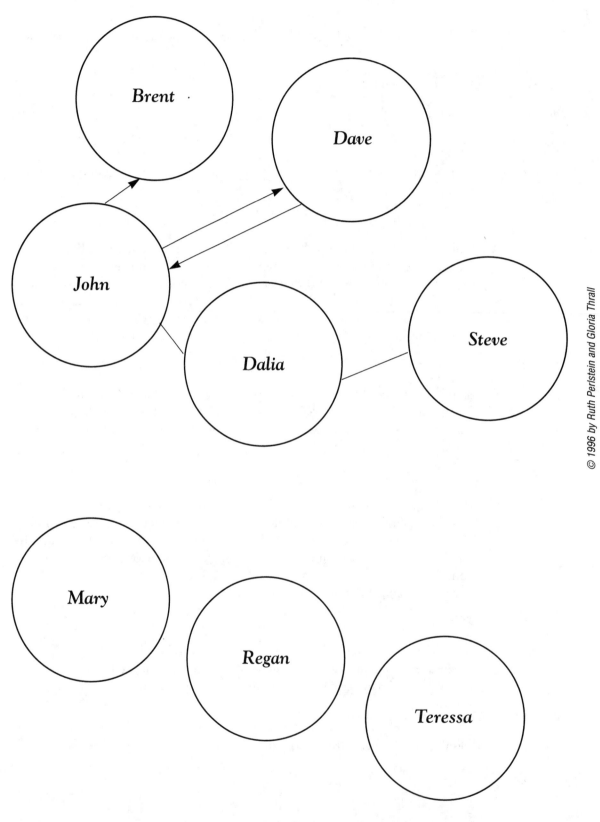

PROM PARTY ANALYSIS

What Is the Problem?

John:

     What does he want?_____

     What does he need?_____

Brent:

     What does he want?_____

     What does he need?_____

Dave:

     What does he want?_____

     What does he need?_____

Dalia:

     What does she want?_____

     What does she need?_____

Steve:

     What does he want?_____

     What does he need?_____

Mary:

     What does she want?_____

     What does she need?_____

Regan:

     What does she want?_____

     What does she need?_____

Teressa:

     What does she want?_____

     What does she need?_____

IMPLICATIONS OF THE PROM PARTY
SCENARIO (7-4)

Defining conflicts can be difficult because figuring out what happened often presents a challenge to the observer.

Determining the needs of the disputants also becomes complicated. For example, in "The Prom Party from Hell," it is really difficult to figure out why Brent landed in the hospital. It appears that he was in the wrong place at the wrong time. Perhaps he would have been better off calling the police and getting help from the hotel security force.

The girls giving the party were angry about having their party ruined and wanted both security and recognition for having provided a party that was fun. To their credit, they came to talk with Ms. T. about managing their anger ("We are afraid of our own tempers.") instead of beating up Dalia.

Most of the players in this scenario are irrational and out of control. The use of alcohol probably played a role. Dalia, the instigator, didn't want her old boyfriend to blow up when she dumped him (security). She also wanted recognition as someone who could have set up a big fight. Dalia spells trouble because she delights in stirring up fights.

Dave got into the conflict because he identified himself with John as his "best friend," but he was the object of John's transferred anger. (John was angry at Dalia for being dumped, but couldn't hit Dahlia because his code of honor prohibited him from hitting a girl. Instead, he punched his best friend.)

All the characters in this scenario need counseling about how to deal with their anger more appropriately. It is interesting to note that John and Dave learned to aim for someone's face when fighting. Hopefully, they might learn how to deal with anger or even wrestle properly as a sport from more appropriate teachers and role models.

The class activities associated with this scenario provide food for discussion that can help prevent violence. Unfortunately, this scenario occurs in many places, and teenagers need to discuss alternative ways of handling difficult situations. Possibilities for all the characters include not scheduling the party in the first place, leaving the party, not drinking, ignoring Dalia, and so on.

What is clear is that it is helpful, but often difficult, to understand conflict. Teachers can use the reproducible "Conflict Observation Sheet" (5-2) for homework assignments. It can be a useful tool for students to use in analyzing conflicts.

Section Three

DEALING WITH CONFLICT
(Background Information)

DEALING WITH CONFLICT
(Background Information)

A good way to begin discussing conflict is to ask people what kind of animal they resemble when they are in conflict. Responses usually range from lions, tigers, and mules to turtles and snails.

Sometimes Styles Vary with Settings

Some people claim they assume multiple animal identities, depending upon the setting. For example, a student might act like a gorilla at home, but become a teddy bear at school. Similarly, another student might describe being a tiger with a sibling, a St. Bernard with a friend, and a mule with parents. Like more aggressive animals, some people actually love a good fight in most settings. They find confrontation stimulating or empowering. Others will consistently flee from conflict and hide in their shells, like turtles and snails.

Five Conflict Management Styles

There are five basic methods of dealing with conflict. These styles are

- ❏ competition
- ❏ avoidance
- ❏ accommodation
- ❏ compromise
- ❏ collaboration

Although one method, collaboration, or cooperatively arriving at a way to meet everyone's needs, produces the most satisfactory long-range conflict resolutions, there is a place for each style. Students need to become aware of their own ways of dealing with conflict and explore more effective means of conflict resolution.

Competition. In our society the authoritarian lions and tigers among us often win the prizes. From toddler days, through Little League and beyond, children learn the importance of winning. They learn to value winning an argument, landing the prize location to display a homecoming float, and even beating someone up in a fist fight.

The thrill of victory lies everywhere. But at what cost? If a competitor wins an argument, he or she risks destroying a relationship with the loser. The cheerleader from Texas, a character in a scenario in this section, faces a competitive captain, Beth, who is determined to have her way. Even if Beth wins, her relationship with her squad and the potential relationship with the cheerleader from Texas will be irreparably damaged.

Using the competitive style is often appropriate when there is an emergency. For example, when a child runs out into the street, someone needs to grab the child before a truck comes. Getting the child out of the street is what matters and there is no time for reasoning or worrying about whether the child will resent the person grabbing him or her.

Competition can also be appropriate when a principle really matters significantly more than a relationship. For example, if a student sees a friend cheat and he really values honor, that student will appropriately report the cheating student, and possibly risk jeopardizing the friendship. People tend to use competition when winning and being right really matter more than the relationship.

Avoidance. Just as some people are naturally competitive, others avoid arguments. The turtles, snails, and shy kittens among us don't like conflicts and choose to run, deny, or hide. This style can be useful when physical danger exists. For example, several of the characters in the scenario "The Prom Party from Hell" would have been wise to leave when they saw trouble ahead. On the other hand, if Brent, a character in this scenario, had not tried to help John and Dave, his relationship with them probably would have suffered.

People need to pick their battles, and avoidance is appropriate when time is limited and a resolution is not really important. Avoidance, of course, does not resolve conflicts. When people avoid, someone usually gets hurt. Not only does someone get hurt, but the problem will probably resurface at a later date.

Accommodation. Accommodation is a kind of avoidance. It is the style practiced by the large friendly docile dog who wants to be loved above all else. If the junior class president is more interested in his or her relationship with the senior class president than getting the best class picnic date on the school calendar, the junior class president will be accommodating and let the senior class president have his or her way.

Accommodation is useful when the other person's needs are greater than the accommodator's. Accommodation is also appropriate when the accommodator doesn't need to win. However, accommodators do run the risk of enabling inappropriate behavior or harboring resentment. The victim accommodates the bully by reinforcing the winner's behavior and resents giving up what he or she wants.

Compromise. The compromiser shares the prize. Like the quick, clever fox, the compromiser works things out so that he can live with the solution, even if he doesn't get what he really wants. If the junior and senior class each decide to sponsor a portion of the September picnic and split the proceeds, the groups are compromising. Compromise works effectively when there is limited time to explore options and the possibility for finding a solution is clear. The only pitfall of compromise is that disputants sometimes become angry after a short-term solution. They may feel they haven't had enough time to explore additional alternatives and work things out. At a later date compromisers may focus on what they have given away.

Collaboration. Collaborative problem solving, practiced by the owls and dolphins and squirrels who explore alternatives, produces the most satisfactory long-term resolutions to conflict. Although this style requires more time than others, it is a useful style when both the task or issue and the relationships between the disputants is important. If the class presidents were to collaborate, they would brainstorm a number of solutions, some of which might be quite creative. When they agreed on a solution through collaboration, they would both be more satisfied with their solution. They would both win.

Summary

In conflicts people argue with each other about what they want. In getting what they want, the competitors have the advantage, at the risk of destroying their relationship with their opponents. The avoiders and accommodators consider, if not maintain, the relationship with the other disputants, but give up what they want. Compromisers do fairly well in walking the tightrope between getting something done and maintaining their relationships with people, but the collaborators win everything. They get what they want and maintain good relationships with one another.

The activities in this chapter help students develop insight into how they personally deal with conflict and help students understand the different ways of dealing with conflict and the related consequences. It is hoped that they will learn to handle conflict more effectively.

8 LEARNING ABOUT CONFLICT MANAGEMENT STYLES

To the Teacher: Although some students will find proverbs too abstract, and the instrument is not a highly reliable measure, this inventory is a useful tool for teaching different conflict management styles. Read the proverbs aloud first to make sure the students understand them.

Objectives: Students will understand the different conflict management styles.

Students will become aware of their own conflict management styles.

Activities:
1. Distribute the "Conflict Styles Inventory" (8-1) and have students fill in the appropriate blanks with respect to a specific setting of their choice. Explain that people sometimes handle conflict differently in different settings. For example, some people are more aggressive at home with their family and more passive in a school or work situation.

2. Distribute the "Scoring Sheets" (8-2) and ask students to score their inventories.

3. Ask students to indicate high scores in each category by a show of hands.

4. Distribute copies of the "Conflict Styles Chart" (8-3) and explain the different styles. Note that accommodation is a variation of avoidance and that the most lasting conflict resolutions result from collaboration, a style which anyone can learn to use.

5. Discuss each proverb on the inventory in terms of the conflict management style it suggests:

   ❏ competition   ❏ avoidance   ❏ collaboration
   ❏ compromise   ❏ accommodation   ❏ accommodation
   ❏ avoidance   ❏ compromise   ❏ collaboration
   ❏ competition

6. Assign students a journal writing to describe how they handled a specific conflict and how they might have handled it differently.

7. Ask students to find new proverbs to illustrate conflict management styles and share them with the class.

CONFLICT STYLES INVENTORY

The proverbs listed below suggest different ways of dealing with conflict. Read each of the proverbs carefully and indicate how typical each proverb is of your attitude toward conflict.

Key: 5 = very typical of the way I think in a conflict
      4 = frequently typical of the way I think in a conflict
      3 = sometimes typical of the way I think in a conflict
      2 = seldom typical of the way I think in a conflict
      1 = never typical of the way I think in a conflict

PROVERB	1	2	3	4	5
1. Give him an inch and he'll take a mile.					
2. A bad peace is better than a good quarrel.					
3. Come, let us reason together.					
4. You have to give some to get some.					
5. It is better to give than to receive.					
6. When you are among the blind, shut your eyes.					
7. Don't wake up sleeping sadness.					
8. Better a diamond with a flaw than a pebble without one.					
9. Two heads are better than one.					
10. He who humbles himself too much gets trampled upon.					

Adapted from materials from the Institute for Conflict Management, 3784 Center Way, Fairfax, Virginia 22033, and the Fairfax County Public Schools Peer Helper/Peer Mediation Curriculum guide.

Name _____ **Date** _____ (8-2)

SCORING SHEET

— CONFLICT STYLES —

The numbers in the key columns (5–1) represent the scores for each item. Please add scores according to the following directions:

Scores for item 2 plus scores for item 7_____Avoidance

Scores for item 1 plus scores for item 10_____Competition

Scores for item 5 plus scores for item 6_____Accommodation

Scores for item 4 plus scores for item 8_____Compromise

Scores for item 3 plus scores for item 9_____Collaboration

CONFLICT STYLES CHART (8-3)

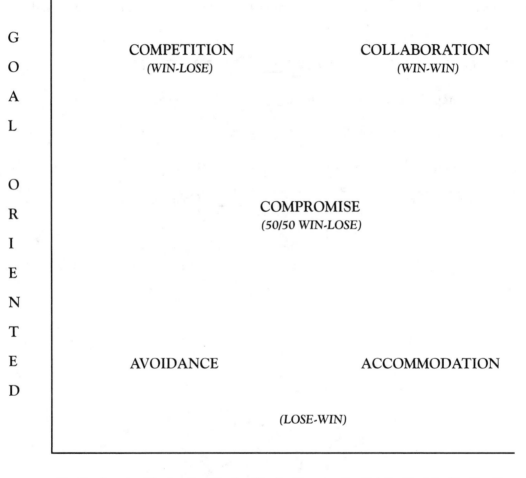

9 DESCRIBING CONFLICT MANAGEMENT STYLES

— "SPOTS ON THE WALL" —

Objective: Students will increase their understanding of conflict management styles and begin to see the consequences of each style.

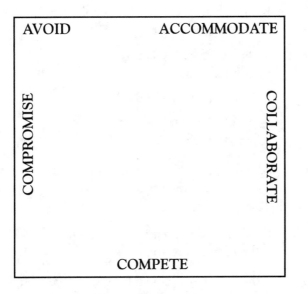

Activities:

1. Tape signs with the words "Avoid" and "Accommodate" on different ends of one wall. Place a sign with the word "Compete" on the opposite wall and place signs with the words "Compromise" and "Collaborate" on each of the remaining walls.

2. Ask students to stand near the sign that applies to their preferred personal conflict management style.

3. Give students in each group ten minutes to plan a brief presentation, explaining the style and its advantages and disadvantages.

4. Ask students to give their presentations.

5. Ask students if they would consider moving to another section of the room after listening to the presentations.

6. Discuss insights students may have acquired from this lesson.

10 **EXPLORING WHERE STYLES ARE LEARNED**

Objective: Students will develop insight into where and how people receive messages about how to deal with conflict.

Activities: 1. Ask students to recall times they experienced, observed, or heard about conflict during their childhood. Ask them to jot notes about their recollections and the messages they received about how to resolve the conflicts.

2. Ask students to select one of the following areas to explore messages about conflict resolution styles.

   a. Growing up in the family
   b. Watching television
   c. Reading fairy tales and books
   d. Listening to songs or popular music
   e. Going to the movies

3. Subdivide the class into groups and ask students to share examples of how people receive messages about conflict resolution in the area assigned to their group.

4. Ask students to summarize their discussion and have a group member present the summary to the class.

5. Ask the class to develop a list of messages people learn about how to deal with conflict.

6. Discuss one of the following issues:

   ❐ How do people receive messages about how to resolve conflict?
   ❐ What is the impact of the media upon conflict resolution?
   ❐ What can be done to send more constructive messages?

Name _____ Date _____ (10-1)

MESSAGES

To the Student: Recall times you have experienced, observed, or heard about conflict during your childhood. Then jot notes about what you have heard in each of the following settings:

Growing up in the family_____

_____

_____

Watching television_____

_____

_____

Reading fairy tales and books_____

_____

_____

Listening to songs_____

_____

_____

Going to the movies_____

_____

_____

What messages did these experiences or observations give you about how one should handle conflict?

_____

_____

_____

_____

_____

_____

LISTENING TO OTHER APPROACHES

To the Teacher: In this lesson students share personal experiences, feelings, and opinions. At no time may students comment on what students have said. This lesson plan often begins with silence. It is worth waiting for a while until someone intolerant of silence eventually begins to volunteer. Students who feel uncomfortable participating have the right to pass. Observers have as much to learn as participants.

Objective: Students will hear where other students are coming from with respect to personal conflict resolution. They will understand how difficult it can be to listen to others when focusing on themselves.

Activities:

1. Arrange students in either a large circle or concentric circles.

2. Ask students to reflect on their own preferred style of conflict resolution and how they think they acquired this behavior preference.

3. Ask students to volunteer to recount their reflections.

4. Ask students to continue to share personal reflections, without commenting on what other students have said.

5. After ten minutes, stop and ask the first person who spoke to tell what other students have said.

6. Ask other participants to describe what they heard other students say.

7. Discuss how difficult it is to hear others when focusing on a topic in which one is personally involved.

8. Discuss the importance of listening to where others are coming from.

12   **ABOUT STYLES**

Objective: Students will understand the consequences of using different conflict management styles.

Activities:

1. List conflict management styles on the chalkboard:

   - ❐ Competition
   - ❐ Avoidance
   - ❐ Accommodation
   - ❐ Compromise
   - ❐ Collaboration

2. Have students brainstorm advantages and disadvantages of each style.

3. Distribute the reproducible "Conflict Management Styles" (12-1).

4. Discuss the reproducible.

5. Ask students to write about a situation in which they would choose a style that is not their preferred style.

CONFLICT MANAGEMENT STYLES

Style	**+**		**—**
	useful when . . .	*consequences*	*characteristics*
Competition	there is a physical threat; a principle is much more important than the relationship	power play; probable loss of long-term relationship	dominating, abusive, arrogant (intensive eye contact)
Avoidance	there is a danger to safety or a job and so on	hurt; mis-understanding	indecisive, apologetic, submissive, timid (poor posture and poor eye contact)
Accommodation	the other person's needs are greater	enabling behavior; possible resentment; no solution	submissive, quiet, friendly (open, good eye contact)
Compromise	there is limited time and an obvious possible solution	possible anger after the short-term solution	direct, poised, skilled at listening (good eye contact)
Collaboration	there is time; parties desire a long-term solution	satisfactory long-term solution	skilled at listening, accepting, competent (good eye contact)

WHICH STYLE WILL WORK?

Objective: Students will understand how to use more effective ways of handling conflict.

Activities: 1. Distribute the reproducible "Comic Strip" (13-1).

2. Ask students to draw a visual representation of a conflict they have experienced or observed in the first frame of the comic strip.

3. Ask students to draw a visual representation of the desired resolution in the last frame of the comic strip.

4. Ask students to fill in the middle frames.

5. Ask students to write about their method of resolving the conflict.

6. Ask volunteers to present their "comic strips."

7. Discuss the comic strips.

COMIC STRIP

To the Student: Think about a conflict you have observed. Draw a visual representation of the conflict in the first frame of the blank "comic strip" below. Then draw a visual representation of the desired resolution of the conflict in the last frame in the "comic strip."

Then fill in the middle frames: What needs to happen between the first and last frame?

Write a paragraph describing how a specific conflict management style is used to resolve a conflict.

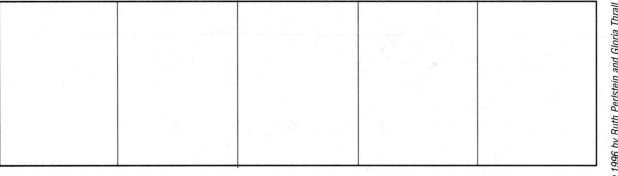

OBSERVING STYLES

Objective: Students will review conflict resolution styles.

Activities:
1. Distribute the reproducible "Styles Scenarios" (14-1).

2. Ask students to identify styles used in the scenarios.

3. Review the conflict management styles (illustrated in the scenarios in the following order):
   - ❐ Compromise
   - ❐ Avoidance
   - ❐ Accommodation
   - ❐ Collaboration
   - ❐ Competition

4. Discuss the consequences of the styles Marianna and Paula use in each of the scenarios.

5. Distribute the reproducible "What Should They Do?" (14-2).

6. Subdivide the class into groups to discuss what the disputants in each of these scenarios should do.

7. Ask a spokesperson from each group to summarize the group suggestions.

8. Discuss the implications of these scenarios for conflict resolution.

To the Teacher: Students need to be reminded that it is difficult to resolve conflict when disputants get out of control. It is far more useful to deal with conflict before it escalates. Once angry people are out of control, students need to seek help in separating the disputants and calming them down.

STYLES SCENARIOS

Marianna (age 16) and Paula (age 14) are sisters who are constantly fighting over the use of the telephone. Their mother is threatening to pull it out of the wall if they don't stop arguing.

a.

Marianna: We always want to use the phone between four and eleven in the evening. Why don't we divide up the time and set up a schedule? I get to use it between four and seven thirty, and you can use it from seven thirty to eleven. If someone calls either of us at the wrong time, we can just take messages.

style_____

b.

Paula (to herself): It's useless to argue with Marianna. I'm going to tell my friends to call me at Toni's house next door. I'll just go over there and visit and Toni and I will do my homework together. Marianna can have that stupid phone . . . I don't even want to be in the same house with her in the evening!

style_____

c.

Marianna: Paula, now that you're a freshman, it's really important for you to make friends, and I know that the best way for you to become popular is for you to be able to talk with friends on the phone in the evening. I guess it's really important for the phone to be available for you. Maybe I can arrange to use Nadia's phone or keep my conversations down to five minutes. My friends are more likely to understand.

style_____

STYLES SCENARIOS
(Continued)

d.

Paula: Look, we both need that phone. Why don't we sit down and figure out why each of us needs it and when? Then maybe we can figure out some way that we can both get to use the phone whenever we need it. After all, there must be loads of possibilities. Can we talk about it and come up with some ideas to consider?

style_____

e.

Marianna: Look, I'm older than you are and I have a boyfriend. No little sister is going to push me around! I get to use the phone when I need it and you can use it for short calls or at any time when I'm not home. You have no right to interrupt my phone calls, so leave me alone and that's final!

style_____

WHAT SHOULD THEY DO? (14-2)

1. Jane and Jim are writers on the yearbook staff. They have just heard that the editors can include only one of two prepared special features sections in the yearbook. Since the editor likes both sections, the editor has given Jane and Jim an hour to decide which article will appear in the yearbook. Jane has written one of the feature articles and thinks that hers is far superior to Jim's. She really wants her article included because it will be her only published contribution in the yearbook. Besides, she is a junior and needs to cite her publication in her college application. Jim, who wrote the other section, thinks his section is far superior to Jane's. He is a senior and wants his mark on his yearbook. Besides, his other articles for the yearbook are all fairly small. What should Jim and Jane do?

2. Marie and Robert have been dating all year. Marie really likes Robert, but she is getting fed up with his showing up late. He is never on time for anything. They've missed parts of movies and have been embarrassingly late to parties. Robert really isn't ignoring Marie. It's just that he's always late for everything. They have been fighting constantly about this issue. Marie wants to tell Robert where to go, but really doesn't want to lose him. What should she do?

3. A group of guys have invited Lewis, a new student, to join them for a snack at their favorite hamburger place. On the way they stop in front of Joanne's house, take out a can of spray paint and proceed to spray racial slurs on her front lawn. Lewis is horrified. What should Lewis do?

4. John walks toward the office to deliver Ms. Partridge's passes. Along the way he sees his friend Joe arguing with Paul in an alcove. Paul is so angry he is out of control and punches Joe. What should John do?

5. All of the boys keep talking to Ellie. Jayne is so jealous of Ellie that in a weak moment she spread some awful rumors about Ellie, and she thinks that Ellie has found out. Now they both want to join the same choral group, and Jayne is petrified about what might happen when they work together. What should she do?

6. Danielle, a new student, has just joined chemistry class. Unfortunately, there are not enough books to go around, and the teacher has told Fred he must share his textbook with Danielle. The sharing of the book has become a problem, and they are blaming each other for having failed the last chemistry test.

ADVOCATING PEACEFUL CONFLICT RESOLUTION

To the Teacher: As an outgrowth of this lesson, students can plan presentations advocating peaceful conflict resolution for younger students. Teachers can arrange to take groups with particularly creative presentations to nearby elementary school classes.

Objective: Students will become more committed to peaceful conflict resolution.

Activities:

1. Tape quotations from the reproducible "Proverbs" (15-1) on different places on the wall of the room.

2. Ask students to read the quotations and stand next to one that appeals to them.

3. Organize groups of students according to the quotations they choose.

4. Give each group ten minutes to organize a presentation advocating peaceful conflict resolution based on the proverb they have chosen.

5. Ask each group to make its presentation to the class.

6. Discuss how students might advocate peaceful conflict resolution.

PROVERBS (15-1)

THE WISE MAN FORGETS INSULTS AS THE UNGRATEFUL
FORGET BENEFITS.

DO NOT SPIT INTO THE WELL . . . YOU MAY HAVE TO
DRINK OUT OF IT.

IT IS EASY TO THROW A STONE INTO THE DANUBE,
BUT RATHER DIFFICULT TO GET IT OUT.

EVERYTHING COMES TO HIM WHO WAITS.

LOOK BEFORE YOU LEAP.

BETTER A COWARD THAN A CORPSE.

KINDNESS BEGETS KINDNESS.

TO LOCK UP MISCHIEF, KEEP YOUR MOUTH CLOSED.

Section Four

UNDERSTANDING DIFFERENT POINTS OF VIEW
(Background Information)

UNDERSTANDING DIFFERENT POINTS OF VIEW
(Background Information)

Failure to listen causes conflict, and the opponent's point of view is often left unheard. Conflicts often occur because disputants fail to consider that others might actually perceive things differently. Consider the teenager who is totally disgusted with her friend who saunters down the hall and constantly makes her wait. Suppose the friend has a muscular disease and cannot walk quickly, but hasn't disclosed the problem. If the teenager knew where her friend was coming from, wouldn't she feel differently and think, "Oh, if I had only known?" Similarly, the insensitive young man who calls all women "honey" might be totally unaware that some of the young women might be offended by that term of address. He might approach these women differently if he became aware of their point of view.

The past shapes our points of view and colors them with all sorts of emotional baggage. As a result, it is difficult to walk in someone else's shoes, particularly when a point of view is tied to a basic psychological need like identity, security, and control. Consider different perceptions of the Confederate flag. Is it a symbol of a proud heritage, a badge of honor, or a symbol of slavery, a badge of shame? Consider various fashion statements, like the wearing of hats, which is often a controversial issue in the classroom. Even teachers disagree about whether students should be allowed to wear hats. Some teachers view the wearing of hats as at best poor etiquette and at worst defiant behavior or a sign of gang membership. Others view hats as a harmless fashion statement, a way to hide hair on a "bad hair day," or a desirable means of expressing individuality. Students in different cultures view clothing differently. According to custom, an orthodox Jewish male wouldn't walk bareheaded before God, and a Moslem woman wouldn't appear in public without her veil.

In an age where political correctness comes and goes as a hot issue and continues to be debated with varying degrees of rationality, the relationship between differing points of view and conflict is obvious. Because they use their own frame of reference, people tend to jump to conclusions about others. The danger that people can become unconcerned about what others think or feel is particularly frightening.

The lessons in this section will help students develop an awareness of different points of view. By encouraging students to listen to different points of view, students will hopefully become more sensitive to others. This sensitivity will help them develop conflict resolution skills.

VIEWING PICTURES DIFFERENTLY

To the Teacher: The reproducibles for this lesson can be enlarged for use as posters or photocopied for use as transparencies. The first represents an optical illusion that different students will perceive differently and offers an effective introduction to increase student awareness of different points of view. As an assignment, students can find other optical illusions in books and share them with the class.

The second reproducible is an illustration that different people perceive differently, depending on the character with whom they identify. Students from different cultures may identify the setting differently. For example, students from a different culture might identify the picture as a party at home because they perceive classrooms as regimented environments.

Objectives: Students will understand that different people can perceive a similar situation differently.

Students will understand that they bring preconceived perceptions with them.

Activities:

1. Show students the reproducible "The Top of the Head" (16-1).

2. Ask students to focus on a cartoon figure and describe the top of the figure's head.

3. Ask students by a show of hands to indicate who sees the bald figure, who sees the figure with hair standing on end, and who sees both.

4. Discuss the implications of different perceptions.

   ❐ What kinds of misunderstandings have you seen based on different perceptions?

   ❐ How can seeing something in a different light be useful?

5. Show students the reproducible "What Is Going on?" (16-2) and ask volunteers to describe the situation and the problem.

6. Discuss how perceptions of the situation vary and whether these perceptions are dependent upon individual experience.

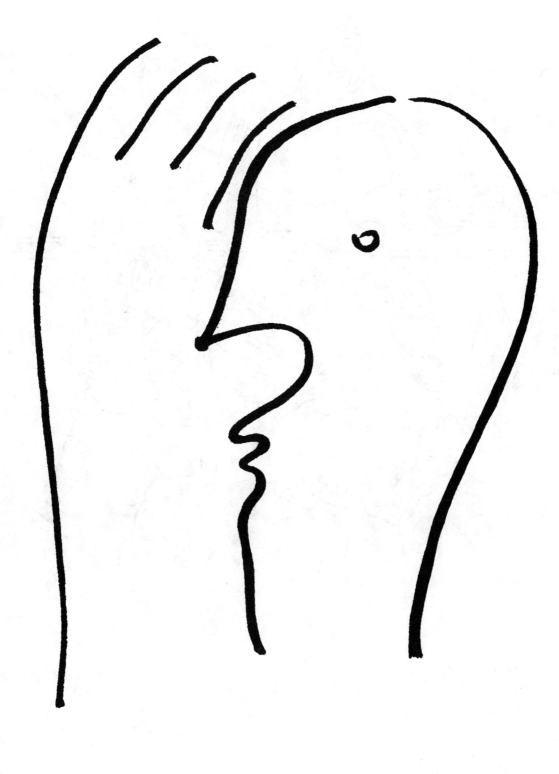

WHAT IS GOING ON? (16-2)

Illustration by Janet Rust.

17   **LOOKING THROUGH OUR OWN GLASSES**

Objective: Students will understand how personal experience shapes perception.

Activities:

1. Distribute the handout "Glasses" (17-1).

2. Ask students to recall significant events or situations that shaped them (e.g., position in their family, important change in their situation, influential institution).

3. Ask students to quickly sketch pictures in the lenses to represent two events or situations that influenced them.

4. Subdivide students into groups of four or five and ask them to share how their "Glasses" affect their perceptions of situations.

5. Ask volunteers to share personal insights with the class.

6. Ask each student to write a journal entry describing an example of how a personal experience shaped how he or she views current situations.

GLASSES

Directions: 1. Think about a few significant events or situations that shaped you (e.g., position in your family, important change in your situation, influential institution).

2. Quickly sketch pictures in each of the lenses to represent two events or situations that influenced you.

LOOKING AT SYMBOLS: POWER OR POISON

To the Teacher: This lesson requires considerable teacher sensitivity and skill. At the end of the lesson students can sort out their thoughts in writing. If a student becomes angry, suggest that he or she assume the role of the character that provokes the anger and write a journal entry from that person's point of view. The teacher can compile and share portions of students' written comments, protecting student confidentiality. This compilation can provide a powerful introduction to the follow-up lesson. Time for processing at the conclusion of the second day is essential.

Objectives: Students will understand that symbols can either empower or offend depending on the connotations different people perceive them to have.

Students will become sensitive to the pain they can cause by offending others with symbols.

Activities:
1. Distribute the scenario "The Confederate Flag" (18-1).

2. Ask students to describe the probable points of view of Joe, Kevin, and Marna.

3. Pose the question, "Should Joe be allowed to wear his Confederate flag tee-shirt in school?"

4. Ask students who think Joe should be able to wear the tee-shirt to assemble in one corner of the room; ask students who think he should *not* be allowed to wear it to assemble in the opposite corner.

5. Ask volunteers to defend their positions.

6. Ask students to write an essay on one of the following topics:

   ❑ Freedom of Speech: Where Do I Draw the Line?

   ❑ Personal Reactions to This Activity (What surprised me? How did this activity influence my thinking? In what way might it influence my behavior?)

   ❑ How Might Each of the Characters Have Handled the Conflict Differently?

SCENARIO:
THE CONFEDERATE FLAG (18-1)

Last week Joe Jones visited a Confederate museum with his grandparents and purchased a tee-shirt featuring a Confederate flag as a souvenir. Thursday afternoon Joe walked into civics class wearing the tee-shirt. His friend, Kevin, a class officer, commented, "Neat shirt!" Marna, an African-American student, found both the shirt and Kevin's comment offensive. She was hot. No doubt about it. And she wasn't about to let Kevin off the hook.

Trying to divert Marna's attention, Kevin said, "Marna, we have business to do. Could we talk about the shirt at another time, in another year, on another planet?"

"Don't even TRY to joke your way out of this one, fly boy," retorted Marna. "HOW could you stand in front of the whole class and condone, even encourage that . . . that person to wear a tee-shirt WITH THE CONFEDERATE FLAG ON IT!?"

Becoming angry, Kevin responded, "The same way YOU condone that friend of yours wearing a Malcolm X hat to school. MARNA, MARNA, let's be reasonable. Let's look at this without your passion, your emotion, your . . ."

"Kevin, forget it. I've had more intelligent conversations with my dog. Just don't you EVER let me hear of your condoning the Confederate flag ever again. You're a class officer; you're supposed to lead the class in a responsible way."

"I DO lead in a responsible manner. And if you want to keep this up, then what IS the difference between wearing the Confederate flag tee-shirt and the Malcolm X hat?"

"A BIG difference. The Confederate flag stands for slavery, something I'm not too fond of, if you didn't know. Malcolm X stood for equality. He . . ."

"Oh, cut it out, Marna. What's the big deal? You know Joe has a perfect right to wear that shirt! I don't understand why you have to get so bent out of shape."

EXPLORING HOT BUTTONS

To the Teacher: Place 3″ × 5″ note cards and the handout "Flag Comments" (19-1) on desks before students arrive. A teacher-made compilation of student comments from their writings can be substituted for the "Flag Comments." This lesson requires considerable skill and is not appropriate for every group.

Objective: Students will become more sensitive to how words can affect others.

Activities: 1. Ask students to list their "hot buttons," names (excluding profanity) that they don't want to be called on 3″ × 5″ note cards. Collect the cards.

2. Ask students for their reaction to the "Flag Comments."

3. Choose names or words that students perceive negatively based on information on cards collected and list them on the chalkboard.

4. Ask students if there are any surprises on the chalkboard.

5. Discuss implications of the "hot buttons" for members of various cultural groups like Native Americans, Asians, and Latinos.

6. Ask pairs of students to share experiences they have had or observed when someone offended a member of a group by using an offensive name.

7. Ask volunteers to share experiences.

8. Discuss what can be done to increase the cultural awareness of other students.

FLAG COMMENTS (19-1)

The following comments are excerpts from student writings about the tee-shirt incident.

"I am the first person to stand up for freedom of speech. I started out on the side to have Joe wear the tee-shirt, but today for the first time in all of our discussions, I could see both sides of the story."

"I am offended by the Confederate flag. However, people do feel proud of their Southern heritage and have a perfect right to wear the flag as a symbol of the South."

"I am a South Carolinian and I am proud of my Southern roots."

"Many people here became upset and have a right to. But that shouldn't mean Joe can't wear the shirt."

"The subject of Joe's shirt obviously hurt a lot of people, and I thought it was interesting that he saw it as symbol of his heritage, but when something hurts people as much as it did, we need to be sensitive to that."

". . . if people are going to wear something like that, they should know that others will be offended. I wouldn't come to school with a shirt like that because it means different things to different people. I know that someone will be offended . . . it's good that people let others know how they feel."

"It is obvious that everyone sees their point of view differently."

"I was so surprised that people got upset."

"Good for Marna! She needs to be assertive and tell people how she feels."

"No one is trying to control freedom of speech and expression, but every intelligent person must realize the need for respecting others and not offending them."

"Too many people consider themselves important and refuse to accept new beliefs and outlooks."

20 LISTENING TO ANOTHER POINT OF VIEW

Objective: Students will practice seeing situations from a different point of view.

Activities:

1. Assign the roles of Marina and Blake to two students and ask them to read the script in the handout "Marina and Blake" (20-1) in front of the class.

2. Ask students to take sides, identifying with a point of view.

3. Ask students who identify with Marina to plan a script from Blake's point of view.

4. Ask students who identify with Blake to plan a script from Marina's point of view.

5. Ask volunteers to stand and assume the role of the character with the opposing point of view and defend themselves.

6. Ask participants how they felt in the other role.

7. Discuss the difficulties and effect of stepping into the role of someone with a different point of view.

8. Brainstorm some possible solutions that Marina and Blake might consider.

ROLE PLAY:
MARINA AND BLAKE (20-1)

Marina: How could you possibly *think* I don't care about you . . . let alone *say* it?

Blake: Because it's true. You know the type of schedule we keep . . . going to different schools, you being so involved in soccer practices . . .

Marina: Wait a minute! YOU being so involved with football practice . . . don't forget that.

Blake: I wasn't forgetting it, but you interrupted me before I could add that. What I'm trying to get across to you is since I don't have a car, if you don't drive over after school before our practices start, then we won't see each other except on weekends. Is that what you want?

Marina: Oh, Blake, we've been over this a million times. You know I want to see you more than only on weekends, but you just don't get it. My coming over to your school takes 45 minutes round trip, 45 minutes that I need to study if I ever dream of getting in State U next fall.

Blake: If you *really* cared, you'd want to come over and see me after school. I'd do it for you if I had a car.

Marina: If *you* really cared, you'd know how unreasonable you're being.

21 EXPLORING CROSS-CULTURAL MISCOMMUNICATION

To the Teacher: Students need to practice being open to different points of view and not jumping to conclusions. Since students usually interpret comments made about them in another language as negative, this situation is one which might easily result in a fight. If English is the primary language of all students in the class, invite a small group of English as a Second Language (ESL) students from another class to participate in the role play.

Objective: Students will become sensitive to their tendency to misinterpret what they don't understand.

Activities:

1. Project a transparency of the reproducible "Hallway Scene" (21-1) as an introduction to the lesson.

2. Set up a role play between one English-speaking student and a small group of students who speak another language in the following manner.

   ❏ Take three English as a Second Language students aside and ask them to chat with one another in their native language, pretending to socialize in a hallway. When the English-speaking student passes them in the imaginary hallway, they should look at the student and comment on the attractiveness of the student's sweater.

   ❏ Ask an English-speaking student to pretend he or she is walking down the hall past the group of students.

3. Distribute observation sheets to students in the class and ask them to record observations. (In the Hallway 21-2)

4. Direct the role players to proceed.

5. Ask the English-speaking student what he or she thinks the group of students said.

6. Ask the ESL students to explain what they said.

7. Ask participants how they felt about the misunderstanding.

8. Discuss the misconceptions arising from the role play with the class.

9. Discuss ways of preventing this kind of misunderstanding.

HALLWAY SCENE

Illustration by Janet Rust.

IN THE HALLWAY

Please jot down notes about the role play you observe.

❐ What do you think the ESL students are saying?

❐ What do you think your classmate thinks they are saying?

❐ How do you feel about your classmate's response?

❐ How would you respond in this situation?

❐ How do you think most students would respond?

22 **EXPLORING ATTITUDES TOWARD CLOTHING**

To the Teacher: Usually the argument about clothing is not about clothing, but about power. The student who refuses to take his hat off in class wants to push his teacher's buttons, and the girl who double pierces her ears to her mother's chagrin sometimes wants to assert her independence.

Objectives: Students will increase their awareness of different points of view.

Students will review basic concepts related to defining conflict.

Activities:

1. Ask students to indicate by a show of hands whether they have had conflicts with parents, siblings, or teachers about their clothing.

2. Distribute the scenario "Fashion" (22-1).

3. Subdivide the class into four groups to work on different presentations related to each scenario.

4. Ask each group to discuss the assigned scenario and discuss the points of view of the characters.

5. Ask each group to prepare a brief skit to illustrate the different points of view.

6. Have the groups present their skits.

7. Ask presenters how they reacted in their roles after they heard different points of view.

8. Discuss what the real problems underlying the conflicts are (identity, security, control, . . .).

9. Discuss ways of resolving these conflicts.

CONFLICT SCENARIOS: FASHION (22-1)

— HATS —

Gerald wears a baseball cap turned backwards wherever he goes. Although Swain High School does not have a dress code, Miss Briar finds the wearing of hats in her classroom objectionable. She sees Gerald as rude, defiant, and ill mannered. Gerald says she has no right to make him take his hat off. Both feel really strongly about this issue. To complicate the issue further, Gerald just found he has ringworm and has had to have a spot of his head shaved. This week he really doesn't want to have to remove his hat in class.

— HAIR —

Mrs. Stace and her son Philip are at it again. Mrs. Stace is simply mortified by Phil's appearance. His hair is down to his shoulders, and she thinks he looks like a "no good hippie." Actually, Philip is rather clean cut, always neat and well groomed. He simply likes his hair long and insists he has the right to keep it that way.

— EARRINGS —

Mr. George thinks the neighborhood has gone to pot. It seems Julian, a young employee, came home from a camping trip with an earring in his left ear. "Is he a druggie, or what?" wondered Mr. George. Julian thinks Mr. George is an old-stick-in-the-mud and decides he'll wear the earring everywhere, even when he's working for Mr. George.

— SKIRTS —

Eleanor loves to look fashionable. This year skirts are short again, and she found a hot pink short skirt that really looks cute. Her older sister Sarah is embarrassed to be associated with Eleanor and can't imagine how their mother let Eleanor out of the house wearing that hot pink mini skirt.

23   EXPLORING CULTURAL POINTS OF VIEW

To the Teacher: Students from different countries often feel like outsiders. Both the language barrier and different customs result in misunderstandings and tension. This activity should increase communication between students and produce projects that may eventually result in schoolwide events to help various ethnic groups to get to know each other better.

As a follow-up activity to the group presentations, ask students to problem solve ways to help students resolve the conflicts presented.

Objective: Students will become sensitive toward the points of view and feelings of students with different cultural backgrounds.

Activities:
1. Ask students if they have observed incidents where students from other countries have been mistreated or misunderstood.

2. Ask students to recount incidents of mistreatment or misunderstanding dealing with foreign students if they have observed these episodes.

3. Distribute the interview "Assignment Sheet" (23-1).

4. Assign students to groups to plan presentations after they have completed their interviews.

ASSIGNMENT SHEET: EXPLORING CULTURAL POINTS OF VIEW

1. Interview a student from a foreign country to learn about that student's experience in the United States. During the interview try to find out what the student's experience was really like. The following sample questions may be used.

   ❒ How were you treated by adults and by students?

   ❒ When you first arrived, how did you feel in your neighborhood? At school?

   ❒ What difficulties did you encounter?

   ❒ Were there any incidents in which you felt misunderstood? If so, what happened?

   ❒ Were there any incidents you experienced or observed where a misunderstanding resulted in a conflict? What happened?

2. Prepare a one-page essay on what you learned about the student's point of view from the interview. Add ideas about how to deal with the problems the student encountered.

3. Write a scenario based on the student you interviewed. It will be used in a classroom presentation designed to help students become more sensitive to the needs of foreign students.

4. Meet with your group and plan a classroom presentation based on your interviews and scenarios.

   Due Dates:

   Interview essay due:

   Group presentation due:

SEEING THE SAME EVENT THROUGH DIFFERENT EYES

To the Teacher: This lesson is less complex than some of the preceding lessons. It reviews the basic concept in this section and encourages students to develop a greater awareness of just how many different ways people can perceive events.

Objective: Students will understand that different people perceive different events differently.

Activities:
1. Distribute the reproducible "The Fire Alarm" (24-1) and ask five students to read aloud the five descriptions of the reactions to the fire alarm.

2. Discuss the different perceptions people might have of the incidents listed: late bus, surprise snowstorm, and championship game loss.

3. Assign a journal writing about different events and how they might be perceived by a variety of people.

THE FIRE ALARM

A fire alarm interrupts fifth period.

The principal is furious. She had warned that if there was one more prank alarm, the students' break would be taken away from them. She feels sure the alarm is a prank, and she is steaming.

One of the math teachers feels frustrated. The class seemed to be catching on to a new concept and now the moment is lost.

One teacher is relieved; one of the students had intimidated him and the student was waiting for his reply. "Saved by the bell," the young teacher thought as he gathered his dignity and led the class out.

One student is angry: she was just beginning to know this new guy in the writing lab, and the stupid alarm went off. She may have lost her chance. The moment had been right to ask him about his weekend plans.

Another student is relieved. He hadn't read the homework assignment last night, and the government teacher was beginning a pop quiz.

The same event is seen through different eyes.

How could different persons view the following events?

❏   The bus is late.

❏   A surprise snowstorm hits town.

❏   The team loses the championship game.

Think of more events and how different people see them differently.

SIFTING THROUGH AN ARGUMENT

Objective: Students will understand how to use writing from another person's point of view to help them deal with their own conflicts.

Activities: 1. Ask students to think about a recent argument they have had with someone. (Assure students that they will not have to share this situation or their writing about it with the class or the teacher.)

2. Ask students to try to place themselves in the other person's position and write several sentences describing the situation from the other person's point of view.

3. Ask students to write a one- or two-page dialogue between the identified person and himself or herself. Begin the dialogue with the other person and discuss the issues involved in the argument.

4. Ask volunteers to share their reactions to this activity by asking the following questions.

   ❐ Has anyone's feelings changed? If so, how?

   ❐ Can the writing help you resolve the dispute?

   ❐ How can you use this tool to help yourself or help your friends resolve conflicts?

Section Five

COMMUNICATING
(Background Information)

COMMUNICATING
(Background Information)

In conflict management, communication is key. The alternatives to violence are really ways of communicating, and unfortunately, people are not born with the communication skills needed to use these alternatives. Students can learn to communicate effectively through frequent, consistent rehearsal as surely as baseball pitchers learn to pitch, ice skaters learn to spin on the ice, and writers learn to write through commitment, repetition, and practice.

Open-Ended Questions

Getting others to talk is an obvious place to begin communicating. Competent communicators are good listeners, and their first step involves looking interested and asking such open-ended questions as "What is happening?" or using open-ended statements such as "Tell me about it."

A closed question such as "How are things going at school?" is *closed* because someone can answer it with a word answer such as "OK," "miserable," or "good." In contrast, an open-ended question such as "What is happening?" or "What do you do when you have a miserable day?" begs a longer answer.

Encouraging responses such as gentle "uh-hum . . . really? . . .oh" keep the speaker talking because he or she will begin to feel heard.

Paraphrasing

To develop effective listening skills, paraphrasing is particularly important. When someone paraphrases, the listener repeats what he or she has heard in his or her own words. As a result, the listener gains the opportunity to reality check the accuracy of the listening. The listener can mentally ask, "Did I get it right?" Paraphrasing also benefits the speaker because when someone hears both thoughts and feelings paraphrased, he or she feels heard and the speaker is ready to communicate.

Paraphrasing content, or repeating the subject matter of what someone says, is important, but insufficient for complete listening. The listener must also hear the emotional content of the speaker. When the speaker hears both content and emotion paraphrased, the speaker thinks, "that person *really* heard me."

Imagine the following situation:

A teacher at Central High School hates seeing students leave their cafeteria tables dirty. She complains to an administrator, "That cafeteria table looks filthy."

If the administrator replies, "It is a mess," the administrator paraphrases content. If the administrator comments, "You are really disgusted," he or she is paraphrasing the teacher's feeling. The teacher would probably feel most accurately heard if the administrator paraphrased both content and feeling. The administrator might say, "Those dirty cafeteria tables really bother you." After feeling accurately heard, a disputant becomes more willing to explore ways to solve problems.

Summarizing, a form of paraphrasing, reflects content and feeling after a longer sequence during a conversation. The listener can summarize at the end of a conversation or at intervals to clarify the speaker's thoughts. This process helps the listener clarify his or her thoughts and reassures the speaker that he or she is being heard.

In teaching conflict resolution, paraphrasing can never be practiced too frequently. Because we think this skill is so essential as a prerequisite to problem solving and mediation, this section contains five separate lessons on the topic.

Laundering Language

When communicating with an angry person or when venting in the heat of anger, people use powerful words. Toning down the emotional intensity of a word in a paraphrase, particularly profanity, can help diffuse hostility. For example, when a speaker says, "That . . .turned this into a pigsty," the listener might paraphrase, "Her messiness really annoys you."

I Statements

No one would disagree that listening is important. We would all also agree that it is important to get others to listen, particularly when you are angry. An "I statement" or "I message" is an effective way to get someone to listen to you.

Suppose the administrator on duty in the cafeteria really feels annoyed when teachers are unwilling to pitch in and help get students to pick up their cafeteria trays. He or she has heard enough complaining from the teacher on duty for an entire career. The administrator might want to say, "You complain about those dirty tables, but you are never willing to help out." This "you statement" accuses the teacher and immediately places the teacher on the defensive. Instead, the administrator might say, "I feel frustrated when people don't help out because I want students to clean up after themselves too." In this way the administrator owns the negative feeling, does not accuse the teacher, and makes a statement the teacher is more likely to hear.

"I statements" are risky because they require careful word choice and sincere willingness to own a feeling. For example, the statements, "I get *furious* when teachers don't help out . . ." or "I get *amused* when teachers don't help out . . ." reflect inaccurate word choice. Because it is natural to want to accuse, rather than own anger, "I statements" can be difficult to use. When someone thinks an "I statement" is too risky in a particular situation, "I need . . ." might substitute. For example, the administrator might paraphrase the teacher and then say, "I need some help in getting these students to pick up their trays."

More than any other learned communication skills, "I statements" require practice. When used poorly, they can sound insincere and contrived. Used skillfully, they are powerful tools for getting others to listen to your point of view. They can diffuse anger and prepare others to listen carefully and resolve conflicts.

Nonverbal Communication

We communicate with more than speech alone. Eye contact, the position of eyebrows, the nod of the head, placement of hands, and the leaning of our body all communicate volumes. Someone can paraphrase beautifully, but the lack of eye contact will indicate failure to listen. Someone can say he or she accepts someone else's point of view, but arms folded tightly across the lap or a body tilted backward in a chair can really signal that the listener is either hostile or couldn't care less about the speaker's point of view.

Mixed messages resulting from conflicting verbal and nonverbal signals really block communication. What student would confide in a teacher or counselor who says, "I'd really like to hear about that," but who looks out of the window while talking to the student?

Cultural differences complicate reading nonverbal communication. We really cannot always assume what people mean by their nonverbal signals. For example, Europeans assume that poor eye contact signifies lack of interest or attention, but many Asians consider the lowering of the eyes a sign of respect.

The most effective way to teach effective nonverbal communication is to provide feedback on videotape. Watching yourself can be a valuable learning experience. Because students are sensitive about criticism, videotaping and student feedback should be carefully handled. When critiquing students, be sure to emphasize positive attributes, and then suggest ways to improve nonverbal communication through practice.

Handling Your Own Anger

When listening to and expressing emotion, anger frequently appears. This emotion is common, normal, but difficult to handle. It presents a challenge for both the angry person and either the person at whom the anger is directed or the person trying to help.

Students need to get in touch with what makes them angry, realize how they generally deal with anger, and explore other appropriate ways of expressing and dealing with anger.

Expressing anger is not always harmful. Sometimes people need to be assertive and explain how they feel. "I statements" are particularly useful when expressing anger. Before using the "I statement," saying something positive can help. For example, in "The Sweater" scenario (28-1), Ian might say to Ilene: "Ilene, you're a really nice person and you've been a good friend. When you wear my sweater I really get upset because people assume I'm two timing my girlfriend. We need to clear up this misunderstanding."

Anger can get out of hand. The most obvious reason for violence is anger, probably because anger is an expression of anxiety and fear and a response to a threat to one's basic psychological needs. We all need to practice stopping ourselves in the heat of anger and mentally saying, "Count to ten," or "Don't get defensive," or "Don't take it personally," or "Consider the source," or "Just let it go." People *can* learn to control their tempers.

Diffusing Anger in Others

The ability to diffuse anger in others with communication skills can help prevent conflict from escalating into violence. To deal with an angry person, it is useful to first let the person vent, then listen, paraphrasing both content and feeling, and then suggest working together to solve a problem. The procedure is almost formulaic:

❐ Listen: Let the angry person vent . . . don't argue.

❐ Relax: Deal with your own emotions . . . don't get defensive.

❐ Paraphrase content and feeling . . . make sure the other person knows you understand.

❐ Problem solve: explore what can be done to make things better

The difficulty with applying this formula is the tendency to get sucked into the emotion and react defensively. As a result, a person interacting with an angry person must beware of getting defensive and irritated. It is important to relax and avoid taking things personally.

The activities in this section can help students develop both verbal and nonverbal communication skills prerequisite to resolving conflict. By no means do they cover the vast topic of communication, but they focus on important concepts, and they can be repeated at various times in many settings.

26 **OPEN-ENDED QUESTIONS**

Objective: Students will understand the difference between open and closed questions.

Activities:
1. Explain the difference between open and closed questions, offering examples.

2. Divide the class into triads.

3. Instruct students in each triad to choose one of the following roles: helper, client, or observer.

4. Ask students in the "client" role to imagine themselves with a problem or concern.

5. Ask students in the "helper" role to try to get their "clients" to discuss their problem or concern. Ask "helpers" on one side of the room to use closed questions and ask "helpers" on the other side of the room to use open questions. (Allow about five minutes for this activity.)

6. Ask "helpers" who used the closed questions, "How did the 'clients' respond?"

7. Ask "helpers" who used the open questions, "How did the 'clients' respond?"

8. Ask "clients" and "observers" to offer their reactions to being asked open and closed questions.

9. Ask students in each triad to switch roles and practice using open questions. (Allow five minutes.)

10. Ask "clients" and "observers" to offer feedback to the "helpers."

11. Ask students to switch roles again and continue practicing the use of open questions.

12. Discuss the use of open questions. If confusion arises, ask students to role play situations in which one student encourages another to start talking. Then discuss the types of questions (open or closed) the student asks and their effects.

27 PARAPHRASING CONTENT AND FEELING

To the Teacher: This lesson plan begins with a demonstration of the activity so that students can more easily understand what to do. If time allows, students in the triads can switch roles so that all students have the experience of expressing something they feel strongly about, paraphrasing content, and paraphrasing feeling.

Objectives: Students will learn how to paraphrase.

Students will learn how to distinguish content from emotion and understand the importance of listening to both.

Activities: 1. Show students the "Paraphrase Chart" (27-1) by drawing it on the chalkboard, using it as a transparency, or by distributing copies.

2. Ask for two volunteers to demonstrate a role play with you.

3. Explain that paraphrasing is repeating what you have heard in your own words. Paraphrasing content requires rephrasing subject matter, and paraphrasing feeling identifies the emotion the speaker communicates.

4. Demonstrate a paraphrase activity in the following manner:
   a. Ask one student (C) to be prepared to paraphrase content; the other (F), feeling.
   b. Describe something about which you have strong feelings (e.g., "Five students tried to cut into the cafeteria line during lunch today.").
   c. Ask the other students in the group to paraphrase your comments as assigned. (C might say, "You saw five people cutting in the lunch line." E might say, "You really get annoyed about that.")
   d. Subdivide the class into triads and ask members of each triad to choose their roles: speaker, content paraphraser, or feeling paraphraser.

5. Ask the speakers in each triad to talk about something they feel strongly about to the two other students for two minutes.

6. Call time and ask the paraphrasers to take turns paraphrasing content and feeling according to their assignments.

7. Ask the speaker to give the paraphrasers feedback. Did they paraphrase correctly?. . . according to their assignment?

8. Ask paraphrasers to indicate by a show of hands how many felt most heard by the content paraphrase.

9. Ask paraphrasers to indicate how many felt most heard by the feeling paraphrase.

10. Discuss the need for paraphrasing both content and feeling.

PARAPHRASE CHART (27-1)

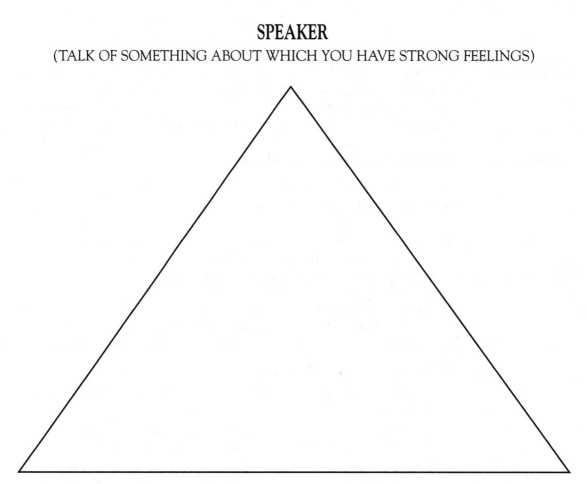

SPEAKER
(TALK OF SOMETHING ABOUT WHICH YOU HAVE STRONG FEELINGS)

CONTENT PARAPHRASER
(PARAPHRASE CONTENT)

FEELING PARAPHRASER
(PARAPHRASE FEELING)

Adapted from Jennifer Beer (1990), *Peacemaking in Your Neighborhood: Mediator's Handbook* (Philadelphia: Friends Suburban).

28   TAKING ANOTHER LOOK AT CONTENT AND FEELING

To the Teacher: In this activity a student paraphrasing Ian might say, "It really annoys you that she assumes you were her boyfriend." Paraphrasing Ilene, a student might say, "This misunderstanding is really humiliating." When students discuss how Ian and Ilene might handle their misunderstanding, they can also learn about ways to respond in difficult situations.

Objectives: Students will become aware of the need for paraphrasing both content and feeling.

Students will become more aware of their ability to respond appropriately in a difficult situation.

Activities: 1. Ask a volunteer to read the scenario "The Sweater" (28-1) to the class.

2. Instruct students to fill in the chart in the reproducible "Ian and Ilene" (28-2) while listening to the scenario being read.

3. Ask a girl to assume the role of Ilene and explain what happened.

4. Ask students to paraphrase "Ilene," paraphrasing both content and feeling.

5. Ask a boy to assume the role of Ian.

6. Ask students to paraphrase "Ian," paraphrasing both content and feeling.

7. Discuss the effect of the paraphrasing. Would paraphrasing be helpful to Ian and Ilene? How?

8. Discuss how Ian and Ilene might handle this situation.

SCENARIO:
THE SWEATER (28-1)

The problem started when Ian noticed Ilene shivering outside at break one day and he offered her his sweater. He always tried to be nice to Ilene; after all, she was his next-door neighbor, and her father was his boss.

Although all their times together had been group dates to the movies or to parties, Ilene hoped they were more than just good friends. And this sweater seemed to symbolize their being a couple. Finally, she had proof of how he really felt!

Ilene could hardly wait to get to school the next day. Everyone would see her in the sweater: in classes, at lunch, at after school practices, and at the games. And Jamie and Jody would be so envious!

The next week Ilene happily waltzed along wearing the sweater, and Ian didn't even seem to notice. They didn't get to see each other that week anyway.

Then one day at lunch, Ilene was horrified to hear her name practically shouted across the lunchroom. "What's this?" Ian blared out as he held the latest edition of the school newspaper. Several of Ian's friends were gathered behind him, smirking. Ilene's picture was plastered on the front page, and, of course, she was wearing Ian's letter sweater.

Ian waved the paper at Ilene and remarked, "Hey, Ilene. I wondered where I'd left that sweater. . . I thought it was in Jake's car. Any idea when I can have the sweater back? Hopefully before my girl comes home from college!"

Ilene felt humiliated. How dare Ian treat her like that, right in front of her friends! Besides, she had worn the sweater everywhere for three weeks now, and people would wonder if she just all of a sudden quit wearing it. What would she say? What could she say?

Name _____ Date _____ (28-2)

IAN AND ILENE

While listening to the scenario being read, fill in the chart below, differentiating between fact and feeling in what is said.

Fact   **Feeling**

If Ilene confided in you about this situation, what would you say?

If Ian confided in you about this situation, what would you say?

How might Ian and Ilene resolve their problem?

29   PARAPHRASING IN CONCENTRIC CIRCLES

To the Teacher: This activity allows students to hear different students paraphrase their own concerns and evaluate the relative effectiveness of the paraphrases.

Objective: Students will develop paraphrasing skills and begin to distinguish the subtle differences between various paraphrasing responses.

Activities:

1. Instruct students to form two concentric circles and pair up so that each student in the outer circle has a partner in the inner circle. If there is an odd number of students, have the extra student function as an observer.

2. Ask students in the inner circle to talk to their partners about something they feel strongly about for about two minutes.

3. Ask students in the outer circle to paraphrase the comments of their partners.

4. After one minute, instruct students in the outer circle to move one place to the right so that students have new partners.

5. Ask students in the inner circle to repeat the description of what they feel strongly about to their new partners.

6. Ask students in the outer circle to paraphrase the comments of their partners.

7. Ask students in the outer circle to move one place to the right and continue the same procedure until all of the students in the inner circle have expressed their concerns to each of their partners, who in turn have paraphrased all of the speakers in the inner circle.

8. Ask students in the inner circle to comment on their reactions to different student's paraphrases. Encourage them to use specific examples of good paraphrasing and its effect.

9. Switch inner and outer circles so that all students can have a chance to hear different students paraphrase them and everyone practices paraphrasing.

30 **PARAPHRASING IN A CIRCLE**

To the Teacher: Although this lesson uses the reproducible "More Paraphrases" (30-1) as a tool for the teacher, teachers can reproduce it and use it as a practice sheet or quiz for students. Practicing paraphrasing in a round, with each student taking a turn to practice with the entire group listening, sharpens the student's paraphrasing skill.

Objective: Students will refine paraphrasing skills.

Activities:
1. Arrange students in a circle.

2. Read each of the statements in "More Paraphrases" and have students take turns paraphrasing each statement after you read it.

3. After each round ask students to choose particularly good paraphrases.

4. Review paraphrasing as a restatement of both content and feeling in your own words.

MORE PARAPHRASES

1. I am so sick of waiting for Tammy that I could scream.

   _____

   _____

2. Terea really thinks she's something! She's always flirting with the guys at the end cafeteria table. She turns my stomach!

   _____

   _____

3. My dad is such an absolute pain. He screams at everything I do. I can never get anything right.

   _____

   _____

4. That English teacher is always picking on me. . . hassle this. . . hassle that. If she doesn't leave me alone, she better watch out!

   _____

   _____

5. I wish he'd shut up. He thinks he knows everything and can monopolize every class discussion we have.

   _____

   _____

6. I shouldn't have told Terri what Anie said. Now everyone will know and Anie will hit the roof. When Anie finds out, she'll come looking for me.

   _____

   _____

7. I'll never be able to catch up. Chemistry is beyond me. I don't even know where to begin. It's over my head.

   _____

   _____

8. I don't know what to do. But if I break one more date with Tim, he's going to dump me, I just know it. But I've got so much to do on finishing my college applications.

   _____

   _____

9. He thinks he is so. . . so whatever, by wearing fishnet hose and a red nose ring. What is he trying to prove? That he's a freak? Well, I won't give him the pleasure of watching him. That's all he wants.

   _____

   _____

10. My mom thinks she's up on what kids wear. She insists on picking out my clothes and they're ugly! She's driving me nuts!

    _____

    _____

11. It really bugs me when people just follow along with the crowd just to follow along, even when they know what they're doing is wrong.

    _____

    _____

12. It was only midnight and that little jerk said he wanted to go to sleep and ruin all our fun at the sleepover. What a twerp!

    _____

    _____

13. Those teachers always gang up on you. They must get their jollies from piling on homework and giving tests on the same day. They must love it when we get bad grades.

    _____

    _____

14. If those guys don't stop picking on me, I'm going to scream!!!

    _____

    _____

SUMMARIZING

Objective: Students will practice summarizing skills.

Activities:

1. Arrange students in a large circle.

2. Begin describing a day in the life of a fictional student (e.g., "Lane missed his bus and showed up in math class ten minutes late this morning. . .").

3. Ask each student in the circle to take turns, continuing the narrative by adding on to the fictional day of the student.

4. Stop every fifth student and ask him or her to summarize the story.

5. Ask students to suggest possible opening statements they might use to summarize a lengthy conversation with a friend.

6. Distribute the reproducible "Summarizing" (31-1) and ask students to add additional opening statements.

7. Ask two students to volunteer to role play a five-minute conversation in front of the room.

8. Ask other volunteers to summarize the conversation, beginning with an appropriate opening statement.

9. Ask students to practice summary skills before the next class meeting and be prepared to discuss their experiences.

SUMMARIZING

Summarizing is really a form of paraphrasing. To summarize, the listener reflects the content and feeling of what the speaker has said until this point. The summary helps clarify what has been said and assures the speaker that the listener is paying attention.

The listener can use summarizing at the end of a conversation or at any time a speaker gets stuck or needs clarification.

The following are possible opening statements for summaries:

"What I hear you saying is. . ."

"Let me see if I heard you correctly. . ."

"So far you have said several things: first, . . . second, . . ."

_____

_____

_____

_____

_____

_____

_____

32 **TONING IT DOWN**

To the Teacher: People in conflict frequently use profanity. It is useful to help students deal with this issue so that they can tone down the language and anger it reflects.

Objective: Students will learn how to apply paraphrasing skills to lessen a speaker's emotional intensity.

Activities:
1. Ask students how they think they would deal with students who rant and rave and use profanity.

2. Distribute the handout "Laundering Language" (32-1).

3. Divide students into pairs and have them practice reading the statements and paraphrasing them without the use of profanity.

4. Ask readers to volunteer feedback regarding the effectiveness of the paraphrasers.

5. Ask volunteers to offer examples of effective paraphrases.

LAUNDERING LANGUAGE

1. I hate that Birdie! She called me the B word again and I'm not going to take it anymore!

   _____

   _____

2. He's nothing but a f.....liar! I never said that and I don't have to listen to that garbage.

   _____

   _____

3. That teacher is a no good.......He's really out to get me!

   _____

   _____

4. That two timing no good Beth! She said she'd go to the prom with me, and now I see her winding herself around that stupid Ben!

   _____

   _____

5. I can't believe that no good Ina blabbed all of that garbage to her nosy loud mouth friends! Now I won't be able to even show up in the cafeteria!

   _____

   _____

33   **I AND YOU STATEMENTS**

Objectives: Students will understand how and why to formulate an "I statement."

Students will increase their vocabulary of words that express feelings.

Activities:

1. Divide the class into triads and distribute the role plays so that each student in the triad has one third of the handout (33-1).

2. Ask the students with the "Speaker" sections of the role play (33-1) to read their scripts to their group members.

3. Ask the students with the "You" roles to read their scripts, responding to the speakers.

4. Ask students with the "I" roles to read their scripts, responding to the speakers.

5. Discuss the probable consequences of the "You" and the "I" scripts. Which is more effective and why?

6. Show the transparency "I Statements" (33-2) and explain how to formulate an "I statement."

7. Ask volunteers to formulate an "I statement" they might use with someone who cuts in front of them in the cafeteria line (e.g., "When you get in front of me, I feel angry because I need to get to class early.").

8. Distribute the handout "Feeling Words" (33-3) and explain how increasing the choice of feeling words can help students express themselves.

9. Ask students to complete the work sheet "Sorting Out Feelings" (33-4).

10. Ask students to volunteer situations in which they felt angry at someone.

11. Ask volunteers to suggest "I statements" they might use in those situations.

12. Ask students to practice "I statements" when they are appropriate before the class meets again.

ROLE PLAY:
I/YOU (33-1)

Situation: The speaker is a member of a group working on a major social studies project which is due on Monday. The speaker has never shown up for the evening meetings because other things always come up. The other members attend regularly in spite of other commitments. One of the other group members has reminded the speaker to attend this afternoon's important meeting.

SPEAKER:

I'll try to come to the meeting tonight, but I don't know whether I can make it.

YOU:

You always find other things to do. You never show up for meetings, and you aren't contributing a thing to our project. You aren't being fair!

I:

When you don't come to meetings, I get upset because we need your contribution to produce a good project and a grade that is fair to all of us.

I STATEMENTS (33-2)

I FEEL _____

WHEN YOU_____

BECAUSE_____

(AND I WANT)

I feel worried when you don't show up after a party because I am afraid you might get into a situation you can't handle and I don't want you to get into trouble.

When you don't show up for our group meetings, I feel upset because I want you to contribute to the group project and I want everyone to get a fair grade.

FEELING WORDS (33-3)

WORDS EXPRESSING ANGER

I feel . . .

aggravated	annoyed	bitter	cranky	riled
appalled	disgusted	dismayed	horrified	nauseated
enraged	exasperated	frustrated	furious	hostile
incensed	infuriated	irritated	outraged	provoked
offended	repulsed	revolted	ticked off	wary
resentful	steamed	troubled	upset	vicious

HAPPINESS

amused	blissful	charmed	cheerful	contented
delighted	ecstatic	elated	excited	fabulous
fortunate	giddy	glad	gratified	high
joyous	jubilant	marvelous	pleased	proud
soothed	thrilled	tickled	turned-on	wonderful

HURT

abused	awful	betrayed	devalued	terrible
crippled	diminished	deflated	forgotten	put down
deprived	deserted	dreadful	intimidated	oppressed
damaged	rotten	insulted	neglected	slighted
ignored	isolated	jilted	defeated	
snubbed	upset	cheated	persecuted	

INADEQUACY

helpless	incapable	incompetent	inadequate	inept
inferior	powerless	useless	unworthy	mediocre

FEELING WORDS (33-3)
(continued)

EMBARRASSMENT

absurd	foolish	awkward	mortified	clumsy
conspicuous	disgraced	silly	uncomfortable	humiliated

CONFUSION

addled	baffled	bewildered	confused	rattled
distracted	dumbfounded	flabbergasted	flustered	jarred
jolted	muddled	mystified	perplexed	puzzled
rattled	anxious	disconcerted	dazed	frustrated

SADNESS

anguished	blue	burdened	dejected	depressed
despondent	disappointed	discouraged	disheartened	downcast
heavy hearted	gloomy	let down	low	melancholy
abandoned	alone	deserted	empty	excluded
lonely	friendless	ignored	isolated	jilted
scorned	lost	rejected	pathetic	slighted
miserable	moody	pained	troubled	weary

FEAR

afraid	boxed in	cornered	fearful	frightened
jittery	jumpy	nervous	panicky	scared
shaken	spooked	terrified	threatened	agitated
uneasy	unnerved	overwhelmed	alarmed	worried

SORTING OUT FEELINGS

To the Student: Look at the following lists of feelings and place them in the appropriate categories below.

amused	tickled	outraged	excited	resentful
cruel	joyous	isolated	elated	aggravated
proud	bitter	pathetic	sad	oppressed
glad	furious	scorned	lost	irritated
vicious	cheery	steamed	jubilant	infuriated
devalued	ignored	desperate	frenzied	cheated
cranky	jealous	terrible	agitated	blissful
content	fantastic	angry	hostile	forsaken
happy	deserted	high	ecstatic	slighted
elated	indignant	awful	delighted	incensed
trapped	charmed	upset	hassled	terrible
enraged	abused	calm	beautiful	turned-on
deprived	pleased	giddy	dreadful	inept
frenzied	thrilled	dismal	snubbed	empty
soothed	annoyed	rotten	rejected	bored

anger_____

belittlement_____

disgust_____

embarrassment_____

fear_____

happiness_____

hurt_____

loneliness_____

sadness_____

34 **DELIVERING I STATEMENTS**

Objective: Students will develop skill in using "I statements."

Activities: 1. Seat students in a large circle.

2. Discuss students' experiences with "I statements" at school or at home.

3. Distribute the reproducible "Scenarios" (34-1).

4. In a round ask students to express "I statements" they might use if they were in the situation described in the first scenario on the handout.

5. Ask students to provide feedback about the "I statements."

6. Repeat the activity for the other scenarios on the handout.

7. Assign a journal writing about students' use of "I statements."

SCENARIOS
A–F (34-1)

Imagine yourself in the following situations, and respond, using an "I statement."

A.

Your friend had promised to meet you in front of the local shopping center a half hour ago. This friend is always late, and you've had it. Here comes the friend, looking as if he or she has all the time in the world. You are really annoyed.

B.

Your girlfriend/boyfriend always seems to be flirting with other people at parties. She/he hardly seems to pay any attention to you and it's getting very aggravating.

C.

Every time you take an algebra test Chase develops cross-eyed vision! Chase's eyes always wander over to your paper. And now Chase has the nerve to ask to look at your algebra homework before class. You just know Chase will simply copy it.

D.

That Jody is simply jealous. Jody told the group that you cheated and went out with someone else behind Sam's back, and it isn't true. Jody said terrible things about you, and you are going to talk to Jody right now!

E.

Mom is always picking out your clothes, and she doesn't have any idea about what's cool. You really wish she'd quit doing this to you.

F.

For the third time in a month your sister has borrowed a shirt from your closet without asking. This business is getting old.

35 NONVERBAL COMMUNICATION

To the Teacher: Noticing nonverbal cues is important, but difficult because one can't always assume what a gesture means. Different people sometimes interpret the cues differently. Cultural differences complicate nonverbal communication too. For example, eyes lowered suggest lack of attention or insecurity to most Americans, but most Asians lower their eyes as a sign of respect.

Objective: Students will become more aware of nonverbal cues.

Activities:

1. Ask students to stand in two concentric circles, with the members of the inner circle pairing with members of the outer circle.

2. Ask students in the outer circle to express an emotion without using words. Then ask their partners to identify the emotion expressed.

3. Have students in the outer circle move one space to the right, thus forming new pairs.

4. Repeat the exercise for a few rounds.

5. Discuss examples of nonverbal communication.

6. Distribute the reproducible "Nonverbal Communication" (35-1) and discuss it with the class.

7. Distribute the reproducible "Reading Nonverbal Cues" (35-2) and give students a few minutes to write responses.

8. Discuss responses to the nonverbal cues. Do students in the class agree? Which nonverbal cues do students interpret differently? To what extent do cultural values influence body language?

9. Assign a journal writing about student's personal responses to and awareness of their own nonverbal communication.

NONVERBAL COMMUNICATION (35-1)

If you are at ease, confident, . . .

your hands might be folded, limp on your lap or on a flat surface.

you might have a smile.

your body would be relaxed, possibly tilted forward toward the speaker.

eye contact would be direct, yet not staring with both eyebrows possibly lifted, and head possibly tilted forward.

If you are uptight, anxious, . . .

your hands could be clenched. You might tap on a table or clutch something tightly.

you might grimace or have tightly pursed lips.

you might fidget, pull at your hair, or perhaps scratch or rub your nose.

If you are angry, . . .

your eyes could be squinting.

one eyebrow might raise.

your hands might crunch into fists or flail around.

your body might be generally stiff or rigid.

If you feel bored, uninterested, . . .

your total body might be slumped over.

your arms might be folded across your chest in a closed position.

READING NONVERBAL CUES

How would you interpret the following body language?

1. Drumming fingers on a desk

_____

2. Leaning forward in a chair

_____

3. Crossing arms tightly

_____

4. Pointing a finger at you

_____

5. Shrugging shoulders

_____

6. Lowering eyes when spoken to

_____

7. Pulling at ears or hair

_____

8. Slapping one's forehead with the heel of one's hand

_____

MIXED MESSAGES

Objective: Students will become aware of mixed messages and the importance of consistency in communication.

Activities:

1. Ask students to share examples of insincere communication they have observed.

2. Ask students what made them think the communication was insincere.

3. Explain that mixed messages often signal insincerity.

4. Distribute the reproducible "Noticing Mixed Messages" (36-1) and ask students to complete it.

5. Ask students to demonstrate responses for the items on the reproducible.

6. Discuss the effects of mixed messages.

NOTICING MIXED MESSAGES

To the Student: Look at the following statements. What would your body language be if you *really* meant the following statements?

What would your body language be if you really didn't mean what you were saying?

How would your voice tone vary?

Forget it. I'm not mad anymore.

_____

_____

Look, that's all I know. That's the truth.

_____

_____

It's okay. Of course. Sure, I understand.

_____

_____

I'm sorry. I really feel bad about the whole thing.

_____

_____

I'm just as upset as you are about what happened.

_____

_____

You can do it. I know you can.

_____

_____

NOTICING MIXED MESSAGES
(Continued)

That's great. Yeah, wow, I'm really excited for you.

_____

_____

No, it's okay. I'm not really scared of heights.

_____

_____

Wow, that's quite a surprise.

_____

_____

Sure, I'll be glad to take your shift at work.

_____

_____

No, I don't mind if you take Jessica home after work. Why should that bother me?

_____

_____

I feel great. Just great.

_____

_____

37 **COMMUNICATION BLOCKERS**

Objective: Students will learn about communication blockers and develop an understanding of their effect.

Activities: 1. Write the following words on the chalkboard: *advise, argue, order, interrupt, threaten, criticize, analyze, use sarcasm.*

2. Assign these behaviors as roles to students in designated rows or sections of the class (Students in row 1 will argue; students in row 2 will give orders, etc.).

3. Ask a student to stand in front of the class and express a concern or explain a problem (e.g., what to tell my parents about my bad grades or what to do when my parents find out I didn't go to the movies like I said I did).

4. Ask students to respond according to their assigned roles.

5. Ask the student presenting the problem how he or she felt about the blockers.

6. Discuss how people block communication.

38 DEALING WITH YOUR OWN ANGER

To the Teacher: This lesson can be divided into several lessons. Let students know that expressing anger can be useful. Before using an "I statement" to express anger, saying something positive can help. Positive self-talk can help students become less defensive.

Objective: Students will understand how to deal with their own anger in more effective ways.

Activities:

1. Distribute two reproducible "Anger Logs" (38-1) and have students fill in one of them.

2. Subdivide the class into small groups and have students share: What makes them angry? How do they react to anger? How do they deal with different degrees of anger? (Students should have the right to pass.)

3. Discuss typical ways students handle moderate anger, developing a list on the chalkboard.

4. Discuss typical ways students handle extreme anger, developing a list on the chalkboard.

5. Discuss which of the techniques are fair or unfair. (To get at appropriateness, ask, "What are the consequences of this behavior?")

6. Ask volunteers to present a situation that someone in the group has described as causing extreme anger. (Request that the person offering the situation not be identified.)

7. Brainstorm ways to effectively handle this situation.

8. Review "I statements" and ask students to demonstrate the use of an "I statement" to deal with the given situation.

9. Brainstorm other ways of dealing with anger (e.g., mental self-talk, writing a letter to be ripped up, punching a pillow, running around the block) and add to the sample list of fair ways to handle anger.

10. Distribute scenarios (39-3) and ask students in small groups to discuss ways to appropriately handle the situation if they were Marge, Frank or Maureen.

11. Ask spokespersons from each group to summarize ideas.

12. Assign students the task of filling in a second "Anger Log" based on experiences during the next week for a follow-up lesson.

ANGER LOG

1. Briefly describe a recent situation in which you were really angry.

   _____

   _____

   How did you deal with it?

   _____

   _____

2. Briefly describe a recent situation in which you were extremely angry.

   _____

   _____

   How did you deal with it?

   _____

   _____

3. What usually makes you angry?

   _____

   _____

4. How do you usually deal with anger?

   _____

   _____

5. Might there be a better way to handle your anger? If so, please describe how you might handle your anger more appropriately.

   _____

   _____

DIFFUSING SOMEONE ELSE'S ANGER

Objective: Students will learn how to diffuse anger.

Activities:

1. Ask students what they do when others express anger.

2. Distribute the reproducible "Diffusing Anger" (39-1).

3. Ask students to share in small groups how they control their own emotional reactions to the anger of others.

4. Ask spokespersons to share some ways of relaxing and avoiding becoming defensive.

5. Distribute the reproducible "Avoiding the Defensive Trap" (39-2).

6. Discuss experiences students may have had with the approaches suggested.

7. Subdivide class into groups of four and ask two students in each group to practice a role play, one person expressing anger; the other, diffusing the anger. The remaining students should take notes and offer feedback.

8. Distribute scenarios (39-3) for students in the groups. Students should discuss how Howie, Rudy and Phillis might diffuse anger, if Marge, Frank and Maureen lose their temper.

9. Ask observers to present observations to the class.

DIFFUSING ANGER (39-1)

❑ *LISTEN:* Let the angry person vent . . .
don't argue.

❑ *RELAX:* Deal with your own emotions . . .
don't get defensive.

❑ *PARAPHRASE* content and feeling . . . make sure
the other person knows you understand.

❑ *PROBLEM SOLVE:* What can be done to make
things better?

Count to ten . . . Tell yourself, "Don't get defensive." . . . Think: "Don't take this personally!" . . . Tell yourself, "Consider the source . . . it's not worth getting upset." . . . Think about how you might feel in the other person's shoes . . . Ask yourself, "Just what is your problem?" . . . Think,"I'm OK and I don't have to defend myself" . . . take a deep breath . . . picture a calm scene . . . pick out a positive feature of the angry person and focus on it . . . figure out what the purpose of the hostility really is . . . find the humor in the situation . . . "LET IT GO!!!"

SCENARIOS:
HANDLING ANGER (39-3)

Marge had really tried to be Howie's friend, but sometimes it was just too much. Howie's so obnoxious, especially around females, calling them names, patting them on their butts in PE class.

Marge asked, "Howie, why do you say those things?"

Howie responded, "You're so cute when you get angry. . . . What's the matter, babe?"

The word "babe" did it. Marge was absolutely furious.

Frank was steaming. His brother Rudy had gone off with the car they shared when he had promised Frank he would take a bus to work today.

Rudy knew that Frank really needed the car to pick up Sally at 2. To make matters worse, Frank couldn't get to Sally's house without a car if he tried.

How could Rudy be so mean?

Maureen really resented her younger sister Phyllis. Phyllis was always borrowing Maureen's clothes. No matter what Maureen said, Phyllis just helped herself to whatever blouse she liked in Maureen's closet.

Unfortunately, Phyllis was the "pretty one" and always received compliments for Maureen's clothes. Whenever Maureen saw Phyllis beaming about the compliments, Maureen burned.

This morning there were no clean blouses left in Maureen's closet as Phyllis slammed the front door to leave for school.

Maureen couldn't wait to catch up with Phyllis and have it out with her.

Section Six

COLLABORATIVE PROBLEM SOLVING
(Background Information)

COLLABORATIVE PROBLEM SOLVING
(Background Information)

Collaborative problem solving involves cooperation rather than competition and produces a positive solution for all parties. An ideal solution to a problem is one in which every party wins. For example, the family arguing about where to eat dinner may eventually decide to go to a popular pizza parlor where the teenager who hates tomatoes can order white pizza and the family member on a diet can order a salad without dressing.

Like the scientific method, collaborative problem solving is a structured process that involves defining a problem, brainstorming possible solutions, and choosing a solution.

Define the Problem

First, problem solvers must *define the problem* they seek to solve. Is the family argument about which restaurant to choose a simple problem of conflicting tastes in cuisine? Or is the problem more complicated? Perhaps the parents have sided with one teenager who wants to go to a restaurant frequented by a particular group or who wants to get dressed up. Suppose the other teenager is angry because he or she thinks the other sibling always gets parental support? Or perhaps the angry teenager associates the restaurant with a particular group of people with whom he or she doesn't want to be identified. Or might the problem be something else?

The problem solver needs to evaluate the size of the problem. Is it too large to tackle? Or is it too narrow? If the problem is too large, it is useful to split it into manageable parts and deal with the least complicated section first. If the family restaurant dispute is complicated and indicative of an ongoing battle, it might be useful to separate the issues and, for one night, focus on preferences for types of restaurants or how to deal with a situation where two family members refuse to sit together. In this way the family will feel they have progressed and be more willing to solve other problems.

Sometimes the problem is too narrow. Suppose the argument about the restaurant is only one example of constant bickering between two siblings and parental favoritism. Perhaps a perception of parental favoritism is the problem, and various arguments related to parental favoritism can be combined and addressed.

When defining problems, it is useful to identify the needs of the disputing parties. What do they want? What do they need? The basic needs of identify, security, recognition, fairness, and control play their role in a dispute about a restaurant dispute just as they do in most conflicts.

Generate a "How to" Statement

After the disputants define a problem, look at the problem and ask, "How might we . . . ?" The questions depend on the definition of the problem. For example, in the family restaurant feud, one might ask, "How might we find a restaurant where everyone can order something he or she likes to eat?" or "How might we find a place where the music isn't going to bother someone?" or "How might we have a peaceful evening in a restaurant?" The "How to Statement" should rephrase the issues defined and address how the needs of the disputants can be met.

Brainstorm Possible Solutions

Without evaluating ideas, problem solvers should generate numerous possible solutions. In developing solutions, consider the following approaches:

❒ *Expand the Possibilities.* Example: Add different kinds of restaurants.

❒ *Consider Rotating.* Example: This month, the family will pick an Italian restaurant, and next month they will go to a Greek restaurant.

❒ *Reduce Someone's Pain.* Example: Reduce Dad's pain by agreeing to sit away from him if you insist on eating with your fingers.

❒ *Combine Options.* Example: If the kids hate sitting still, and the parents want to eat in a restaurant, choose one with a playground or crayons and paper placemats as well as good food.

Choose an Alternative

After exploring possibilities, begin evaluating them and choose an option that will meet everyone's needs. It is important to ask, "What will happen . . . how will everyone feel . . . if we do this?"

Develop a Follow-up Plan

For a solution to stick, explore implementation plans. If the family decides on a monthly procedure for selecting a restaurant and agrees not to start arguments during dinner, the family members need to address what will happen if someone begins bickering before or during the evening. "What if . . ." is the important question to explore. To really solve a problem, plan implementation, monitoring, and updating procedures. Address the following questions: How will we check to see whether the plan is working? If not, when, how, and where will we meet to reevaluate our plan?

Necessary Conditions

To solve a problem collaboratively, the parties involved need to be committed to the problem-solving process. Unfortunately, not all people are interested in solving problems. If family members do not want to resolve the family restaurant conflict, it could conceivably be unresolvable. In order to collaborate, family members must be willing to deal with the problem, get beyond the win-lose idea, and provide an opportunity for all parties to save face. Trust and the ability to be rational are also necessary.

Sometimes people can be convinced to be reasonable. Although the win-lose idea sometimes dies hard, people can frequently accept the notion that solutions are in their best interest. Total alienation cannot be converted to trust, but relationships are often important enough to motivate people to seek solutions to problems. Whatever is behind the restaurant problem, family members usually really care about their relationships with one another. In the scenario "Antoine and Francisco" (41-1), the lack of trust seems to block any hope of exploring alternatives to violence. Yet if Antoine and Francisco could listen to each other and really explore their points of view, they might begin to see common interests and develop the trust that is prerequisite to dealing with problems. Even in the *Carmen* story in this section (44-1), Carmen and Don José probably share an interest in staying alive. Carmen is not interested in solving problems; she is interested only in stirring up trouble. However, Don José does have other interests. He might be convinced that Carmen's affairs are always short, and he doesn't have to buy into her schemes.

Implications

Collaborative problem solving offers endless creative solutions. With increased input from several group members, possibilities can increase. In the courts judges have offered creative sentences. For example, a judge in Washington State turned over two teenagers convicted of assault and robbery to a Native American tribal court, which proposed banishing them to a southeast Alaskan island with tools and a few week's provisions. After considering this recommendation, the judge had the teenagers released from jail, examined by a physician, and flown to the Alaskan island. In many areas the police department, school administrators, and community groups have collaborated to address difficult problems of school violence and created excellent programs. Similarly, communities have collaborated to resolve conflicts about many issues from swimming pool use to enforcing leash laws. Although all problems cannot be solved, the possibilities for creative problem solving are limitless.

This section provides students with the opportunity to practice problem solving with different kinds of material. The scenarios are also useful for teacher in-service training to facilitate better problem-solving procedures.

COOPERATION VERSUS COMPETITION: ROPE AND SQUARE

To the Teacher: This activity requires a large open space, masking tape, and two ropes tied together in the center or joined by a carabiner. With the masking tape draw a three-foot square on the floor. Place the carabiner in the center of the square with the ropes extended through the corners of the square. The object of this game is for the teams to get to the opposite corner without letting their own team members into the square. If students communicate and collaborate, they can walk around the square, holding their rope and reach their destinations. In this way every team can win.

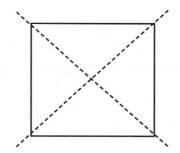

Objective: Students will understand that a win-win can result from collaborative problem solving.

Activities: 1. Subdivide the class into four teams, and line up each team next to the rope behind each corner.

2. Tell students the purpose of this activity is to see which team can reach the opposite corner within ten minutes. The rules are as follows:

a. Students may not let go of the rope.

b. Team members may not allow their own members into the square.

3. Give the students a signal to begin.

4. Process the activity by asking the following questions:

Which approach was more effective: competition or cooperation? Why? Was there collaboration? If so, how did it help? Can you think of examples of how you have solved problems and helped produce success for everyone in another setting?

UNDERSTANDING PROBLEM-SOLVING PREREQUISITES

Tips for the Teacher: This activity offers an opportunity to review learning in Section I (Defining Conflict) and Section V (Communicating). Questioning the characters about what the problem really is, paraphrasing, and diffusing anger are relevant skills.

Objectives: Students will understand the conditions required for collaborative problem solving.

Students will begin to develop problem solving skills by finding ways to encourage others to consider alternatives to violence.

Activities:
1. Distribute the reproducible "Antoine and Francisco" (41-1).

2. Ask students if Antoine and Francisco are likely to find alternatives to fighting. Why not?

3. Ask students to suggest conditions required for collaborative problem solving and develop a list.

4. Using the reproducible "Collaborative Problem-Solving Requirements" (41-2) as an overhead transparency, share commonly accepted conditions, compare them with the student-generated list, and discuss (e.g., If someone says something irrational, does that mean the person necessarily lacks the ability to be rational?).

5. Brainstorm ways of encouraging these young men to find alternatives to fighting.

6. Role play conversations with each of these characters.

ANTOINE AND FRANCISCO

Antoine sat sullenly in the corner of the room, seemingly trying to slink right into the wall. Francisco sat as if his whole body had been starched. His face was rigid and cold.

Francisco yelled, "Your older brother hit my little cousin. If he hadn't been driving so fast, that wouldn't have happened. What'd you have to say for yourself?"

Antoine retorted, "Look, man, I didn't do it! Why you got your people comin' after ME? Let the law take care of it."

"Yeah, right. The law . . . I don't have time for the law. Here my cousin's hurtin' in the hospital and you sit there all dumb and happy. I ought to . . ."

Antoine became furious. "What do you mean, dumb and happy? I'll take you down right now and. . ."

A fist fight was about to occur.

— REVIEWING SKILLS —

What is the problem?

If you were Antoine, how might you deal with Francisco?

If you had a chance to speak with Francisco, how might you help diffuse his anger?

COLLABORATIVE PROBLEM-SOLVING
REQUIREMENTS (41-2)

WILLINGNESS TO DEAL WITH THE PROBLEM

WILLINGNESS TO GET BEYOND THE WIN-LOSE IDEA

OPPORTUNITY TO SAVE FACE

TRUST

ABILITY TO BE RATIONAL

SOLVING PROBLEMS: DEFINING, EXPLORING, CHOOSING

Objective: Students will understand the collaborative problem-solving process.

Activities: 1. Distribute the reproducible "Collaborative Problem-Solving Process" (42-1) and discuss.

2. Distribute scenarios "Speaker" (42-2) and "Retreat" (42-3) and ask students to write responses.

3. Discuss responses.

4. Distribute the reproducible "Elections" (42-4).

5. Acknowledge that no administrator can allow discrimination in an election campaign.

6. Subdivide the class into small groups and ask them to find a solution to the problem of community animosity and prejudice using the collaborative problem-solving approach.

7. Ask spokespersons from each group to describe their solution and comment on their process.

COLLABORATIVE PROBLEM-SOLVING PROCESS (42-1)

Define the Problem:

❒ What *is* the problem?

❒ How complex is the problem?
  – Can it be subdivided?
  – Can it be combined with other problems?

❒ What basic psychological needs are involved?

Generate a "How to" Statement:

❒ Rephrase the problem and ask "How might we . . ."

Brainstorm Possible Solutions:

❒ Expand the possibilities.

❒ Consider rotating.

❒ Reduce someone's pain.

❒ Combine options.

Choose an Alternative.

Develop a Follow-up Plan.

SCENARIO:
SPEAKER

Dan and Kim are responsible for getting a speaker for the school service banquet. Dan wants everyone to have a good time and would like to engage his neighbor Mr. Cain, a stand-up comedian who is well known for his off-color jokes. Kim is sensitive about possible criticism of poor taste. Besides, community service is a serious endeavor, and her uncle, Mr. Humane, is well respected for his inspirational speeches, which Kim thinks will appropriately commend the service-oriented students. They are both absolutely convinced that their choice is the only one.

What is the problem?_____

_____

_____

      from Dan's point of view?_____

      _____

      from Kim's point of view?_____

      _____

Write a "How to" statement._____

_____

_____

Brainstorm several possible solutions._____

_____

Choose one solution and explain why you would choose this alternative._____

_____

Jot notes about a possible follow-up plan._____

_____

© 1996 by Ruth Perlstein and Gloria Thrall

Name _____   Date _____ (42-3)

SCENARIO:
RETREAT

Steve and Houng are presidents-elect of the student government and the senior class, respectively. Their sponsors have assigned them the task of suggesting a site for a summer student leadership retreat. The PTA has had a huge, successful fund-raising drive and can provide for a four-day retreat, including ample funding for rooms (four students sharing a room) and food. Picking a place for the retreat seems like a dream assignment, but Steve and Houng couldn't be more annoyed with each other. Steve loves the beach. He thinks the beach is the perfect place for team-building exercises and bonding. Besides, the group will need breaks and he loves to swim. But Houng really wants the group to have their retreat in the mountains. He thinks hiking activities are great team builders and the mountains would provide the best environment for group bonding. The sponsors would accept both ideas, but Steve and Houng must recommend one place. What can they do?

What is the problem?_____

_____

_____

Write a "How to" statement._____

_____

_____

Brainstorm several possible settings for a leadership retreat that will satisfy both Steve and Houng.

_____

_____

Choose one solution and explain your choice._____

_____

_____

What follow-up procedures need to be considered?_____

_____

_____

SCENARIO:
ELECTIONS (42-4)

For the first time in many years it seemed everyone was excited about the student government elections. Teachers, parents, even the students were talking about how many people were involved in the campaigns. Previous apathy seemed to have disappeared and in its place, a healthy competitive spirit had taken over . . . that is, until someone put up those ugly posters about Jeff, a Native American running for student body president.

"I don't understand," Jeff said as he sat with his counselor. "Calling me names. I'm as much a regular guy as everyone else. Why me?"

It was a good question. And the problem was that the issue was tearing the whole school apart. Everyone denied involvement in the smear campaign, but the posters still kept appearing as quickly as the administrators took them down, until one night someone got caught.

"You punish me and there's gonna be a big problem in this school. A BIG problem." Nick's voice was almost threatening, but the administrator sat still, amazed that it was Nick who had been behind the whole smear campaign.

"Nick, whatever possessed you?"

"We had a great school here until all these minorities started taking over. Ask my dad about it. He talks about when he went here and there were NO minorities. Just us. Now it's bad enough we have to go school with them. But SGA president? No way. I don't think so. And if there is . . ."

"Nick, don't feel so free with those threats. They work both ways. Now you've got the Native American population in our community all riled up, and they are as angry and threatening to you as you are toward them. This thing can get totally out of hand."

43 FINDING MORE WIN-WINS

To the Teacher:

This lesson plan can be repeated, using the Industrial Plant (43-1 and 43-2) role plays for one lesson, the Tip Top Peak role plays (43-3 and 43-4) for the second lesson, and Auditorium Hall Mural role plays (43-5 and 43-6) for a third lesson. If time does not allow for three separate lessons, distribute different role plays to different groups and have the groups explain their problem-solving process in a group presentation.

An ideal solution for the Industrial Plant problem is the joint purchase of the Voltaire estate by the power and chemical companies. The chemical company can use and process the water for its chemical needs and return it for use in generating power. Another solution might be to move the chemical plant somewhere else if the power plant promises to employ the personnel who don't want to move with the chemical plant.

The following are some possible solutions to the real estate problem: community purchase and management of the mountain; an agreement that the home-owners will help market the new lots if the developer keeps the trees and builds on side roads; creating a profitable resort attraction on an adjacent area and limiting development.

Students might solve the mural problem by changing $1 + 1 = 2$ to $a + bx = c$ or $E = mc^2$, removing the mural and asking the artist to display it elsewhere, or creating additional murals. This simulation works well with small groups.

Objective:

Students will develop more insight into the collaborative problem-solving process.

Activities:

1. Divide the class into pairs and explain that pairs will participate in a problem solving exercise. The mural scenarios can also be assigned to small groups of three or four.

2. Distribute role plays to students. Each pair should have one student with an "A" role and another student with a "B" role. Tell students to read their role descriptions silently. They may not share their written role descriptions.

3. Instruct students to assume the roles described on their handouts, introduce themselves to their partner, and begin discussing and problem solving.

4. Ask each pair of students to tell the class what solutions they chose.

5. Discuss how well students arrived at win-win solutions.

ROLE PLAY:
INDUSTRIAL PLANT A (43-1)

Your name is Sandy Smolkey, and you represent the Panoramic Power Plant based in City, Somestate. You are here to negotiate the purchase of a thousand acres of land on the Voltaire estate in rural Somestate for your company.

The Voltaire estate is the only parcel of land of its kind in Somestate. It is perfectly situated near a fast-flowing stream that your company can use to generate power in a new hydroelectric plant.

By obtaining the Voltaire estate property, your company will be able to close down its nearby nuclear power plant, thereby creating a power network that is more environmentally safe. A quarter of a million people live in the City Valley area and are, of course, dependent on Panoramic Power for heat and electricity. The population of the City Valley is a young one, and families are strongly opposed to the threats the nuclear power plant presents. Health and environmental issues are very important here.

You are really committed to the need for converting Panoramic Power to a hydroelectric plant. Your father-in-law died as the result of a nuclear power plant accident, and the mere thought of continuing to work for a nuclear power company causes considerable tension at home. Unfortunately, you have no employment prospects elsewhere, and you just have to be successful in getting the Voltaire estate for Panoramic Power.

You have been authorized to spend up to $2 million for the land, which includes a thousand acres, the stream, and an old family vacation house.

ROLE PLAY:
INDUSTRIAL PLANT B (43-2)

Your name is Chase Carrier and you represent the management of PHARMIS, a chemical company in Hillsdale (population 75,000), in the City Valley area of Somestate.

Hillsdale is a fairly prosperous company town. Sixty thousand residents are families with at least one member working for PHARMIS, which recently developed a food additive that neutralizes carcinogens. The company is on the cutting edge of the fight against cancer.

The future of the PHARMIS plant is seriously threatened because its water source on the Vein River has been contaminated. After much research, PHARMIS has determined that the only nearby available water resource it could use for its work in producing cancer prevention food additives is on the old Voltaire estate, which is currently for sale.

You are here to make sure that PHARMIS gets to buy the Voltaire estate. Unfortunately, Paramount Power wants to purchase it to build a hydroelectric power plant. Paramount Power really doesn't need to build this plant because its nuclear power plant produces power quite efficiently. Besides, those Paramount people all live on the other side of the valley and could care less about Hillsdale.

If you can't convince the Paramount representative that you need the land more, you are in serious trouble. PHARMIS will close, and the entire city will be devastated. Because many of the jobs at PHARMIS are highly technical and narrow, and because employees have worked there for many years, displaced employees will have considerable difficulty relocating.

If PHARMIS can purchase the Voltaire property, the community will be saved. The company could even use the old vacation house on the estate for a management training retreat.

PHARMIS is prepared to spend up to $2 million for the land, which includes a thousand acres, the stream, and an old family vacation house. You are really concerned that Paramount might outbid you.

ROLE PLAY:
TIP TOP PEAK A (43-3)

Your name is Jordan Marsh and you represent the residents of Tip Top Peak, a resort community in the mountains. The residents love Tip Top Peak. When they drive up the mountain, they feel they are entering another world, one filled with untouched forest and clear air. Even the houses on the back roads blend into the woods, creating a total contrast to the bedroom communities the residents left behind in the suburbs where they spend the rest of their time.

Last summer a new developer, Dragnet Properties, bought the undeveloped land from the former owner. Dragnet's managers are building the least expensive homes they can to make a quick profit. As a result, they are building prefabricated tract houses on the main road up the mountain, cutting down trees, and creating what looks like another subdivision. They aren't even maintaining the roads properly. The Tip Top residents are furious.

As a Tip Top resident, you are seriously interested in preserving the environment and wildlife. You moved here to escape the suburbs and you feel betrayed by Dragnet. It is changing the community, threatening the environment, and reducing the value of your land.

The Tip Top homeowners are relatively affluent. They have friends who are interested in buying lots and building houses on Tip Top Peak, but Tip Top homeowners are now discouraging friends from joining them. They are really angry at Dragnet for ruining their beautiful community. They are upset about having the value of their investment in Tip Top property devalued. And they are furious about Dragnet's irresponsible failure to maintain the roads and water system.

The homeowners have asked you to meet with a Dragnet representative to discuss the possibility of the firm's preserving the trees, maintaining the road and water systems, building on side roads only, and building houses that fit into the setting more appropriately.

ROLE PLAY:
TIP TOP PEAK B (43-4)

Your name is Sydney Ripper. When your company, Dragnet Properties, purchased Tip Top Peak, a resort community in the mountains, it thought it bought a lovely community that offered both potential profit and a good working relationship with a popular community. Dragnet looked forward to profit and a pleasant experience with a well-maintained, prestigious vacation community. Although Dragnet had to borrow considerable funds, management thought the investment was worth the risk.

Unfortunately, your company has had nothing but trouble since it acquired Tip Top Peak. The roads and the water system were in worse shape than expected, and the real estate market has all but caved in. Dragnet has not been able to pay the interest on its loans and is feeling quite desperate.

In an attempt to sell lots and houses, Dragnet has started an advertising campaign, complete with billboards in front of the main entrance. You think these are quite tasteful, and they encourage people to look at property.

Meanwhile, Dragnet has built some small country homes as models to attract more permanent residents. Since some of these houses have sold, Dragnet would like to build more. You rather like these houses and think building more can save Dragnet from bankruptcy.

The homeowners have been a real pain. They have blocked every attempt Dragnet has made to recover from its almost destitute position. They don't like the houses Dragnet builds, even though they look much nicer than those contemporary "lean-tos" they hammer into those cliffs. Their demands are outrageous. Dragnet cannot possibly afford to repair the roads and maintain the water system in its current economic state. To make matters worse, the homeowners have hired an attorney and threaten to sue Dragnet for chopping down trees and not maintaining the roads and water system properly.

As Dragnet Properties general manager, you are going to meet with some representatives of these disagreeable homeowners to try to keep them from blocking your sales.

ROLE PLAY:
THE AUDITORIUM HALL MURAL A (43-5)

You are Alyse Treasure and these are some of your thoughts:

"When our principal asked our art class to design a mural to represent the different departments in the school, our art teacher divided us into teams and asked each team to submit a mural design. The winning design would be painted on the wall next to the school auditorium.

"Our team submitted a series of caricatures of students, each representing a different department. We planned carefully, and the mural design was balanced and attractive. The group of caricatures even reflected the diversity of the student body and we were really proud of the design. No one seemed surprised when we won.

"After the contest, we worked for three weeks to paint the mural, and everyone seemed to like it. I really felt proud of the creative work.

"A month after we completed the mural, a student stopped to look at the mural and said that it contained a racial slur. He got a group of his friends together and they asked the principal to have the mural removed. They insisted we paint over it. We couldn't believe our ears!

"When I asked what was wrong with it, the student said the mural makes African Americans look stupid.

"Actually, I had drawn an African-American student to represent the math department, one of the academic departments, and I drew Caucasian students as representatives of the physical education department and vocational departments. I asked how could my choice of where to place the African-American student make African Americans look stupid.

"The student pointed out that the African American student was looking at a tablet that says 1 + 1 = 2.

"I used the formula 1 + 1 = 2 because it is the universal math symbol, and all the departments are represented similarly.

"I refuse to remove or alter my work of art."

ROLE PLAY:
THE AUDITORIUM HALL MURAL B (43-6)

You are Jerry Stone and these are some of your thoughts:

"On my way to an assembly the other day I stopped to look at the mural the art class painted. There were striking pictures of students involved in school. I looked at the pictures, and suddenly I was horrified.

"Right in the middle of this bright mural is an African-American student writing $1 + 1 = 2$ on a chalkboard tablet. $1 + 1 = 2$! What is this saying about that student? Can't he even do baby arithmetic? in high school? How insulting!

"As an African-American student I am offended and I can't believe the administration would allow this mural in the school. What kind of racist message is this school condoning?

"Since I saw the mural, I've pointed it out to several friends, and they all agree that the mural is racist. A few of our parents checked it out last night at the band booster's meeting, and they too are really upset.

"This mural has upset so many of us that it is really important to erase the mural. I don't know whether the artist is really racist or not, but the mural has hurt so many people that it must be erased."

A VISIT TO THE OPERA

To the Teacher: Literature can lend itself to rewriting. Pick a story or novel with a tragic ending, consider the needs of the characters, and ask how the plot might end differently. Bizet's opera *Carmen*, available on videotape, offers appropriate material for foreign language, music, and humanities classes. It also offers students the chance to explore alternative ways to solve a problem. The legendary temptress Carmen succumbs to the dagger of her jealous former lover, Don José. Both Don José and Carmen need control and their identity: Don José as Carmen's lover, Carmen as a free-spirited conqueror of men in the limelight. Don José wants Carmen and needs to save face. Carmen desires a new conquest and a public audience. Don José also wants forgiveness from his mother and status in his company. Because Carmen really wants to stir up trouble, there probably cannot be a win-win, but need there be an absolute loss? Several alternatives students might suggest include finding a way for Don José to stay away from the bull ring and having Carmen self-destruct, asking Don José to consider what might happen if Carmen stubbornly insists on following Escamillo, or convincing Carmen to wait for a different and better bull fight. The reproducible can be used as an optional activity with the lesson plan. Students can find creative ways to rewrite plots to come closer to win-wins.

Objectives: Students will practice creative problem solving.

Students will become aware of the importance of dealing with anger and thinking about consequences.

Activities: 1. Ask students to review the plot of *Carmen.*

2. Develop a list of characters on the chalkboard.

3. Discuss the needs of each of the characters.

4. Subdivide the class into several small groups and ask the groups to rewrite the last act of *Carmen.*

5. Ask spokespersons of each group to present their "final acts."

6. Review ways to prevent anger from escalating.

7. Discuss how Carmen might have handled Don José differently.

8. Discuss how someone might have intervened to prevent the tragic ending.

9. Assign a project: Summarize a movie, story, novel, or play and rewrite the ending to resolve a conflict in a better way.

CARMEN (44-1)

Plot Synopsis:

1. Micaela comes to the tobacco factory with a message from Don José's mother. Zuniga and Don José lead soldiers to the factory. When Zuniga asks Don José about the flirtatious cigarette girls, Don José seems interested only in Micaela. Although Carmen, a cigarette girl, brazenly throws a flower at Don José, Don José and Micaela speak and pledge to marry.

   When Carmen and another cigarette girl fight, Zuniga orders Don José to investigate the quarrel. When Carmen refuses to speak, Don José obeys his orders and takes her to jail, where he falls in love with her and Carmen tricks him into letting her escape.

2. Zuniga, Don José, and Carmen appear at a tavern. Carmen tries to persuade Don José to desert his troop and join her with the gypsy smugglers in the mountains. When Don José refuses to desert his troop, Carmen becomes angry. Then Zuniga tries to woo Carmen, and thereby infuriates Don José. Don José changes his mind and leaves with Carmen.

3. Don José and Carmen argue about smuggling. Escamillo arrives, telling Don José that he seeks Carmen, who loves him. Don José and Escamillo fight, and Carmen intervenes. Then Micaela tells Don José his mother is dying and she implores him to go with her. Carmen tries to get rid of Don José, but he tells Carmen he will return. The smugglers warn him to stay away from Carmen.

4. Don José appears at the bull ring, where Carmen is awaiting Escamillo's victory. When Carmen and Don José meet, Don José pleads with Carmen, who rejects him. Jealous and raging, Don José kills Carmen with his sword.

Characters:

Micaela: What does she want?_____

What does she need?_____

Zuniga (dragoon captain):_____

_____

Carmen:_____

_____

Escamillo:_____

_____

Don José:_____

_____

Rewrite Act Four of *Carmen* so that most needs are met.

Section Seven

MEDIATING
(Background Information)

DEFINING MEDIATION
(Background Information)

Mediation is a process in which a third party helps disputants solve their problems by guiding them through the collaborative problem-solving process. In a way mediators serve as police officers directing the disputants as drivers, offering them directions, and helping them get their bearings as they drive toward their destination. If disputants feel threatened, mediators help them navigate toward safety as they work through the mediation process. If they feel a loss of control, mediators help them find a place where balance exists. If they feel insignificant, mediators can help them find a place to feel important.

Student mediation programs are becoming popular in schools across the country and yielding promising results as measured through reduced suspension rates. Mediators work in pairs to help each other stay on task by sharing responsibilities and chiming in when one mediator drives in the wrong direction. Although they usually work with two disputants, they occasionally find it useful to work with larger groups of disputants, as long as each disputant agrees to work with the larger group.

Training programs include frequent role playing because practice is essential for mediators to hone their skills. Student mediators should practice mediation throughout the year. If at all possible, they should keep journals and videotapes for feedback.

When to Use Mediation

Mediation is not appropriate for all conflicts. It is inappropriate when the disputants have committed a crime or when they are not rational. Some conflicts require litigation rather than mediation. Since theft is a crime, it is not a situation to be mediated. Conflicts involving drugs, alcohol, and violence are likewise inappropriate for mediation.

Mediation *can* resolve relational problems that affect classroom behavior. The conflicts most frequently handled by school mediators are those involving behavior and property. For example, disputes resulting from behavior such as spreading rumors, gossiping, name calling, racial putdowns, bullying, or disputes involving the borrowing of hats, pencils, or books lend themselves to mediation by a third party. They are the disputes that can erupt into fights and violence. Often these conflicts have a history of other difficulties, and mediators can help disputants to sort them out. Mediation *must* be voluntary and confidential. It cannot substitute for suspension, but can often be offered as an opportunity to solve problems after suspension.

Mediators work both formally and informally. Once mediators acquire skill in the mediation process, they can apply their skill informally in daily life. One of our student mediators claims that when she stops in the library and hears students bickering, she walks up and quietly asks, "What is happening . . . what do you think the problem *really* is?" Somehow she ends up walking them through the mediation process and conflicts get resolved without formal mediation. As a result, the potential for mediation as a method for reducing conflict is even greater than reduction in suspension statistics indicate. Students can use these skills every day.

This section contains several activities that help students learn about mediation. The activities vary in complexity and include the application of mediation to groups. The activities assume good communication skills, which students can practice with the activities in Section V. The acquisition of these skills will serve students well throughout their lives.

A THIRD PARTY

To the Teacher: Students sometimes ask, "Why do we need a mediator? We can work our problems out by ourselves." Of course, sometimes they can and, hopefully, will. The following activity will help students realize that it is sometimes useful to have a third party to help them solve their disputes. This activity makes a good introductory lesson to mediation.

Objective: Students will recognize that a third party can help them solve disputes.

Activities:

1. Divide the class into two groups, one of girls, the other, boys.

2. Distribute copies of the "Suzi and Ellen" role play (45-1) to the girls and copies of the role play "Mel and Matt" (45-2) to the boys.

3. Divide each group into pairs.

4. Ask students to role play the characters described in the handouts and resolve the conflict.

5. Ask pairs to join to form groups of four and answer the following questions:
    a. How did you solve the problem?
    b. What solution did you choose? Was it satisfactory? Why? Why not?
    c. Would it have helped to have a third party help you solve the problem?

6. Ask spokespersons from each small group to report findings to the class.

7. Discuss whether a third party might have been helpful or when a third party might be helpful.

8. Assign a journal describing times when a third party helped them resolve a conflict with another person. (Alternatively, make a journal entry about a situation in which disputants need a third party.)

9. Ask students to share insights about problem solving and the role a third party might play in helping disputants solve problems.

ROLE PLAY:
SUZI AND ELLEN (45-1)

Suzi and Ellen, seniors at Central High, have been best friends since the seventh grade. Recently they combined their savings and bought a used car together.

Buying a car together had seemed like such a great idea, but now Suzi was having second thoughts. "Let's face it, Ellen's a slob," she muttered as she picked up the trash in the car. "Yuk. Wiping up catsup and . . . was that orange juice? . . . off the dashboard was no fun. The car looks and smells like a moving hamburger bar."

After school, Ellen came bounding out of her car, a huge grin on her face. She was the happiest slob Suzi had ever known, always smiling, always upbeat. Sometimes Suzi envied her carefree manner. Just then she spotted some open mustard packets in the back seat and Suzi suddenly wanted to murder Ellen.

Ellen smiled and waved. "Suzi, wait 'til you hear what happened in old man Henry's class today. You know how he always snorts when . . ."

"Ellen," Suzi said with hesitation. "The car . . ."

"Don't worry, Suzi. I know it's a mess, but I'll . . ."

"Clean it up later? Like when? . . . next month? Ellen, it's always . . ."

"Look, Suzi. You've known me for five years now, since seventh grade. You've *always* known that I'm not a fanatic like you are about keeping things straight. I mean I've never wanted to perform open-heart surgery on the floor of a car and . . ."

"Hold it right there! A fanatic? Wait a minute. I just would like to be able to drive MY car without having birds and stray cats following me hoping to get a bite to eat off THE TRASH TRUCK you've created."

"Look, I've paid half of all of the expenses. Did I ever agree to undergoing a personality/habit change also? I'm sick of your insults!"

ROLE PLAY:
MEL AND MATT (45-2)

The football team members elect their own captain. This year Matt and Melvin tied for captain. Although they have been close friends, Matt and Mel have very different ideas about football strategy. They are both bright, knowledgeable, and very competitive.

When they are playing a defensive game, Matt is very aggressive. He tends to play close to the line to cover the opposing team's receivers. He is absolutely convinced that an aggressive defensive plan is the only one to use. After all, if the defensive backs play aggressively, the opportunity exists to force mistakes on the part of the other team, allowing their team to take advantage of the situation.

Although Mel is just as fast as Matt, he prefers to play back about ten yards, giving himself a few additional seconds to react to the play of the opposing team. He insists that the aggressive play Matt proposes will cause them to make mistakes and allow the opposition to create big plays, thereby creating an advantage for the other team.

Next week's game is pivotal because it decides the division championship. The opposing team has two outstanding running backs and a split-second advantage could put Mel and Matt's team to a disadvantage.

Mel and Matt are each so sure that their defensive strategies are correct that they are barely talking to each other. The team as a whole is suffering because they are spending so much time fighting and the team is not working together. Team morale is at an all-time low.

46 **A GOOD MEDIATOR**

To the Teacher: After students understand that a third party might be useful in resolving conflict, students can brainstorm characteristics of good mediators.

Objective: Students will recognize which qualities good mediators must possess.

Activities:

1. Subdivide the class into small groups.

2. Distribute the reproducible "A Good Mediator" (46-1).

3. Ask students to share their thoughts about the kind of person who might help them solve a conflict with someone else. What qualities does that person have?

4. Ask students to describe what qualities a helpful mediator would not have.

5. Ask spokespersons to share characteristics of good and bad mediators.

6. Distribute the reproducible chart (46-2) and compare results with the lists they generated.

A GOOD MEDIATOR

Directions: Individually or with your group, decide what qualities you think are characteristic of a good mediator and a bad mediator.

List these qualities below.

— A GOOD MEDIATOR —

IS	IS NOT
_____	_____
_____	_____
_____	_____
_____	_____
_____	_____
_____	_____
_____	_____
_____	_____

A GOOD MEDIATOR CHART (46-2)

IS	IS NOT
a person you can trust	someone who gives orders or advice
a good listener	a judge
a fair person (does not take sides)	a person who talks about other student's conflicts
a person who will maintain confidentiality	a person who interrupts or focuses attention on himself or herself

47   THE MEDIATION PROCESS

To the Teacher: To understand the mediation process, students need to see it in action. Role plays are helpful, and students need a script to begin mediation. They can fill in details with improvisation. To explain the mediation process, try the procedure in the following lesson.

Objective: Students will begin to understand how the mediation process works and develop good observation skills.

Activities: 1. Distribute the reproducible handout "Steps for Mediation" (47-1).

2. Ask four students to volunteer to role play a mediation, with two students role playing disputants and two role playing mediators.

3. Distribute the handout "Student Government Officers" (47-2) to the role players and place them in front of the class or in the center of a fishbowl. (Arrange role players in a circle with the rest of the large group surrounding them in a concentric circle.)

4. Ask students to role play the mediation.

5. Ask students observing the role play to critique the mediators.

❒ What did a mediator say that was helpful?

❒ What nonverbal messages did mediators give?

❒ What were the problems?

❒ How else might the difficulties have been handled?

6. Ask students who role played disputants to report their reactions to the mediation.

❒ Did they feel listened to?

❒ How did the mediators encourage problem solving?

7. Comment on the role play.

❒ Point out open and closed body positions. Good mediators usually lean forward slightly, do not close arms, smile, nod their heads appropriately, and have excellent eye contact.

❒ Reinforce good paraphrasing skills.

❒ Point out that repetition of the question, "What do you think the problem *really* is," often helps disputants zero in on their problem.

❒ Point out the importance of shared interest.

STEPS FOR MEDIATION (47-1)

— I. INTRODUCTION —

Hello, I'm _____ and this is _____. We're school mediators. We are not judges. We are here to help you resolve your conflicts, and we are interested in everyone winning.

Before we begin, we need to agree on some ground rules. Most people suggest the following:

- ❒ Agree to try hard to identify and solve the problem.
- ❒ Agree not to put down the other person.
- ❒ Agree to let the other person finish talking.
- ❒ Agree to try to tell the truth.
- ❒ Agree to keep this conference confidential—what we say must stay in this room.

Are these rules acceptable? Do you have any additional suggestions? Do you agree? Are we acceptable as your mediators?

— II. LISTENING —

(Disputant A), tell us what happened . . . why are we here?
  (paraphrase what you heard)

(Disputant A), how do you feel about what happened?
  (paraphrase feelings)

(Disputant B), will you tell us what happened?
  (paraphrase what you heard)

(Disputant B), how do you feel about what happened?
  (paraphrase feelings)

— III. PROBLEM SOLVING —

(A), what do you really think the problem is?

(B), what do you really think the problem is?
  (If problem is complex, break it into parts and start with the simplest part.)

What interests do you share?

What are some ways you might both get what you want?

(A), what can you do to solve this problem? *(B)?*

What other possible solutions can you think of?

STEPS FOR MEDIATION (47-1)
(continued)

— IV. Choosing a Solution —

(A), which solution do you prefer? What are the consequences?

(B), which solution do you prefer? What are the consequences?

Which would you both agree to adopt?

— V. Implementing Plans —

How might we make sure the solution works? What if you have trouble?

Adapted from Children's Creative Response to Conflict Materials (Arlington, VA).

ROLE PLAY:
STUDENT GOVERNMENT OFFICERS (47-2)

This year Melissa and José tied in the student government elections, and they have decided to be co-presidents. They share an office at the end of the math hall and quickly discover that they really have some problems.

Melissa is a slob. She not only leaves her stuff all over the office, but invites her friends to leave their books, pom-poms, and athletic bags in the office. One day she left her makeup bag on José's desk.

José is a neat freak. He lines up his books in his book bag, puts student government forms in folders and files them in a file cabinet, and places books on shelves according to subject area.

Melissa and José recently had to work on the student government budget, and they are so angry at one another that they can't agree to sit and meet. José thinks that Melissa would develop a budget as sloppy as the office has become, and Melissa thinks José would spend hours counting pennies and miss the big picture of the budget.

PRACTICING MEDIATION

To the Teacher: Mediation requires constant practice. Our student mediators tell us that actual mediations have offered them their very best training. At first, students sometimes think the mediation script is artificial and the process contrived. Once they see it in action, they quickly become advocates of the process.

"It's amazing," reported one first-time mediator. "They [the disputants] seemed to be getting nowhere and we kept asking them what the problem really is and all of a sudden a light bulb went on . . . they came in ready to kill each other and walked out smiling."

After mediators get their feet wet in real mediations, role plays take on a new relevance, and their use becomes even more important. Teachers and trainers will find the following procedure useful.

Objective: Students will strengthen mediation skills.

Activities:
1. Subdivide the class into groups of five.

2. Distribute the reproducible "Mediation Menu" (48-1) to review the mediation process.

3. Organize the small groups into pairs of disputants, mediators, and an observer.

4. Distribute role plays (48-2, -3 or -4) and ask participants to role play mediations.

5. Ask participants to process role plays with the observer. What worked? What didn't work? What else could have been said?

6. Ask observers to report learning to the class or large group.

7. Ask experienced student mediators to share experiences.

8. Explain that although this process may seem contrived at first, it really works.

This lesson can be repeated with assigned roles changing until all students have practiced being mediators. The handout "Steps for Mediation" (47-1) can also be used.

MEDIATION MENU (48-1)
(An Alternative to "Steps for Mediation")

— I. INTRODUCTION —

We are your mediators, and we are here to help you resolve your conflict. We cannot make you do anything, but we will help you decide for yourselves how to resolve your conflict. We will not take sides.

Before we begin, will you agree

- ❏ To try to identify the problem?
- ❏ To try to solve the problem?
- ❏ Not to interrupt each other?
- ❏ Not to put each other down? (no name calling)
- ❏ To tell the truth?
- ❏ To keep this conference confidential? (We will not tell anyone.)

— II. LISTENING —

- ❏ Please tell us what happened. (Paraphrase content and feeling.)

— III. PROBLEM SOLVING —

- ❏ What is the problem?
- ❏ What are some possible solutions?

— IV. CHOOSING A SOLUTION —

- ❏ What are the consequences of each solution?
- ❏ Which solution do you prefer?

— V. CONCLUSION —

Can you live up to your side of the agreement?

ROLE PLAY:
CHEERLEADERS (48-2)

The junior varsity squad for the school year is exceptionally competent. Questions start to buzz about just how many juniors will be allowed to join the varsity squad, which has been traditionally dominated by seniors.

Elie and Sherry are the junior varsity cheerleader captains and think that the varsity squad could be better if there were more juniors on the squad. Besides, they're pretty good and why shouldn't they be varsity cheerleaders?

None of the senior cheerleaders wants to allow additional juniors on their team. If Elie and Sherry were to join, it might be possible for the juniors to dominate the team. Lucinda, the varsity captain, is particularly upset about the idea of juniors joining the squad. After all, the seniors have been around longer and it's their last year. They certainly wouldn't put up with two more juniors on the squad.

Lucinda and another senior, Rae, have threatened to quit the squad if the sponsors allow Elie and Sherry to join the squad. The girls are taking sides and practices are tense.

Key Questions to Consider

❒ What is Elie and Sherry's position?

❒ What do they want?

❒ What is the position of the seniors? What do they want?

❒ How do each of the parties feel?

❒ What are their interests?

❒ Which interests do they share?

❒ How might they both win?

ROLE PLAYS (48-3)

— YEARBOOK —

John Teague and Milly Bigham have both wanted to be yearbook editors since their freshman year. Ms. Specscript, their sponsor, has chosen John to be editor and Milly is miffed. Milly thinks that she is more capable than John and believes that Ms. Specscript is partial to boys. Every time Milly sees John, she becomes irritated.

John has some new ideas about yearbook themes and layout and is anxious to get the group going. He likes working with the staff, but wishes Milly would leave the staff because she pouts too much.

Every time John comes up with an idea or assignment, Milly thinks she has a better one and stands up to offer what she considers a superior idea. Then Milly proceeds to try to point out why John's ideas won't work. Before long, John and Milly's factions build up, and there's so much tension in the yearbook room that everyone dreads showing up and nothing is getting done.

— FOOD FIGHT —

Six English as a Second Language students congregate outside of their transitional English class after fourth period. Since two of them speak limited English, they feel more comfortable chatting in their native language. During this time they happily share their experiences of the day.

While the students laugh and share their stories, a young girl walks by and assumes they are laughing at her. She turns to look, and one of the English as a Second Language students smiles.

Later the girl sits at a table adjacent to where the ESL students are eating lunch. One of the girls points to her tee-shirt logo and comments about how attractive it is. The girl now really thinks the group is saying negative things about her. She becomes incensed and throws her pretzel and mustard at the girls in the group. One of the boys at that table defends the girl and food flies everywhere.

ADDITIONAL ROLE PLAYS (48-4)

— THE COUPLE —

Jamie insists that Bob, her boyfriend, drive to her house to see her every night after work. Bob is taking a number of academic courses, and he cannot get his homework done if he visits Jamie. They look forward to being together, but by the time Bob gets to Jamie's house he is so tired and she is so angry that they spend their time together fighting. The prom is coming up and both of them wonder about the commitment they've made to one another.

— PASSING NOTES —

Melissa saw Sandy, her best friend, pass a note to Joe, Melissa's boyfriend, in algebra class. "Why, of all the nerve," thought Melissa, as she fumed all through class. After class Melissa walked up to Sandy and slapped her.

— SPORTS REPORTING —

It's happened again. For the third straight year, the wrestling team at Sam's high school has brought home the state championship. Also, for the fourth straight year, the basketball team has come in fourteenth in the regionals. It infuriates Sam and the rest of the wrestlers that in spite of their efforts and accomplishments, the school newspaper makes the basketball team's loss front-page news and mentions the wrestling team's victories as an afterthought on a back page. Of course, the winning brings plenty of satisfaction, but they would like some recognition too. Besides, they think that wrestling is an important sport that requires even more skill than basketball. Sam wonders if they should raise a stink about it or let it go.

— THE SWEATSHIRT —

Paul borrowed a sweatshirt from Miguel last week and finally returned it. Miguel is angry at Paul because the sweatshirt now has a stain on it. He'd like the shirt replaced, but even more than that, he wants to punish Paul for being so careless. Paul doesn't understand why Miguel is being so petty. After all, it's only an old sweatshirt, and the stain can be removed.

49 SHIFTING FROM POSITION TO INTEREST: A TROUBLE SPOT

To the Teacher: As students acquire experience in mediation, they soon discover several trouble spots. The first challenge usually occurs in making the jump switch from defining a problem to developing solutions. This difficulty usually arises from the failure to switch from position to interest.

Even though their positions differ, the cheerleaders share an interest in recognition for themselves and the squad. In the "Yearbook" role play, John and Milly obviously share an interest in getting recognition for producing an excellent yearbook. The ESL role play is more complicated because students can define the problem in a number of ways. Their positions might be that "the Hispanic value of honor requires boys to protect girls" versus "ESL students should not speak their own language." Only the disputants' points of view matter. Only they can identify the problem, but before they generate solutions, they must also focus on a common interest. Might they not all share an interest in being respected? . . . not being suspended from school? They might also see other possibilities.

This lesson can help students distinguish between position and interest and understand how to shift from one to the other. In the role play "Friend or Gossip" (49-1), the first role play that accompanies the lesson, Lorene and Mickey really have different positions. Lorene really believes that as Mickey's friend, she must tell Mickey that her boyfriend was flirting with another girl. On the other hand, Mickey's position is that she trusts her boyfriend, and Mickey has no right to interfere. Although Lorene and Mickey have different positions, they do share some interests, the most obvious being the desire to remain friends. They also plan to go on a ski trip together. Once Lorene and Mickey see their shared interest and focus on it, they can more easily generate ideas for solutions. In the role play, "He Keeps Staring at Me," Molly and Terry differ in their positions about whether Dan has the right to stare at Molly. They share an interest in remaining friends and avoiding consequences for fighting.

Understanding how to shift from position to interest is an important skill for mediators to acquire. Watch students carefully as you try the following lesson.

Objective: Students will learn to discriminate between position and interest and apply this learning to mediation.

Activities: **1.** Explain the difference between position (what you believe) and interest (what you really want).

2. Describe a situation in which a mother and daughter frequently quarrel about clothing. The mother's position is that her daughter should not wear jeans to school. Ask what the mother's interest is.

3. Describe a situation in which a father and son quarrel about whether the son can take money from his savings account to pay for his car repairs. What might their positions be? Their interests?

4. Distribute a role play, either "Friend or Gossip" (49-1) or "He Keeps Staring at Me" (49-2).

5. Subdivide the class into groups (two mediators, two disputants, an observer in each) to role play the situation described in the role play.

6. Ask students to discuss the disputants' positions and interests. What interests might they share? Have these issues been explored in the practice session? If not, how might this exploration have been useful? If so, how was it useful?

7. As an assignment, ask students to write a description of a conflict they have experienced or observed with statements describing the positions and interests of each party.

ROLE PLAY:
FRIEND OR GOSSIP (49-1)

Mickey has been away from school for a few days visiting her grandmother, who is in the hospital in another city. She just returned to school today and stops to have lunch with her friend Lorene at their usual table in the cafeteria.

Just after Mickey settles down at the table, Lorene hits her with the news. "When you were out of town, I went to a party and I saw your boyfriend, David, and he was all over this other girl!"

Mickey is furious and retorts, "Lorene, you're just jealous because you don't have a boyfriend. Maybe if you had a life you wouldn't have to go buttin' in other people's stuff and causin' trouble!"

Lorene replied, "But if my boyfriend were cheating on me, I'd want to know."

The girls continue to bicker, and a teacher on lunch duty comes over and refers them to mediation.

Mickey really believes that Lorene has no right to say anything to her about her boyfriend, especially in the cafeteria where everybody has an ear tuned to gossip. She also thinks Lorene has a tendency to exaggerate anyway. If it weren't that she and Lorene have arranged to go on a ski trip together next week, Mickey would like to avoid Lorene forever.

Lorene really thinks that as Mickey's best friend it is her duty to tell her about David.

ROLE PLAY:
"HE KEEPS STARING AT ME" (49-2)

Terry has rounded up a group of friends and is making plans for them to beat up Molly after school. After all, somebody has to teach that Molly a thing or two.

It all started in math class when Molly got annoyed with Ron. Molly complained, "This boy in math class keeps staring at me. Just staring and staring . . . I told the teacher to make him stop, but she's done nothing. He just keeps staring and smiling."

Then Molly told her boyfriend about Ron, the boy in math class. Right after that Ron heard that a bunch of older guys, friends of Molly's boyfriend, were planning to beat him up at the bus stop.

Ron confides in Terry, who has been Molly's best friend since the fifth grade. Terry would like to get to know Ron better, and she wants to defend him. After all, there's no law that says a guy can't look at a girl.

Before long, the school tongues waggle about the upcoming fights. One of the guys tells an administrator about the situation. The administrator refers Terry and Molly to mediation.

Terry would like to get to know Ron better, even though she knows he has a crush on Molly. At least she can be Ron's friend and meet more people through him. She sees no reason why Ron can't look at Molly in math class, and Molly needs to learn she can't control everything. Otherwise, she'd like to remain friends with Molly.

Molly really finds Ron's staring annoying. She knows she should have kept her boyfriend out of this, but she didn't mean to cause trouble.

IDENTIFYING THE INTERESTS

To the Teacher: This activity helps students imagine how to guide disputants from position to interest so they can brainstorm solutions from a more common ground. The activity should also reinforce student understanding of how it is the disputant who can define the problem.

Objectives: Students will understand how to shift from position to interest.

Students will become more sensitive to the numerous possibilities that under-lie conflict.

Activities:
1. Distribute the reproducible "Positions and Interests" (50-1).

2. Ask students to complete the handout.

3. Ask a student to read the first "position" aloud.

4. Ask volunteers to read their interpretations of that position.

5. Discuss the responses.

6. Repeat the activity with the remaining items on the sheet.

7. Share thoughts about how this exercise might help mediators.

POSITIONS AND INTERESTS

To the Student: For each item read the position expressed and imagine what interests might be related to the position stated. Describe probable interests in the spaces provided.

1. Position: If you shave your head, our relationship is over.

    Interest: <u>(I want, I need)</u> _____

2. Position: You gave me that bracelet and you can't have it back just because we broke up.

    Interest: _____

3. Position: You should apologize first.

    Interest: _____

4. Position: Beating him up is the way to teach him a lesson.

    Interest: _____

5. Position: You didn't even notice I got my hair cut. Why should I go to the dance with you?

    Interest: _____

6. Position: I don't care if she is one of the football managers. I still don't want you giving her rides home from your football practices.

    Interest: _____

7. People who borrow things and don't return them on time can't be trusted.

    Interest: _____

FINDING SOLUTIONS: ANOTHER TROUBLE SPOT

To the Teacher: Once disputants determine a common interest, finding solutions becomes easier. Nevertheless, the answer to the question, "How might you both win" is tough. Not all disputants are particularly creative, and occasionally mediators find themselves facing disputants who are no longer angry or hostile, but are still clueless about how to find solutions. The mediators face blank faces and wonder what to do.

Objective: Students will learn ways to encourage problem solving with disputants who get stuck.

Offer the following suggestions for encouraging problem solving:

Activities:

1. Restate the problem and the shared interest clearly so everyone is discussing the same issue.

2. Have everyone brainstorm as many solutions as they can.

3. Ask disputants to explore the consequences of their suggestions. ("What would happen if you were to try this suggestion?")

4. If disputants are truly stuck, move to another issue where it is more likely that they will agree and return to the troubling problem later.

5. Point out that the disputants have agreed to try to solve their problem. Given their desire to change, where can they go from here? ("You really *do* want to solve the problem and we know you can be creative. What are some possibilities to think about next?")

6. Offer several ideas *impersonally* ("Some people find that . . . works well; others have suggested . . . ," etc.).

7. Before giving up, meet separately and urge disputants to come up with possible solutions.

8. Before accepting a solution too quickly, ask disputants how many possibilities have been considered ("It looks like you have a plan that might work, but so far it's the only one you considered. We would like you to relax and see if you have any other ideas.").

9. Have disputants talk through the consequences of their proposals ("Will this really work? How? Will it work six weeks from now?").

10. Use the reproducible "Evaluating Proposed Solutions" (51-1).

EVALUATING PROPOSED SOLUTIONS

Ask these questions to evaluate whether proposed solutions are "doable."

1. Can this be accomplished?

2. Does the solution meet the shared needs of all parties?

3. Does it meet individual needs?

4. Does the solution favor one party over another?

5. Have all parties participated?

6. Does it permit parties to save face?

7. Does it help improve the overall relationship of disputants?

Remember: Disputants cannot always find the perfect solution and must come up with the best alternative.

Adapted from Dudley Weeks (1992). *The Eight Essential Steps to Conflict Resolution* (New York: St. Martin's Press).

52 **REFINING SKILLS: THE INTRODUCTION**

To the Teacher: The more students practice mediation, the more skilled they become. Since complex mediations and feedback require more time than a class period, break mediations into sections, focusing on the different components. This activity is designed to help students refine their skills in introducing mediation, a crucial part of the mediation process that requires more skill than is obvious. Videotaping is an extremely useful tool in this activity.

Objective: Students will refine their skills in introducing mediation.

Activities:
1. Review introductions (47-1, 48-1) and explain that styles vary.

2. Suggest that students might want to include a brief explanation of the mediation process with a visual chart or an outline on the chalkboard: introduction, defining the problem, finding solutions, choosing a solution, conclusion.

3. Distribute the reproducible "The Introduction" (52-1) and ask students to formulate an introduction as directed.

4. Subdivide the class into groups of four, two mediators and two disputants.

5. Ask mediators to introduce the mediation process to the disputants in their group.

6. Ask the disputants to offer feedback to the mediators:
   - ❑ How did the mediators make you feel?
   - ❑ What did they do or say to convey their ability to help you resolve a conflict?
   - ❑ From the introduction, did you understand what mediation is about?
   - ❑ How did they clarify the mediation process?
   - ❑ What else could they have done to appear helpful?
   - ❑ Did they appear sincere?
   - ❑ Comment on their nonverbal communication and its effect.

7. Ask volunteers to share what they learned with the class.

8. Ask volunteers to demonstrate effective introductions.

9. Videotape role plays if possible and discuss the tapes.

THE INTRODUCTION

To the Student: All introductions to mediation contain these basic elements: an explanation of mediation, the role of the mediator, and ground rules. However, individual styles of presentation vary. It is important to look genuinely interested in helping the disputants solve their problems. How successful you are is largely determined by how you set the stage in the introduction.

In the space provided, write out an introduction that you would feel comfortable using as you begin a mediation.

_____

_____

_____

_____

_____

_____

_____

_____

_____

_____

Notes from feedback:

53 THE CAUCUS

To the Teacher: A caucus is a brief "time out." Sometimes a mediation isn't going anywhere and mediators might choose to speak with each party separately for a short period of time. Mediators can add a brief comment about caucusing in the introduction. They might say, "Sometimes it becomes necessary to stop the mediation and speak with each of you briefly. If we think this is advisable, we will ask your permission, grant equal time to both sides, and keep our conversation with you confidential unless you ask us to share what we have said."

In this scenario the mediators meet with each disputant separately. They will ask what the disputant wants, help him or her to see the other point of view, and find out which solutions each party can accept. Mediators will ask the disputant who is waiting for a turn to write a list of possible ways to resolve the conflict.

Students should use the caucus with caution because it takes time, and sometimes disputants get almost paranoid about what they think the others are saying about them.

Objectives: Students will understand how to use a caucus during a mediation.

Activities:
1. Ask students who have mediated whether they ever wanted to call time out and talk with individual parties during a mediation.

2. Explain that a caucus is a kind of strategy meeting. In a mediation it is an opportunity to take a brief "time out" with individual disputants. Ground rules follow:
   - ❏ Obtain permission to caucus from both sides.
   - ❏ Be brief.
   - ❏ Grant equal time to both sides.
   - ❏ Keep conversations confidential unless given permission.
   - ❏ Ask the party waiting his or her turn to use the time to plan problem-solving strategies.

3. Distribute the scenario "Split Personalities" (53-1).

4. Ask students to assume they are mediating the conflict in the scenario. During the mediation Becca and Tim start shouting at each other. You are getting nowhere and you call for a caucus. You meet with either Becca or Tim. Plan your strategy.

5. Discuss what students think will happen in the caucus.

6. Ask students to form pairs and role play the caucus. Each pair can choose whether they will work with Becca or Tim.

7. Ask two pairs, one that involves Becca and the other that involves Tim, to role play the part of the mediation that follows the caucus.

8. Discuss the effects of the caucus.

SPLIT PERSONALITIES

Becca and Tim have been dating for a year. Recently they have been fighting quite a bit, and a friend convinced them to meet with mediators.

After the mediators ask Becca and Tim what their problem is, Becca accuses Tim of being thoughtless when he's with his friends.

Tim says, "Oh, so THAT'S what this is all about. My friends. What's wrong with my friends?"

Becca replies, "NOTHING'S wrong with your friends. It's YOU. Every time you're around them you become a different person. Someone I don't really know or like."

Tim snaps, "What's THAT supposed to mean?"

Becca responds, "The jokes, the innuendoes about other girls, the guy talk. It makes me sick . . ."

"Wait a minute," shouts Tim. "How about when you're around YOUR friends? You make me feel so . . . so unnecessary. You even kidded about the shirt I had on the last time we were with them."

Tim and Becca continue to shout, and the mediators are getting nowhere. Finally, the mediators stop the mediation and ask Tim and Becca if they will meet separately with each of them for a few minutes. They agree.

What would you ask Tim?

What would you ask Becca?

How will you begin to continue the mediation?

54   **DEALING WITH DIFFICULT PROBLEMS**

To the Teacher: Some mediations offer special problems. The scenarios in this section present challenging situations for the mediator. The reproducible "Suggestions for Difficult Situations" (54-2) can be kept for reference when mediators meet for follow-up training. Students should understand that there are times when mediation simply cannot work.

Objective: Students will learn some strategies for dealing with extremely emotional disputants, nonstop talkers, disputants obsessed with establishing fault, and timid disputants.

Activities:

1. Distribute the reproducible "Scenarios: Difficult Situations" (54-1). These situations would challenge mediators to maintain control, handle nonstop talkers, deal with students who lie, and deal with timid disputants, respectively.

2. Subdivide the class into small groups to discuss how they might handle each of the scenarios if they were mediating.

3. Discuss strategies group members have suggested with the class.

4. Distribute the reproducible "Suggestions for Difficult Situations."

5. Discuss the suggestions and add additional ideas students have mentioned to the list.

SCENARIOS:
DIFFICULT SITUATIONS (54-1)

— DORA SPILLS THE BEANS —

Dora saw Wes, Lee's boyfriend, in a compromising position with another girl. When Dora told Lee what she had seen, Lee became angry at Dora. A teacher saw the girls arguing and referred them for mediation.

After the mediators introduce the mediation process, Lee emotionally accuses Dora: "You're just jealous!"

Dora shouts back: "Wait a minute . . . . Don't you try and put this off . . . ."

Lee interrupts: "You don't have a guy. If you did, you'd stay out of my business . . . that's why you hang on to me so much. Get a life."

Dora gets up, knocks over her chair, and yells, "You wench . . . I could have had Wes if I'd stoop that low. He's made it with every other . . ."

At this point, Dora and Lee are in each other's face, almost ready to fight.

— MORE GOSSIP —

Two mediators are working with a group of four girls and a boy who are angry about a rumor that two of them have started about one of the girls, Lori. Another girl, Toni, is incensed that the rumors have spread about Lori. Toni keeps interrupting and dominating the discussion.

"You all wait a minute," says Toni, " I heard all about it in the cafeteria the other day, and the rest of you don't know what people have been saying. You just don't know what happened anyway. Now listen to me . . ." (proceeds to talk quickly without stopping).

— THE BABY-SITTING JOB —

Tiffany says Leah "stole" Tiffany's daily baby-sitting job by telling the mother that Tiffany entertained male visitors while on the job.

Leah caused this trouble because she wanted to get even with Tiffany because Tiffany spread rumors about Leah's sleeping around.

Leah accuses Tiffany, "Where do you get off sayin' I stole your baby-sitting job? YOU lost the job because you were late so many times and . . ."

Tiffany replies, "Oh, yeah? Well, that's not what I heard. Talia said that you and she were waiting for the bus one day and she heard you say I had boys over in the afternoon when I was supposed to be just watching that baby. She . . ."

Leah replies, "I never said that!"

Tiffany shouts, "Oh, yeah . . . it's all your fault that I lost that job."

Before long the girls are accusing each other of lying, and each wants to get even.

— CROWDED CAFETERIA —

When a counselor on cafeteria duty saw Evan push and threaten Paul, he referred them to mediation.

During the mediation Evan accuses Paul of deliberately bumping into him. "He bumped into me. Then made some smarta– – comment. My friends heard him. He can't deny anything," explains Evan.

Paul timidly says, "I didn't mean to. Geez, it's crowded in there. You were cutting in line and I accidentally . . ."

"No accident . . . my friends saw it all," retorted Evan.

Paul replied, "You pushed me back and THAT was on purpose. And you wouldn't let me near my locker in gym this morning."

Evan puffs up his chest like a rooster and scowls at Paul, who lowers his head and shrinks into his chair.

SUGGESTIONS FOR DIFFICULT SITUATIONS (54-2)

— MAINTAINING CONTROL —

of the mediation process . . .

- ❏ Stand up, bang on the table, yell over the commotion.
- ❏ Ask each person, "Do you want to continue?"
- ❏ Call for a caucus or separate meetings.
- ❏ Stop the mediation.

when disputants get extremely emotional . . .

- ❏ Stay calm, keeping a low voice and relaxed body posture.
- ❏ Arrange a caucus: ask angry disputants whether they came to work on a problem in good faith.

— DEALING WITH NONSTOP TALKERS —

- ❏ Say, "We need to hear what others think."
- ❏ Interrupt and direct the group back to the task.
- ❏ Take a break and speak with the person.
- ❏ Ask, "Can you state that in just a few words?"

— DEALING WITH DISPUTANTS WHO LIE OR WISH TO ESTABLISH FAULT —

- ❏ Remind disputants that mediators cannot be judges, but that they assume that disputants really want to resolve the conflict.
- ❏ State that no one can really know exactly what happened, and that focusing on what can happen in the future is really important.
- ❏ Arrange a caucus and clarify what parties want to gain from the mediation.
- ❏ Acknowledge the desire to "get even," but explain that mediation cannot do this. If they insist on getting even, the case needs to be handled by the courts.

— DEALING WITH TIMID DISPUTANTS —

- ❏ Offer the timid person the chance to speak first.
- ❏ Use separate meetings.
- ❏ Arrange for an advocate to come to the sessions if this is acceptable to all parties.

Adapted from Jennifer Beer (1990). *Peacemaking in Your Neighborhood: Mediator's Handbook* (Philadelphia: Friends Suburban Project), pp. 38–39.

55   MEDIATING WITH A GROUP

To the Teacher: The role plays accompanying this lesson take a long time to resolve because of the larger number of characters. They provide excellent training for experienced mediators at a half-day training session.

In all three role plays there are issues to be separated and common interests.

In all the role plays, the mediator will need to focus on maintaining the control of the mediation. Some will need to stand and shout over the fray; others will call "time out." Others will be lucky and simply need to clarify the rules.

The reproducible "Mediation Observation Sheet" (55-4) is an optional tool you might wish to use.

Objective: Students will increase their skill in mediating with groups.

Activities: 1. Discuss how group mediations can be handled.

2. Share the following suggestions:

   ❐ Follow the basic mediation format.

   ❐ Give each disputant a chance to speak.

   ❐ Be sure to control the mediation process.

   ❐ Have faith in the process; if it is working, the mediators will have to say little.

   ❐ Summarize carefully, particularly in the conclusion.

3. Subdivide the class into groups of six to ten students.

4. Assign each group a role play, designating two mediators and specific disputants. Additional group members can be observers. If there is more than one observer in a group, assign each observer a specific task like observing one mediator, noticing paraphrasing, maintaining control of the process structure, separating issues, focusing on common interests, encouraging problem solving, exploring consequences, or concluding.

5. Observe the groups and take notes to share for feedback.

6. Ask groups to report their experiences.

7. Share feedback.

ROLE PLAY:
QUARREL WITH THE QUARTERBACK (55-1)

Jules, the hotdogging quarterback, goes for the dramatic move and it works. Most of the time. Unfortunately, in the regional playoffs, the biggest game the school had seen in 12 years, Jules made a mistake. Time and time again, he chose to go for the big throw instead of plodding through, making first in 10 by passing it off.

The team walked away from the defeat divided. Some blamed Jules. Others supported him. Frustrated players defended their views, and skirmishes here and there developed into a confrontation between supporters of Jules and his newly found enemies. When Jules found his car vandalized, he confronted Mike with a push and a shove in the lunch room. The situation was beginning to get out of hand.

Jim and Jake, supporters of Jules, join Ivan and Mark, supporters of Mike, at a mediation arranged by an administrator.

Mike thinks Jules was "stupid for hotdoggin' the most important game of our lives!"

Ivan thinks Jules is stuck on himself and resents his arrogant manner.

Mark is quiet and follows along with Mike and Ivan. He thinks Jules deserved more than a messed-up car.

Jules thinks Mike and his friends are just jealous. After all, the team elected *him* captain.

Jim is Jules's loyal friend. He overheard Ivan berating Jules in the gym locker room, and he thinks Ivan is a jerk. He'd like to teach him a thing or two.

Jake knows who vandalized the car, but he won't talk.

ROLE PLAY:
THE ELECTION SCANDAL (SS-2)

Bart and Ben ran against each other in a class election. After Bart won by a narrow margin, a rumor about rigged election results spread at school. Ben, Bart, and their friends are at each other's throats. Ben and his friends are demanding a vote recount, and Bart and his friends refuse. The voting machines are no longer available, and reorganizing an election would be difficult.

The following cast of characters assemble at a mediation.

Allison was in charge of arranging the election poll watchers. A responsible person, she finds the allegation that some students voted twice insulting. She takes the accusation personally and is absolutely furious.

Bart won the election, and he thinks the people asking for a new vote are sore losers. He doesn't know whether voting was regulated honestly, but he doesn't see why the issue is such a big deal. After all, real politics is pure sleaze.

Claire is Bart's girlfriend, and she feels duty bound to defend her man. She sees the challengers as "spoiled, snooty, and downright devious." She questions their motives. They're just angry that Bart made an ethnic slur before the election. After all, Bart didn't mean what he said. He even apologized and the remark is history.

Ben lost the election to Bart and wished to challenge the results. He heard that the results were rigged. Some students voted twice, and a few students who had moved to another school district stopped by to vote. Since the election was close, Ben is certain that he should have won.

Robert is aghast at the election results. How could that pompous Bart get those votes . . . especially when he made that dumb joke right before the election? Everyone's so hyped up about the election and irritated by Bart's arrogance. If only the class could vote again, Ben would surely win.

Doug is a hot head. He is really angry at both Robert and Ben. "An election is an election . . . who do they think they are!" Doug also thinks that if there is a recount, some students will bring up the ethnic slur issue and different groups will accuse each other of being racist.

ROLE PLAY: CATSUP (SS-3)

Everyone at the back two cafeteria tables stands up and starts shouting. It all started with some catsup that squirted from Erin's tray onto Marie's new white sweater. Marie's boyfriend, Rod, sat at the next table and saw it all happen. He blames Rusty for deliberately squeezing the catsup carton, and he is going to make sure Rusty pays for a new sweater for Marie.

Mindy, one of the girls at the table, sees the administrative staff closing in and convinces the group to settle this at a mediation.

Marie thinks Rusty deliberately squirted the catsup on her sweater. She knows her mother will be furious because it is an expensive sweater that she has just purchased.

Rusty did not squeeze the catsup carton. He doesn't know who did, and he has no intention of getting stuck with a bill for Marie's sweater. Besides, he couldn't afford to pay for the sweater if he wanted to.

Mindy thinks that accidents happen. She feels sorry for Rusty. After all, he's always had a crush on Marie and it's not his fault that Marie flipped over Rod.

Rod loves to stir up trouble. He has always disliked Rusty, and he really did see the catsup fly from his direction.

Erin's tray was the one with the catsup, but she is oblivious to what really happened. She is simply upset that everyone is ready to fight.

MEDIATION OBSERVATION SHEET

— 1. THE INTRODUCTION —

❏ What did the mediators do or say that made the introduction effective?
❏ What could have been done to improve the introduction?

— 2. LISTENING —

❏ Which paraphrases were particularly effective?
❏ What suggestions for improvement can you offer?

— 3. DEFINING THE PROBLEM —

❏ How did the mediators encourage the problem definition?
❏ How did the mediators focus on common interests?
❏ How did they combine or separate issues as appropriate?

— 4. DEVELOPING SOLUTIONS —

❏ How did the mediators encourage brainstorming?

— 5. CHOOSING A SOLUTION —

❏ How did mediators encourage the evaluation of ideas?
❏ How did mediators encourage exploring consequences?

— 6. PLANNING IMPLEMENTATION —

❏ How did the mediators encourage implementation?
❏ Does the solution appear doable?
❏ How did the mediators summarize and conclude?

MEDIATION OBSERVATION SHEET
(continued)

— 7. SPECIFIC SUGGESTIONS FOR IMPROVEMENT —

_____

_____

_____

_____

_____

_____

_____

56 EVALUATING WITH COLORED PAPER

To the Teacher: Reproduce "Observation A" (56-1) on white paper and "Observation B" (56-2) on colored paper. This structured approach helps every student get involved in the observation process and gives all students an opportunity to provide feedback.

Objectives: Students will gain more insight into mediation skills.

Students become more aware of nonverbal communication in mediation.

Activities:
1. Arrange students in a large circular seating plan.

2. Distribute observation sheets (56-1 and 56-2) to students, alternating the sheets so that every other person receives "Observation A" and the remaining students receive "Observation B."

3. Ask four volunteers to role play a mediation in front of the room, while observers make notes on their observation sheets.

4. Stop the mock mediation about 15 minutes before class ends and ask students with "Observation A" sheets to share their observations.

5. Ask students with "Observation B" sheets to share their observations.

6. Discuss how mediators can build cooperation between each other, develop trust in the disputants, and move the mediation process forward.

OBSERVATION A

To the Student: Observe what mediators *say* in this mock mediation carefully. Make notes on this sheet as you observe the mediation. Notice how the mediators work together, how they build trust with the disputants, how they paraphrase and summarize, and how they move the process along.

Record some particularly effective comments made by the mediators. How were the comments helpful?

1. _____

   _____

   effect_____

2. _____

   _____

   effect_____

3. _____

   _____

   effect_____

4. _____

   _____

   effect_____

What did the mediators say that could have been improved? How?

_____

_____

_____

_____

_____

Name _____ Date _____ (56-2)

OBSERVATION B
(colored paper)

To the Student: Observe the *nonverbal* communication in this mock mediation carefully and make notes on this sheet as you observe.

Pay close attention to how the mediators work together, how they build a relationship with the disputants, and how they move the process along with their facial expressions, gestures, and posture.

Participant_____   nonverbal signal_____

Participant_____   nonverbal signal_____

Participant_____   nonverbal signal_____

Participant_____   nonverbal signal_____

Participant_____   nonverbal signal_____

Participant_____   nonverbal signal_____

Participant_____   nonverbal signal_____

What are your suggestions for improvement?_____

_____

_____

_____

_____

_____

_____

_____

_____

_____

MEDIATING INFORMALLY

To the Teacher: Mediators frequently observe conflicts and use their skills informally. Both their personal relationship with the disputants and the physical environment will affect how they deal with the situation.

Objectives: Students will develop informal mediation strategies.

Students will become aware of when it is or is not appropriate to intervene in a conflict.

Activities:
1. Subdivide the class into groups, some with seven members and some with five members.

2. Distribute the scenario "At the Locker" (57-1) to the groups of four, asking two students to play the roles, one to act as a peer mediator, and one to be an observer.

3. Distribute the scenario "Music in the Parking Lot" (57-2) to the groups of seven, asking four students to play the roles, two to act as peer mediators, and one to be an observer.

4. Ask group members to act out the scenarios.

5. Ask observers to summarize what happened in their groups.

6. Ask a particularly successful group to demonstrate their role play for the large group.

7. Discuss when it is or is not appropriate to intervene.

8. Brainstorm strategies for helping (e.g., Ask, "What is this really about?" or "Slow down . . . is this really worth getting all bent out of shape for?" or "What do we need to do to keep this from getting out of hand?").

9. Ask the class to assume that one of the disputants in the scenario says, "I want to settle this . . . just you wait until after school." What can the mediator do to diffuse the disputants' anger and get them to think about the consequences of acting (fighting) before investigating?

10. Discuss how physical environment and the relationship between the mediators and the disputants affect finding solutions.

11. Distribute "Tips for Secondary Peer Mediators (57-3)" and discuss, adding additional suggestions generated from the discussion.

SCENARIO:
AT THE LOCKER (57-1)

Tabitha was standing at her open locker, just about to put the finishing touches on her lip gloss when she saw Jessica through her mirror. Before Tabitha could speak, Jessica slammed the locker shut and pushed Tabitha against the wall.

A peer mediator, a mutual friend of Jessica and Tabitha, happens to walk by and hears them argue:

"Look here, Tabitha, if I ever catch you near Chad again, it'll get really ugly!"

"What are you talking about, Jess?" Tabitha tried to smile.

"You know what I'm talking about! I heard about you at lunch."

"Jessica, I never would . . ."

"Don't mess with me, Tabitha. Emma saw you. Do you think I'm stupid? Just watch it," Jessica added with a shove.

SCENARIO:
MUSIC IN THE PARKING LOT (57-2)

It was spring at Fairview School, and spirits and tempers both ran high. Sara and Joe sat in his car, rehashing the same old argument.

"But Joe, if you'd just listen. Every time I . . ."

"No, YOU listen. You never . . . . Geez I can't hear myself think. Who's playing the loud music?"

Parked not far from them were Manuel and José. As they waited for their sister to come out, they contented themselves by playing a tape of Latino music.

"Hey," Joe called over, "Can you turn it down?"

Manuel and José continued to enjoy the music, oblivious to everyone and everything around them.

"Joe, just ignore them. Just tell me what . . ."

"I can't hear myself think. I'm going over there and . . ."

"Joe, no, you'll just start something. You always . . ."

"Don't start on me, Sara." With that, Joe was out of the car and slamming the car door. Sara froze.

"Hey, can't you hear me?" Joe yelled as he approached the guys' car.

"What's your problem, buddy?" José yelled over the music.

"Your music's the problem—turn it down!"

"What?" José yelled back.

By this time Joe was livid. He ran over to José and yelled at him, "You turn your stupid music down or else."

All of a sudden people swarmed around waiting for something to happen. Joe and José were nose to nose and anything could happen.

Two trained mediators who happen to know the students walk by. What can they do to help?

TIPS FOR PEER MEDIATORS

1. Think before you get involved. What is likely to happen if you intervene? If you do not intervene?

   ❐ Sometimes it is wise to avoid getting involved in a conflict.
   ❐ Consider reporting the situation to an administrator.
   ❐ Try to remove one of the disputants from the scene if you can.

2. Diffuse anger with paraphrasing. ("Sounds like these comments about . . . really upset you.")

3. Set ground rules. ("Could we agree to stop and let the other person finish and not attack each other?")

4. Encourage problem solving.

   ❐ Ask, "What do you think the problem really is?"
   ❐ Ask, "What might make things better?"
   ❐ Ask "what if" questions (e.g., "What if you were to take time out to cool down and then talk about this . . . ?").

_____

_____

_____

_____

_____

_____

_____

58   ONGOING TRAINING

The following activities are useful in ongoing training of mediators.

Journals

Students will find keeping conflict logs or journals useful for both understanding conflict and brainstorming ways of handling conflict differently. Students can also record questions and concerns for discussion at meetings with mediators.

Journals also produce an excellent way for students to become aware of their personal progress in handling conflict. One student wrote the following journal entry:

> *I had my pet names for all the guys in the class, and I really thought that was cool. Yearbook class should be fun, and I could always get a rise out of somebody. It was fun to stir up a fight. Now I'm not sure.*
>
> *I guess I finally see that I just wanted to be a big shot . . . someone important that people could laugh at. I guess not everybody thinks the same things are funny.*
>
> *I really don't like it when people don't like me, and I guess I'll have to find other ways to be somebody. Maybe I'll write my jokes down before I say them . . . or write a good article . . . or try out my jokes before class. Maybe I can get Jason to give me the high sign when I get out of hand.*
>
> *I'll really have to stop calling Judy "honey" or "babe." It finally hit me that she doesn't think that's cute. I don't know why, but I'll practice calling her "Judy." That's better than getting dirty looks, staying after school, or getting a bad class grade.*

Brainstorming

To practice brainstorming, students may review any of the role plays with which they have worked and brainstorm possible solutions. Sharing lists of possible solutions and evaluating consequences will help them as mediators and problem solvers in many settings.

Reference Material

If students keep the reproducible pages in Part One of this book in a three-ring notebook, these pages will make valuable references as they continue working with mediation.

Part Two

APPLYING CONFLICT RESOLUTION CONCEPTS IN SCHOOL SETTINGS

Section Eight

CONFLICT IN THE COUNSELOR'S OFFICE
(Background Information)

COUNSELOR AS MEDIATOR

Conflict appears hourly in the counselor's office. Even routine questions like, "Which electives shall I take next year?" or "Which college should I attend?" reflect the student's inner conflict. They challenge the counselor to help students develop problem-solving skills.

Conflicts between peers and groups also frequently appear at the counselor's door. Since the school counselor is in the unique position of being a trained listener who often maintains a position of neutrality, the role of mediator is usually a comfortable one, placing the counselor in an excellent position to deal with conflict. Given the absence of a classroom audience and the ability to collaborate with other staff members, the counselor possesses real conflict resolution power.

Although skilled counselors often use the steps in the mediation process intuitively, awareness of the mediation structure can greatly facilitate constructive problem solving and save considerable time. The counselor can move through the steps in the mediation process, questioning, listening, reflecting, and facilitating appropriate problem solving. When the going gets tough, the counselor can use counseling skills to manage anger and help disputants understand different points of view. As in both mediation and counseling, listening is key. The counselor builds rapport to set the stage for conflict resolution.

The concepts in mediation are so relevant to the counselor that counselors might consider posting visual aids related to mediation in their offices. Since most students and adults are visual learners, we have found visual aids most helpful in keeping counselees in conflict on task. Students will often glance at the visual and consider where they are going. When convenient, counselors can refer to items on the chart to either remind disputants of ground rules or move them along in the mediation process. We recommend that counselors post the following reproducible chart (59-1) in their offices. It can easily be enlarged into 11″ × 17″ size on a copier.

This seven-step chart is a bit more sophisticated than the five-step mediation menus presented to beginning students in Section VII because of its greater emphasis on defining problems and finding common interests. However, the structure of the mediation process remains consistent. This chart may also serve as a model for experienced peer mediators.

RESOLVING CONFLICT (59-1)

— INTRODUCING THE PROCESS —

Ground Rules:
- ❏ Try to identify and solve the problem.
- ❏ Don't interrupt.
- ❏ Maintain confidentiality.

— FINDING OUT WHAT HAPPENED —

— DEFINING THE PROBLEM —

- ❏ What do you want?
- ❏ What do you need?

(*Note:* basic needs: security, recognition, identity, control, fairness)

— FINDING COMMON INTERESTS —

— EXPLORING SOLUTIONS —
(*Brainstorm possibilities*)

— CHOOSING A SOLUTION —
(*What are the consequences of each idea?*)

— CONCLUDING —

SEVEN STEPS FOR MEDIATING A DISPUTE: "AMY AND SHELLEY"

The steps in the mediation process really serve the counselor well. Consider the following scenario.

— AMY AND SHELLEY —

Amy and Shelley sit in Mr. Dan's office, trying to avoid each other's eyes. It isn't hard; they sit at separate ends of the counselor's office. Both girls seem hesitant to speak, yet anxious to talk at the same time. Shelley speaks first, "How does she get off talking about welfare and blacks in civ class? Who told her that most blacks abuse the system? What gave her the right to insult us with inaccurate information?" Shelley's comments are articulate, as usual, and Amy sits with her head down and her eyes staring at the floor.

Finally Amy responds, "I only said that *most* blacks abuse the system; I wasn't talking about *you*. Anyway, whatever I said shouldn't make you get your friends together to beat me up."

Shelley sneers, and Amy looks absolutely terrified as she explains that she heard a group of girls were going to beat her up.

To the Counselor: The following description of how a counselor, Mr. Dan, handles Amy and Shelley illustrates in detail how counselors can use the mediation process in working with two disputants. This section also shows how the counselor can handle typical problems in this kind of conference.

The description contains more steps than indicated in the general model on the chart (59-1). Additional optional steps, *handling trouble in the beginning* and *using a caucus*, are included to match this situation.

Step 1: Introducing the Process

Beginning with a simple paraphrase, Mr. Dan introduces his mediation structure: "You two really look upset. I know it's really tough to take a deep breath and try to calm down, but I know you both would really like to work this out. Look, I'm not a judge, but I'd like to listen and help you find a way to resolve this problem.

"Let me tell you how I can help. I'll listen to both of you tell me what happened and how you feel and I'll help you define what the problems really are. Then I will help you explore and pick ways to resolve the problem.

"Most students having conflicts suggest that it's important to agree to these ground rules: let the other person finish talking, try to identify and solve the problem, and make sure that what we say in this room stays in this room. So many students have suggested these rules that we've listed them on the chart.

"Would you be willing to accept them as your rules as you tell me more about what happened? Are you willing to give this process a try?"

(Adding an optional step)

Handling Trouble in the Beginning. Amy and Shelley not only look skeptical, but they are unwilling to cooperate. After all, they were forced to sit together by that English teacher who dragged them to Mr. Dan's office. Mr. Dan continues, and asks several key questions:

❑ What will happen if you don't resolve this conflict?

❑ What are the advantages of working things out?

❑ What do you think might happen?

❑ How do you feel about this conflict? How do you think the other person feels?

Soon Amy and Shelley agree that resolving this conflict is really in their best interest. Shelley notices the visual and thinks about what she wants. She really doesn't need trouble. If she has anything to do with a fight, she might lose her election for student government secretary. And Amy will do anything to avoid getting jumped. She is really in a panic about the rumors she's heard. The girls agree to give Mr. Dan a try.

Reinforcing the Ground Rules (Step 1 Again). Mr. Dan asks Amy and Shelley whether they have any additional suggestions for the ground rules. When they offer none, Mr. Dan asks whether they will accept the suggested ground rules as their own. When they agree, Mr. Dan knows he can refer to the chart to remind them of "their rules." He looks at their simmering nonverbal gestures and knows that time spent on establishing these rules is time well spent.

Step 2: Finding Out What Happened

Mr. Dan asks, "Who would like to begin?" Shelley angrily retells what happened as Mr. Dan listens intently, head slightly tilted forward. "You really felt offended by Amy's remark," paraphrases Mr. Dan. "Definitely," affirms Shelley, finally feeling heard. Then Amy says, "But I wasn't talking about *you!*" Mr. Dan calmly asks Amy what happened. Amy then blurts out her fears about Shelley's friends and seems clueless about how she might have upset Shelley. Shelley interrupts and Mr. Dan quietly reminds Shelley about the ground rules, offers her paper to take temporary notes if she would like, and allows Amy to continue. Mr. Dan paraphrases, "You're afraid that Shelley's friends will beat you up because they thought you were insulting Shelley?"

Step 3: Defining the Problem

Mr. Dan asks what the girls really think the problem is, and the girls begin to talk to each other, laboring at restraining their hostility. Shelley asks, "What makes you think that most blacks abuse the welfare system? I think the problem is you stereotype blacks and I'm not going to stand for it!" Amy avoids Shelley's questions and says she thinks the problem is that when Shelley gets upset, she sends her friends out after people and that kind of behavior isn't right. "Wait a minute," interrupts Shelley. "None of my friends have threatened you. No one that I know of. If you listen to idle chatter, then that's your problem."

Step 4: Finding Common Interests

Mr. Dan asks, "Am I hearing some agreement on two problems . . . the effect of Amy's statement about blacks and welfare and a rumor about a plan to fight Amy?"

The girls might have agreed and allowed Mr. Dan to focus on one problem at a time, but this wasn't destined to be a simple conference. Both girls start to quarrel again.

(Adding an optional step)

Using a Caucus for Time Out. Maintaining control of the conference, Mr. Dan stands up slowly and quietly says, "Time out . . . let's take a five-minute break. I'd like to meet with each of you for five minutes. While I'm meeting with one of you, I'd like the other to jot some notes about what you think the problem really is and how the other party feels. Is this OK?" The girls agree and Mr. Dan asks, "Who would like to go out first?"

Mr. Dan begins with Shelley and allows her to vent for several minutes before paraphrasing, "You really think she thinks most blacks abuse the welfare system, and this really infuriates you." Shelley nods her head and says that Amy's lack of sensitivity is the real issue. She also claims that no one will attack Amy. After all, Shelley knows that if she gets involved in a fight, she'll lose her election. Mr. Dan asks Shelley for permission to share anything said in the caucus with Amy. Shelley agrees and returns to the room with an assignment: make notes about the problem and Amy's point of view.

When Mr. Dan meets with Amy, he asks her how she came to the conclusion that blacks abuse the welfare system. When she cites hearsay, Mr. Dan asks, "What if you were to check out the statistics in the library?" Amy doesn't respond, and Mr. Dan comments, "Amy, you're really frightened about the possibility of being hurt and you think a physical response to something you said without meaning to hurt someone is terrible, don't you?" Amy at last feels heard. Mr. Dan asks, "Why do you suppose Shelley found your comment so upsetting?" Amy mutters, "She has hangups." "So Shelley feels hurt when someone pushes a sensitive button?" paraphrases Mr. Dan.

Then Mr. Dan asks Amy to mention groups with which she identifies. Among a few, Amy mentions "cheerleaders." He asks, "What if Shelley said cheerleaders were dumb blondes?" Time is up, Amy gives Mr. Dan her consent to share what they talked about if necessary, and they return to the counseling office.

Mr. Dan wishes he had asked to see Amy first so that she would have more time to reflect. She doesn't really understand Shelley's point of view and needs more time to think about where Shelley is coming from.

Defining the Problem (Returning to Step 3). "What do you think the problem really is?" asks Mr. Dan. He allows a few minutes of awkward silence, after which Amy sheepishly offers, "I guess I really don't know any facts about blacks and welfare, and even if I did, I didn't understand that a statement like I made would hurt you, Shelley." Shelley hesitates, looking at first surprised, and then unsure. After a few moments of silence, one of them says, "I guess neither of us likes to get threatened."

Step 4: Focusing on Common Interests (Again)

With an encouraging nod, Mr. Dan comments, "Then you agree that the real problem is one you both share: a real threat . . . you, Shelley, feel your identity and pride is threatened, and you, Amy, feel unsafe?"

Step 5: Exploring Solutions

"How might you both feel comfortable?" asks Mr. Dan. "What are some of your thoughts?" The girls seem to relax a little and brainstorm some ideas. Mr. Dan is prepared to encourage them to explore alternatives with a few "what if" statements, but none seems necessary. Eventually the girls produce the following list of possible ways to resolve their conflict:

Amy could apologize for being insensitive.

Shelley would find a way to assure Amy that no one would beat her up.

The girls could have lunch together to show everyone that they have no hard feelings toward each other.

Amy could offer a public apology to Shelley in civ class.

Shelley could talk directly to Amy if she hears an inadvertent insensitive remark.

To prevent further problems, both girls could write up their impressions of this conference from the other girl's point of view and describe what they learned and share it with each other.

Step 6: Choosing Solutions

Amy and Shelley explore the consequences of each proposed solution. As their discussion progresses, the tension between the girls decreases, and slowly they begin moving closer to each other. Amy apologizes and confesses that she learned a painful lesson, and Shelley assures her that she had nothing to worry about. The girls who spread the rumors are all talk and have nothing to gain by beating up Amy. Both girls agree to try several of the suggested solutions.

Step 7: Concluding

Mr. Dan praises the girls for their maturity and ability to resolve their conflict. He summarizes their conclusions and asks the girls how they might deal with any future unforeseen problems. With a slight grin, Shelley replies, "Oh, we can talk to each other, but if we can't, we'll take a deep breath and check in with you."

"Yea," nodded Amy.

Although this procedure may appear lengthy, it actually takes less time than a less structured counseling session. In addition, the process offers good long-term results. In addition, it makes the disputants more aware of each other's feelings and teaches them new ways to handle conflict.

To the Counselor: If Amy persisted in being oblivious of Shelley's feelings, Mr. Dan might have deviated from the standard mediation procedure and tried another procedure to facilitate conflict resolution. The following activities, "Two Chairs" (60-1), "From the Other Chair" (60-2), "Taping the Talk" (60-3), and "Including the Group" (60-4), can help students more effectively define problems and understand themselves and others. They may be scheduled as follow-up counseling activities to prevent further conflict.

TWO CHAIRS (60-1)

To the Counselor: The counselor may choose to ask students to fill in the handout "From the Other Chair" (60-2) before proceeding with this strategy.

Objective: Students will understand another point of view.

Activities:
1. Ask the two disputants to switch chairs.

2. Ask each to assume the role of the other student. You may use the handout (60-2) as a tool at this point.

3. Ask each to state his or her side of the conflict and describe how he or she feels from the point of view of the person whose role he or she is playing.

4. Ask students to return to their original seats.

5. Ask students to respond to the role play: Were the situations and feelings accurately described? If not, how should they be corrected? How did it feel to be in someone else's seat?

6. Ask the disputants to discuss how this activity feels.

7. Ask students what they learned from this activity.

FROM THE OTHER CHAIR

Imagine yourself sitting in the chair of the other person. Try to imagine what he or she is thinking and how he or she is feeling.

1. Assume the role of the other student.

2. State your side of the conflict and describe how you feel.

_____

_____

_____

_____

_____

_____

_____

_____

_____

_____

_____

_____

_____

_____

_____

TAPING THE TALK (60-3)

Objectives: Students will be able to clarify the causes of their conflicts.

Students will develop increased insight into the interaction between someone else and themselves.

Activities:

1. Ask students permission to audiotape their discussion for personal feedback. Agree to keep the tape confidential.

2. Ask students to take turns describing what they think their problem really is and how they feel about the situation.

3. Replay the tape, allowing students to take notes about what they say and how they respond.

4. Ask students to describe their reactions to the audiotape. Ask, "Did you hear anything you weren't aware of? Did you learn anything about the other person's reaction to your point of view?"

INCLUDING THE GROUP (60-4)

To the Counselor: Sometimes the only way to really have disputants solve a problem is to invite all of the parties involved. When mediating with a group, be sure to see that both sides are balanced so that one disputant doesn't feel ganged up upon. Mediating a group of disputants involves more skill than mediating a dispute between two students because the stories become more involved, but the results can be extremely rewarding. The counselor should consider the following suggestions:

1. Be sure to spend enough time on the introduction, clarifying the group rules.

2. Reaffirm the advantages to resolving the conflict. (Ask, "What would happen if this conflict is not really resolved? What will happen to anyone who might love to stir up a fight?")

3. Follow the same mediation rules, allowing each person to state his or her side of the story in turn.

4. Allow students to take turns taking notes to keep track of what is being said, but insist that the notes be destroyed at the conclusion of the conference.

5. When stuck, use the group process. Ask the group, "What is happening here? How might we move forward?" "Remember, we agreed to try to resolve the problem . . . what is this like for you now? . . . how do you think they feel about this?"

6. Use the subgroups to explore feelings and expose different points of view. For example, if insensitivity is an issue, ask each subgroup to discuss how they think the other group feels.

7. Ask spokespersons from each subgroup to share their responses.

8. Ask individuals to respond to what they heard (What did you learn? How can what you learned help to resolve this conflict?).

9. Ask each member to summarize the solutions the group selected.

10. Affirm students for their commitment and problem-solving skill.

61 ## CONDUCTING A PARENT-TEACHER-STUDENT CONFERENCE

Counselors frequently counsel the student who is referred as a result of inappropriate behavior. Many difficult students cause conflict and are not mature enough to participate in a mediation session until another time. Like the teacher, the counselor must consider what is causing the behavior. What does this student want? What does he or she need?

Consider the following scenario:

— TRAVIS THE TERRIBLE TROUBLEMAKER —

Travis's mind was consumed with plots to stir up a fuss. Here he sat in math class and the ways to get Ms. Smith's goat seemed endlessly intriguing. He could easily lift her calculator without her noticing. That used to be fun. Or he could sit in that "off-limits rocking chair" and wink at the girls, especially Karen, "Miss Prom Queen . . . nose so high in the air". Or he could mess around with the ball cap that sat precariously on studious Josh's head. His eyes sauntered across from the calculator to Karen to the rocking chair to Josh to . . .

"Travis . . . Travis. Why do you insist on *not* paying attention?" Travis tuned in to hear Ms. Smith bark at him.

"What a sweet snort you have, Ms. Smith," grinned Travis.

"Travis," Ms. Smith said almost solemnly, "we, that is the rest of the class, are getting ready for tomorrow's test. Would you care to join us?"

"You bet," Travis returned, as he headed for the forbidden rocking chair with his pencil and paper. "Now I can rock and look down at Karen baby . . . so I can better see what her hairdresser did with bleach!"

"Enough!"

Thankfully, the bell rang and Ms. Smith sent a discipline report to an administrator and stopped by the counselor's office to request a parent conference with his counselor, Ms. Teague.

Preparing for the Conference

Although Ms. Teague rarely has the time to have preconferences with students, she feels that a brief conference with Travis might be crucial before meeting with him, Ms. Smith, and Travis's parents, Mr. and Mrs. Jacks. She wants to have Travis understand that she isn't going to let people gang up on him. Instead, she genuinely wants to get to know more about him. She is particularly interested in the goals of his behavior. As she writes out a pass, she mentally explores the possibilities, noting that status is more easily achieved through inappropriate behavior than by accomplishment.

1. Does the student want to be left alone because he has academic difficulty, which is painful?

2. Is control really the important issue? For what purpose?

3. Was the student hurt in the past by someone at home or by someone in the class? Does he want to get even?

4. Does the student want the teacher's attention? Why? Does it make the student feel important in the group?

Travis arrives, and Ms. Teague observes without judgment, "Gosh, Travis, you really do enjoy getting Ms. Smith's goat . . . what's going on?"

Travis comments that the class is a total bore and Ms. Smith is a total buffoon. Ms. Teague asks, "What would you really like to have happen?" "Get fat lady Smith out of my face," Travis mumbles.

"It would be nice if there were an easy way out, but if that's not possible, what do you really want?" When Travis shrugs, Ms. Teague asks, "Honestly, would you feel better if you could get credit in this class and get it over with?" Teague shrugs again. "That Ms. Smith won't pass me anyway. What's the point?"

"So would you like to pass the class?" Travis nods an "I guess" response, and Ms. Teague comments that she will try to see how things can get better after the conference. She thanks Travis for stopping by and compliments him on his insight.

Before the conference she checks with Ms. Smith to see whether Travis can possibly pass the math class. Thankfully, there seems to be some hope.

Ms. Teague warns Ms. Smith not to get defensive. "There's probably going to be some anger, and it's in your best interest to let the angry people vent. We'll eventually think about some creative solutions to the problems."

Tips for Teacher: 1. Don't get defensive. Allow people to vent their anger. The problem will get solved or the angry people will hang themselves by having their irrationality unmasked.

2. Bring grade books and notes if relevant. Don't place yourself in a position where you appear not to know what happened.

3. Be sure you know where a student stands academically.

4. Be prepared to offer several positive suggestions for resolving the problem. Be creative.

5. Allow the student to save face.

6. Remember: The purpose of the conference is to make things better.

Step 1: Beginning the Conference: Introducing the Process

Ms. Teague introduces Ms. Smith to Mr. and Mrs. Jacks and begins: "The purpose of this conference is to see what is happening with Travis in math class and to see how the situation can be improved. Since all of us share an interest in having things work out, can we agree to give everyone a chance to talk without interruption and really try to solve the problem?"

All nod, but Travis lowers his head. Travis's parents and Ms. Smith look angry.

Step 2: Finding Out What Happened

Ms. Teague usually would proceed with the question, "Who would like to go first?" However, Travis's parents look ready to attack (either Travis or Ms. Smith), and she chooses to ask Ms. Smith to begin.

Ms. Smith describes the incidents: low test grades, constant disruptions (playing with someone's hat, disrespectful comments to the teacher and students, picking up calculators, sitting in the wrong seat, etc.), failure to pay attention in class, failure to hand in homework. Ms. Teague paraphrases, "You seem exasperated by the disruption and frustrated by the lack of academic progress."

Ms. Teague turns and asks, "Travis?" Travis sits still, eyes glued to the floor. Silence. An indolent shrug.

Step 3: Defining the Problem

"Travis," asks Ms. Teague, "what do you think the problem really is?" More shrugging. "Can I go now?"

Mrs. Jacks interrupts sternly, "Now Travis . . . you tell her what the problem is . . . RIGHT NOW!!!"

Travis heaves a huge sigh and implores, "Mom, get off it!" He then retreats into the corner and Ms. Teague holds her hand up, gently signaling to Mrs. Jacks that she withhold her comments.

Reinforcing the Ground Rules (Returning to Step 1). Ms. Teague states (at once maintaining control and reassuring), "Remember, we're here to find out what is happening so that we can make it better. Sometimes figuring out what is going on is both tough and intimidating . . . that's OK."

Step 4: Finding Common Interests

"Travis," Ms. Teague continues, "let's separate the issues. Let's deal with academics first. What about passing, Travis. Is this worthwhile?"

Travis mumbles affirmatively and thinks he's heard this nonsense before.

Ms. Teague turns to Ms. Smith for a reality check. Ms. Smith comes through: "After checking my grade book, I think it is still possible for Travis to pass." Seizing the opportunity, Ms. Teague comments: "Passing is possible and preferable. Obviously, there is some common ground here. All of us, including Travis, would like to see Travis pass math." The atmosphere in the room lightens.

Separating the Issues (Returning to Step 3). "Sounds like we have two major issues: academic success and appropriate behavior . . . (Ms. Teague looks around and all agree with nonverbal expressions of frustration, anger, annoyance, and quiet acceptance.) Let's look at the academic problem first. What's happening, Ms. Smith?"

Ms. Smith opens her grade book and explains exactly what work is missing and what Travis needs to do to pass the class. Her suggestions include his coming in after school for a tutoring session on Tuesday and the opportunity to make up a test. After some discussion, Travis seems to see some real hope, but doesn't seem interested in coming in after school and spending time with Ms. Smith.

Ms. Teague adds information: Travis's academic record indicates strong problem-solving skills and the ability to succeed in mathematics. Everyone, including Travis, agrees that he could catch up, but that he has some gaps in his math background. The group discusses strategies for success, and Travis finally reluctantly agrees to come in after school one day a week. He also agrees to do his homework every day this week.

Ms. Teague asks Travis what it would take to follow through. Travis simply says, "I'll just do it." (Anything to get them off his back.) When Ms. Teague asks the group how others might help Travis this week, Mr. and Mrs. Jacks agree to remind Travis to stay after school on Tuesday and allow him to negotiate a reward with them if he completes his homework every day this week.

Focusing on a Different Issue (Still Step 3). "I like what I see . . . there is some real hope here. Travis can pass math, and he is willing to work on some specific ways to pass. I also see a pair of parents who care and will be supportive." Ms. Teague reinforces the progress in the conference and checks to see that the mood of the group is more positive.

Ms. Teague continues, "What about the other issue, the behavior? What seems to be the real problem here?"

Unfortunately, Travis continues to shrug and Mr. and Mrs. Jacks' only comment that "Travis has always been trouble." It would be nice if the group could suggest what Travis needs or share some successes, but neither causes nor strategies emerge. Ms. Teague decides to narrow her focus.

Separating the Problem into Smaller Parts (Step 3 Continued). It would be useful to look at one example of inappropriate behavior. Ms. Smith, can you mention just one small example of inappropriate behavior in class yesterday?"

Ms. Smith pauses and finally says, "Travis was fiddling with Josh's hair."

Finding Out What Happened (Returning to Step 2). "Let's take some time to focus on that one incident. Travis, try to remember what was going on in your head when you were fiddling with Josh's hair . . . tell us about it."

Travis shrugs again.

Defining the Problem (Proceeding to Step 3). Ms. Teague asks, "Is it fun to upset Josh? . . . were you trying to get his attention for some reason: Is this the only way you can get attention in class? Or weren't you even aware that you were doing this?"

Travis looks up at Ms. Teague and slowly says, "I really don't remember."

Ms. Teague paraphrases, "So you really weren't aware of what you were doing at that particular moment?" Travis nods affirmatively. He actually looks sincere.

Step 4: Finding Common Interests

Ms. Teague offers the group an opportunity to chime in. All seem to agree that it's possible that sometimes Travis gets carried away and doesn't realize this. Recognizing that getting to the bottom of the many possible issues is unrealistic in a short period of time, she chooses to go with this corner of the problem. She takes the time to affirm: "Looks like we all understand that sometimes you don't mean to get carried away . . . and we'd all like the situation to get better." At a later date Ms. Teague plans to explore Travis's need for attention and control and to affirm exactly what is not acceptable . . . no lectures now.

Step 5: Exploring Solutions

Looking directly at Travis, Ms. Teague asks, "Tell me, Travis, how do you think Ms. Smith should have handled that?" Travis shrugs again. Ms. Teague opens her question to the group, adding, "Ms. Smith is really interested in what works . . . can you think of any examples of success with Travis that might be relevant?"

Mr. Jacks shifts his seat and declares, "If Ms. Smith wouldn't allow Travis to fiddle with Josh's hair, he wouldn't do it!" Ms. Teague considers asking Mr. Jacks how he might suggest Ms. Smith do this, but decides against this because she intuitively senses he would produce no constructive suggestions, only expressions of anger and frustration. She makes a mental note that she needs to explore Travis's ownership of the problem in subsequent counseling sessions.

Using "What If" Statements to Find Solutions. Ms. Teague senses that she is about to hit a blank wall and gently starts planting some ideas: "I've been in hundreds of these conferences, and sometimes students come up with ideas that really work. Some of them may sound silly, but for some students, they work. Let me see whether I can remember a few suggestions students like you have made. What if Ms. Smith placed a prepared red card with the message 'You've gone too far . . . next time you'll stay outside the room and make up time after school'? Or what if she tapped you on the shoulder to signal 'Enough'? Or what if she called home? Or does anyone else have any ideas?"

Step 6: Choosing a Solution (Checking Out Consequences)

Ms. Teague smiles at Travis and says, "Look, you're the final word on Travis Jacks. Ms. Smith cannot and will not put up with your behavior. What is it you'd like her to do? What do you think might work?"

Travis says, "I want out of her class." Ms. Teague responds, "Since that is not an option, what would work?"

Travis shrugs again, pauses, and Mr. Jacks interrupts, "Look, I think Ms. Smith should send him to the principal!"

Ms. Teague asks, "And would happen then?" Mrs. Jacks darts an angry expression at her husband and mutters, "Oh, Travis has spent half his life in principals' offices."

"Travis?" asks Ms. Teague once more. "Oh, I think the red card might work. If she gets off my back and quietly hands me the card, I'll stop what I'm doing. But she can't look at me."

"And why do you suppose this will work?" questions the counselor. No response. "What makes the red card better than whatever Ms. Smith usually does?" Travis responds, "It's less hassle. She won't bark and stare at me."

"And if you ignore the red card, what should she do?"

"Well, I won't," insists Travis.

"Oh, just to make the situation more comfortable, what should she do in the unlikely event that the red card doesn't work?"

"Well, she can send me outside to sit in a chair and do my work alone." Ms. Teague asks, "What if you had to make up the time after school?" Travis stares at the floor and mumbles, "OK."

Ms. Teague continues to explore the red card suggestion and asks Ms. Smith how she feels about Travis's idea. Ms. Smith says she is willing to give it a try.

Involving the Group. "I think it's really great that you are willing to try a new approach to help you with your behavior in class, Travis. I also think it's wonderful that Ms. Smith is willing to try the new approach too. After all, trying a new approach when the school expects students to behave is extra trouble for her. What might the rest of us do to help the red card to work?" asks Ms. Teague.

It would be nice if everyone agrees and offers support. Perhaps the Jacks might suggest consequences for success and failure; perhaps Ms. Smith might compliment Travis on an alternative to their usual confrontation.

No such luck.

Mr. Jacks stands up and yells, "Oh, this is garbage! No red card is going to solve the problems of this no-good kid. He belongs in a special school. (Certainly Mr. Jacks is unwilling to foot the bill for special services.)

Diffusing Anger and Returning to the Agenda. "Being a parent does get frustrating, Mr. Jacks. But unfortunately, our resources are really limited. It would be nice if we could all decide on the ideal classroom and school for Travis and provide it, but we can only do the best we can. There are positive things happening here . . . I don't see Ms. Smith looking at Travis negatively, and he's offered a suggestion for improvement. We did agree that we'd like to see things be better. Isn't his idea worth a try?"

Mr. Jacks starts to calm down. Ms. Teague notices a smirk on Travis's face and she nods in his direction. (Is Travis shifting his need for attention from Ms. Smith to his father? Ms. Teague might discuss this with Mr. Jacks later, but this is not the time.)

Choosing a Solution (Returning to Step 6). "Do you see the problem in math class any differently than you saw it when you first came here, Travis?"

"Well, I know I can pass and Ms. Smith might get off my case. I guess I still don't want to be there (in class), but maybe it's worth trying to work and use the red card if I forget."

Step 7: Concluding

Ms. Teague continues. "We've agreed that if Travis forgets and behaves inappropriately, Ms. Smith will place a red card on his desk to remind him that he must shape up. Travis will remind himself to pay attention to class and behave appropriately.

"We all understand that Travis's behavior has not been acceptable. If what we try isn't working, we need to be willing to try something new. If Travis's behavior doesn't improve, can we agree to meet and try again?

"I'm not taking off work again," declares Mr. Jacks.

"Hopefully, Travis will find a way not to make that necessary," says Ms. Teague. "Breaking behavior patterns is tough, and I really appreciate the fact that all of you have been willing to get together to discuss how Travis can improve his performance and behavior in math class. Travis, I particularly appreciate your willingness to think positively."

To the Counselor: This conference follows the basic steps in mediation as outlined in the chart (59-1). Unlike the conference with Amy and Shelley in this section, the counselor does not use a caucus. However, the counselor inserts additional steps to separate issues, explore solutions, and deal with this difficult group. Not every approach the counselor tries works, but she keeps returning to her general outline of seven steps and the conference progresses.

Travis Jacks is, of course, the teacher's thorn. No one wants Travis around. No teacher wants him in class, the counselor does not have hours to spend with him, and his parents have given up on him. But Travis is sometimes likable and can be coaxed into cooperating. The red card might work if it is introduced late in the year and the student feels some ownership of the idea. It's important to always keep in mind what the student wants and what he or she needs.

Sometimes it *is* possible to change classes. Travis might function better with a teacher with a different personality, in a classroom with different chemistry, or at a different time of day. We could build a case advocating placing Travis in an alternative school. Sometimes that is not possible, and Travis does need to learn to behave more appropriately. The best we can do is look at the options possible and collaborate to explore solutions. With follow-through, they usually work. Old habits die hard, but they can change.

TEACHER'S TIPS FOR FOLLOW-UP (61-1)

Tips for the Teacher:

1. Follow through. (Remember to follow the procedure and enforce consequences agreed upon every day.)

2. If the procedure isn't working after a reasonable trial period, be prepared to renegotiate.

3. Keep in mind what the student wants and needs (not all students respond positively to praise in class).

4. Keep notes about the student's behavior. They will help if punitive consequences become necessary.

5. Try to look at the troublemaker positively. Think of one thing you actually find appealing about the student and think about this when you interact with him.

6. Try not to take the student's negativism personally. We don't need to have everyone love us.

COUNSELOR'S TIPS FOR FOLLOW-UP (61-2)

1. Follow up. (Block out times to see both the student and teacher.)

2. Set up counseling sessions with the following goals:

   ❐ The student learns to understand and accept the behavioral expectations in the classroom.

   ❐ The student has an opportunity to explore how to look at the teacher differently and practice techniques to change his interior dialogue.

3. Use other resources.

   ❐ Team with an administrator who can enforce appropriate consequences.

   ❐ Suggest that parents explore family and/or individual counseling.

   ❐ Offer Travis the opportunity to join a counseling group.

   ❐ Consider what possible positive reinforcements might be appropriate for Travis: staff members whose opinions or attention he might care about, privileges his parents might grant, and so on.

62   USING MEDIATION TO PREVENT SERIOUS TROUBLE

Problems in the neighborhood often spill into the school and appear in the counselor's office. The following scenario involves a complex, potentially violent conflict with a history of tension in the neighborhood.

— NEIGHBORHOOD ALARM —

Golden Hills and Glen Forest are two adjacent apartment complexes. Glen Forest is a little newer looking, and it is obvious to most people in the community that there are a number of unemployed young adults living in Golden Hills.

The kids from the complexes have generally gotten along well, and they have formed informal basketball teams. Recently, however, the parents from Glen Forest have been complaining that the kids from Golden Hills threaten their children. The atmosphere in the neighborhood has become tense.

Last spring the guys from the area were shooting baskets and little Jules, a Glen Forest 12-year-old, joined some teenagers in their informal basketball game. When Jules accidentally bumped into Frank, a Golden Hills teenager, Frank jumped and yelled, "Get out of my face, kid, or I'll get you!"

Jake, who was shooting baskets nearby, heard and then saw what was going on. He rushed to his younger brother's side, and punched Frank in the face. Then Jake and Frank circled each other, shoving, as a group gathered around them. The fight ended when a police car drove by and both Jake and Frank left, muttering to themselves. The battle was over, but not the war.

During the summer there were several threats and fist fights and when someone saw a gun, the neighborhoods mobilized to protect their own kids.

When school started in the fall, Jake heard snickering and rumors on the bus, all meant for him to hear. Sometimes he was in a cold sweat by the time he got on the bus, and he eventually swallowed his pride and asked his mother to drive him to school.

Jake kept hearing rumors that Frank's older friends who live in Golden Hills have threatened to gang up on him. When Jake heard some Golden Hills guys had weapons, he stopped coming to school.

Jake and Jules's mother, Mrs. Goins, wanted to go to the police, but Jake was afraid of retaliation. Besides, he couldn't press charges against Frank because he couldn't prove a thing. He continued to hide at home.

Finally, Mrs. Goins dragged Jake to school and sat stone faced with him outside the guidance office.

— SETTING UP THE MEDIATION —

Ms. Church, the counselor, convinces Jake to give her permission to include Frank in the conference. While Jake and his mother, Mrs. Goins, wait in Ms. Church's office, Ms. Church gets Frank out of his science class and persuades him to join the conference.

Step 1: Introducing the Process

Ms. Church explains her procedure, referring to her wall chart on conflict resolution (59-1). Mrs. Goins agrees to be a silent observer and maintain confidentiality. Both students agree to allow her to stay.

Step 2: Finding Out What Happened

Both Jake and Frank tell their sides of the story, and Ms. Church paraphrases both content and feeling. Both Frank and Jake listen intently and eventually begin to hear each other.

Step 3: Defining the Problem

Frank explains that "little Jules made me mad when he put his hand in my face . . . he should know better and when I get mad, I punch." He acknowledges that he felt Jules threatened his status in the game.

Jake explains, "You have no right to hit my little brother!" He acknowledges his need to preserve his status as the older brother, protector of Jules.

Step 4: Finding Common Interests

Ms. Church affirms the young men for listening and points out an important area of common interest: they both don't like their security threatened. She asks, "What do you think the problem really is?"

Frank says he won't put up with "little kids getting in my face," and Jake admits he wants to be safe. Both admit they're into revenge and are used to fighting to solve problems. Frank says, "When Jake gets jumped, I'll feel better. I'll know he won't hit me again and my friends will know I won't put up with Jake's butting in my business!"

Step 5: Exploring Solutions

Ms. Church reminds Frank and Jake that they probably both want to feel safe and have a chance to save face. She asks them to consider other ways to get what they want. When Frank says fighting is the only way, she asks both about other consequences of fighting. "What will happen after you fight?" They finally reluctantly agree that future problems might result for both, and they eventually admit that they want to be safe and maintain their reputations of strength more than they really want to fight.

They brainstorm a few alternatives, including wrestling, carving out territory, and crossing to the other side of the street when they see each other.

Step 6: Choosing a Solution

They eventually suggest that they call a truce and avoid each other. Frank agrees to tell his friends to "cool it." He can save face by telling them he settled the problem himself. Jake agrees to warn his little brother about Frank and to avoid starting fights.

Step 7: Concluding

Ms. Church commends Frank and Jules for being creative enough to come up with ways they can both win and plans follow-up conferences with both of them.

63 DISTINGUISHING MEDIATION FROM COUNSELING

How Do the Processes Differ?

Mediation is a specific structured process used to help disputants resolve a conflict. Unlike most mediation, counseling is a process involving an ongoing relationship that helps the counselee learn more about himself or herself and make appropriate decisions in many areas, only some of which may involve conflict. Depending on the theoretical background of the counselor, counseling techniques vary. In all counseling, empathy is extremely important. In mediation, there is a place for empathy, but impartiality is paramount. Although active listening is a significant component of both processes, active listening is much more prevalent in counseling, where a primary goal is self-discovery.

Using the Example of Amy and Shelley (Lesson 60)

Looking back at the case of Amy and Shelley, Mr. Dan sometimes walks the tightrope between mediator and counselor. As the mediator, he is careful to define his impartiality and encourage problem solving as efficiently as possible. When he takes time out for a caucus, he briefly becomes more of a counselor by carefully reflecting feeling. When he empathizes with Shelley, "You really think she thinks most blacks abuse the welfare system and this really infuriates you," he is clearly in her corner. Even as he pushes Amy to see Shelley's point of view and understand the irresponsibility of her statement, Mr. Dan makes a strong active listening statement to Amy: "You're really frightened about the possibility of being hurt . . . ." Mr. Dan, the counselor, encourages insight more than problem solving here. Throughout the conference Mr. Dan, as both counselor and mediator, continues to use active listening by paraphrasing content and feeling. When he is mediator, he focuses more on finding common interests and generating solutions. At all times the counselor maintains professionalism by respecting confidentiality and not taking sides.

Using the Example of Travis (Lesson 61)

The difference between mediation and counseling is more obvious with Ms. Teague and Travis the Troublemaker. In the teacher-parent conference Ms. Teague functions as a mediator. Presumably she would follow up in her counselor role with the goal of increasing Travis's self awareness. Travis could benefit from family counseling to help the family work together more effectively. After continued counseling, Travis would be a more forthcoming participant in a mediation.

Using the Example of the Neighborhood Alarm (Lesson 62)

Like Travis, Jake and Frank are insecure young men who need to solve conflicts more effectively. All three can also benefit from counseling to help them improve their self-concepts and handle anger more effectively. In a mediation session it is important to shift from portion to interest. Frank's position is that he must seek revenge through his friends. Jake's position is that he must defend his younger brother with his fists. The mediator can help them shift from their positions of "I must fight" to interest: security, identity, and recognition. Unlike the mediator, the counselor will focus on why Frank and Jake maintain their positions, hoping that they will be better prepared to consider alternatives to fighting.

The Mediator-Counselor Chart (63-1), designed for faculty in-service presentations and community meetings, illustrates the similarities and differences between the roles of mediator and counselor.

MEDIATOR-COUNSELOR CHART (63-1)

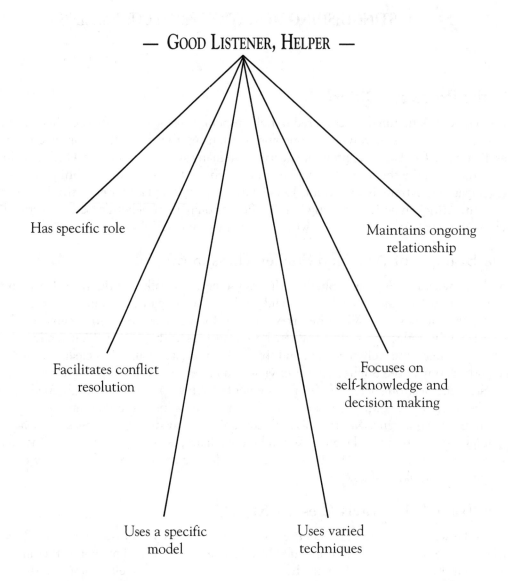

— GOOD LISTENER, HELPER —

Has specific role

Maintains ongoing relationship

Facilitates conflict resolution

Focuses on self-knowledge and decision making

Uses a specific model

Uses varied techniques

Section Nine

CONDUCTING COUNSELING GROUPS
(Background Information)

ORGANIZING GROUPS

Many school guidance departments offer students the opportunity to meet in small groups for support, growth, and skill building. At the beginning of the school year, counselors inform students and their parents about the availability of groups and offer students a chance to sign up. Teachers, parents, and administrators may refer students.

Group Size, Leadership, and Duration

Ideal group membership size varies from 8 to 12 students. The facilitator should be trained in group counseling and plan to meet with the group weekly for a class period on a rotating schedule, during a lunch period or after school. Frequently co-facilitators, comprised of a counselor and social worker or psychologist, team to lead groups. Although some groups meet for an entire year, groups usually meet for 6 to 10 sessions.

Member Selection

Group composition is important. Group members should have similar needs, but the groups should not be too homogeneous. No group member should be totally out of field. For example, a student who is irrational and has extremely poor impulse control or who always monopolizes groups is not a good candidate for a counseling group, unless the facilitator is extremely skilled in handling disruptive group members.

Before organizing groups, it is desirable to screen group members through an interview. The interview offers a chance to assess commitment to joining a group and offers a chance to ask questions about the group process. In addition, information obtained about student schedules and needs can form the basis for setting up and scheduling groups. In the screening interview, the interviewer might cover the following topics:

- ❏ Expectations and concerns
- ❏ Scheduling
- ❏ Confidentiality
- ❏ Responsibility about notifying teachers about class meetings, makeup work, and classroom assignments
- ❏ Meeting attendance and promptness
- ❏ Parent permission slips

The selection of group activities depends on the characteristics of the group. Usually students who will sign up for groups dealing with conflict fall into four categories: bullies, victims, students who want to help their friends, and students who are interested in learning more about how to handle their own conflicts. Sometimes principals may require group membership after a disciplinary action.

Types of Conflict Resolution Counseling Groups

Although it is a good idea to place a mixture of different kinds of students in a group, group members should share common needs. It is useful to place victims together so that they can learn to become more assertive in an atmosphere where bullies are not there to intimidate them. Since the "victim" label can humiliate students, this group should not be identified as a "victim group." The sample plans for Group A in this section offer suggestions for working with these students.

Since bullies tend to reinforce each other, they should be mixed with other students, excluding the victims, who do not need to be attacked. This mixture is important because some group members need to question the bully value system that says resolving conflicts by talking is "for wimps." The sample plans for Group B provide useful ideas and materials for this kind of group.

When different groups are antagonistic toward each another, consider forming two different homogenous groups as support groups and later combining them to define and resolve conflicts. For example, if two different ethnic groups threaten to fight over what kind of music to play at the prom, why not meet with the groups separately before combining the groups to resolve the conflict? The last portion of this section describes this procedure and offers some relevant suggestions.

Recruiting Group Members

Group members can be recruited in a variety of ways. The following are some effective recruitment ideas.

- ❐ Publicize groups at orientation sessions: Tell students the groups will help them learn more about conflict resolution.
- ❐ Survey students through classrooms. See the Sample Group Survey (64-1).
- ❐ Request referrals from teachers. See the Sample Teacher Memo (64-2).
- ❐ Inform parents about groups informally, at evening meetings, and through newsletters.
- ❐ Write articles for the school newspaper.
- ❐ Ask selected students to join an advisory group about conflict to suggest ideas for the principal.
- ❐ Offer group members status through special duties, like escorting guests to the office.

Distributing Forms

During the initial student interview, distribute both the Sample Permission Slip (64-3) and the Counseling Group Meeting Schedule (64-4). In this way students can return their signed permission forms on the first session and plan for meetings on their calendars.

Planning Sessions

Before the first meeting, the facilitator or co-facilitators should plan activities and discuss their evaluation procedure. All groups need an orientation phase, where students develop trust and a sense of community. Then group members can begin practicing new skills and reaching their goals. After the work phase, the group needs to summarize and conclude.

Activities should match different phases of the group process. A list of resources for group counseling appears in the appendix to this book.

Evaluation

Although many facilitators evaluate groups informally, it would be useful to assess what students learn by following their progress after the group concludes. For example, counselors can observe students frequently involved in fighting and find out whether these students fight less after participating in a group. Group members can also submit written evaluation forms or take pre- and post-tests about their comprehension of conflict resolution concepts. We have included a Sample Evaluation Form (64-5) and a sample Pre- and Post-Checklist (64-6).

Name _____ Date _____

SAMPLE GROUP SURVEY

The guidance department is offering students the opportunity to join small groups to discuss common concerns and learn related skills.

A counselor and the school social worker will lead the groups of 8 to 12 students, who will meet for six weeks on a rotating schedule so that you will miss only one of each of your classes.

The following groups are available on a first-come, first served basis. Please place a check next to the group you would be interested in joining.

Managing Conflict_____

Coping with Grief_____

Study Skills_____

Alcohol and Substance Abuse Prevention_____

Coping with Divorce_____

Other_____

SAMPLE TEACHER MEMO (64-2)

TO: XXXXX Faculty

FROM: Marianne X, Counselor, and Joel Y, School Social Worker

SUBJECT: Conflict Resolution Groups

TARGET DATE: October 10, 19__

We are offering students the opportunity to join a small counseling group focusing on conflict resolution.

All students interested in this topic are welcome. We are particularly interested in recruiting students who are frequently involved in conflicts with other students and teachers. We are also interested in recruiting students who are the objects of aggression and teasing and students with the communication and leadership skills to help others resolve conflict.

The groups will meet for six weeks on a rotating schedule so that students will miss your class only once. They will be responsible for all assigned work and make up work.

Please submit names of students you recommend for these groups by October 10.

We really think these groups can make a difference in our school climate. Thank you so much for your support.

Name   **Reason for Referral**

_____   _____

_____   _____

_____   _____

_____   _____

SAMPLE PERMISSION SLIP (64-3)

Dear Parent,

We are offering students the opportunity to join a small counseling group to discuss strategies for conflict resolution.

The group will meet for six sessions on a staggered schedule and students will be responsible for making up work for classes missed.

Materials and session outlines are available if you would like to review them. Actual student discussions will be kept confidential. If you have any questions, or would like to discuss the group with us, please call us at xxx-xxxx.

We think that students can benefit greatly from participation in these groups.

If you would like your son or daughter to join a conflict resolution group, please sign the permission slip at the bottom of this page.

We look forward to working with your son or daughter.

Sincerely,

Marianne X
Counselor

Joel Y
School Social Worker

I_____, parent of_____, give my son/ daughter permission to participate in a counseling group dealing with conflict resolution this fall.

Signature_____

COUNSELING GROUP MEETING SCHEDULE (64-4)

Dear_____,

Our counseling group will meet in the guidance conference room on the following dates during the periods designated.

Session I	period 2
Session II	period 3
Session III	period 4
Session IV	period 5
Session V	period 6
Session VI	period 7

Please show this schedule to your teachers so that you may obtain appropriate makeup work. You will be responsible for assignments due on meeting dates.

We are looking forward to having you join our group.

Sincerely,

Marianne X
Counselor

SAMPLE EVALUATION FORM (64-5)

— CONFLICT RESOLUTION GROUP —

Please evaluate what you learned about the following topics:

	Not useful	Useful	Very useful
Defining problems	_____	_____	_____
Ways to deal with conflict	_____	_____	_____
Problem solving	_____	_____	_____
Other	_____	_____	_____

Please tell us what was the most valuable outcome of this group for you.

_____

_____

_____

_____

_____

Please offer suggestions for improvement for this kind of group.

_____

_____

_____

_____

_____

PRE- AND POST-CHECKLIST

To the Student: The statements below relate to conflict resolution. Circle the appropriate response for how you think or feel at this time.

		Never				Always
1.	When I observe a conflict, I understand what the problem is.	1	2	3	4	5
2.	I frequently get into fights.	1	2	3	4	5
3.	When I have a conflict with someone, I usually talk things out.	1	2	3	4	5
4.	I think of different ways to solve problems.	1	2	3	4	5
5.	There's really only one good way to solve a problem.	1	2	3	4	5
6.	I understand what makes me angry.	1	2	3	4	5
7.	I just can't control my anger.	1	2	3	4	5
8.	I listen to other points of view.	1	2	3	4	5
9.	I pick on other people.	1	2	3	4	5
10.	I get picked on.	1	2	3	4	5
11.	I have a right to express how I feel.	1	2	3	4	5
12.	I can express how I feel effectively.	1	2	3	4	5

65 **CONDUCTING GROUP A (FOR "VICTIMS")**

Whom to Include

Although "victim's groups" should include different kinds of students from different backgrounds, avoid the inclusion of aggressive members. Bullies can intimidate victims. Victims need to feel that they are not alone as people who have difficulty handling teasing and aggression, and they need the freedom to talk about how they feel without overly aggressive members dominating them.

Although victims do need to be grouped together for support, it would be useful to include some supportive group members who are not victims. In this way the group members who are not victims can offer suggestions, encouragement to try new strategies, and positive reinforcement. The helping students will acquire skill in helping others resolve conflict and develop more insight into how to handle any of their own conflicts. As a result, all group members can benefit.

What to Call the Group

It is important not to label this group a "Victim's Group." The title "Conflict Resolution Group," "Conflict Resolution Advisory Group," or "Lunch Bunch" will suffice. Group members can also name their group. When inviting students to join this group, it might be useful to suggest that the purpose of the group is twofold: to understand how to deal with conflict and to generate ideas for the school administration. The second purpose serves two functions. First, it indicates that the administration values the opinions of these students and can motivate them to join the group. Second, the feedback from this group can actually provide the school administration with useful insight.

Activities

The group begins with the establishment of a common trusting environment and concludes with reflection and positive reinforcement through acclamation.

Each session begins with a "check-in" and offers students the opportunity to suggest strategies to students who report difficulty with conflicts. When students get comfortable in a counseling group, they will often share more than enough material for the group to use to develop skills. The majority of the sessions include assertiveness training through practicing "I statements" and role playing. After group members become comfortable with role playing, videotaping can be an extremely useful tool for group members to use for practicing assertive behavior and getting feedback. As victims learn not to look like victims, they cease to be treated like victims.

Ongoing Planning

The suggested outline of six group sessions that follows is a sample. It contains more material than a facilitator needs for six sessions.

Activities can and should be varied to match the group as it forms. Part One of this book offers numerous activities that can be used during group counseling sessions. After each session the facilitator should evaluate the group session and reevaluate the plans for the succeeding session.

— Session One (Group A) —

Objectives: Students will understand ground rules.

Students will develop a sense of community and shared purpose.

Activities:

1. Ask students to introduce themselves with an ice breaker. For example, ask them to name an animal beginning with the same letter as their name (e.g., "I'm Ruth, the Rhinoceros").

2. Ask students to indicate what animal they resemble when they are in a conflict at home, school, or in extracurricular activities.

3. Ask students to share their expectations for the group.

4. Agree upon ground rules: maintain confidentiality, no interruptions or putdowns, arrive on time, and so on.

5. Ask volunteers to describe a conflict they experienced or observed.

6. Discuss what the problem really is.

7. Share ideas about how the disputant's needs might be met.

8. Review the meeting schedule.

— Session Two (Group A) —

Objectives:
Students will develop problem-solving skills.

Students will learn how and when to use "I statements."

Activities:

1. Check in: Ask students to share how their week has been (on a scale of 1 to 10) and ask volunteers to share difficulties with conflicts that they have experienced or observed.

2. Choose a suitable conflict presented by a group member.

3. Check to see whether all group members can relate to the situation presented. (Ask, "How many of you have seen or experienced something like this?")

4. Ask the group to brainstorm possible ways to handle the conflict the student described.

5. If appropriate, ask the student who presented the situation to evaluate the suggestions, choose one to try, and plan to report back to the group during a future "check-in."

6. Distribute the scenario "On My Case in the Cafeteria" (65-1) and ask a student to read it aloud.

7. Ask students how they might respond if they were in Maria's situation. How would they feel? What would they say?

8. Distribute the handout "I Statements" (33-2) and explain.

9. Ask students how they might use an "I statement" if they were in Maria's situation (e.g., "I get mad when people call me names because I don't need to be blamed for an accident" or "When I get yelled at for something that was an accident, I really get angry.").

10. Discuss appropriate uses of "I statements" (see Lesson 33).

11. Ask students to practice "I statements" during the week when they seem appropriate.

To the Counselor:
This lesson contains more activities than can be covered in a single session. The selection of which activities to use depends upon the group. If students are unfamiliar with "I statements," the lesson needs to be divided into two sessions, with one focusing on identifying feelings and using "I statements."

SCENARIO:
ON MY CASE IN THE CAFETERIA

Maria sat in the administrator's office and picked at her nails. That cafeteria incident had been really tense. She proceeded to explain what happened.

"All I know is that I was outside the cafeteria eatin' lunch with my friends. We were foolin' around with the ice in our drinks—throwin' it and stuff—and it hit this jerk's friend. Next thing I know, this jerk is in my face sayin', "Listen, sweetheart . . ." and I want to say, "Don't call me sweetheart," but I was scared to death! Thank goodness the awareness aide showed up cause I don't know what could have happened."

If you were Maria, what would you do?

_____

_____

_____

_____

_____

_____

_____

— SESSION THREE (GROUP A) —

Objectives: Students will acquire some insight into why students tease other students.

Students will learn strategies for dealing with teasing.

Activities:
1. Check in: Ask students to share their strategies for dealing with conflict during the week, including the use of "I statements."

2. Practice using "I statements" (see Lesson 33-2).

3. Distribute the scenario "Arthur and Roy" (65-2).

4. Ask students why students pick on other students. How do each of the parties feel?

5. Discuss ideas about how to deal with teasing.

6. Distribute the handout "Teasing" (65-3) and discuss it.

7. Ask volunteers to role play the scenario "Arthur and Roy."

8. Discuss what Arthur can do. (The suggestion that Arthur might take a karate course might be a useful addition to the list on the handout.)

Tips to the Counselor: Because students frequently have trouble expressing feelings, it is useful to encourage the group to discuss how the characters in the role plays feel.

Role playing is extremely useful for students in the group, but younger students need coaching. It is acceptable for the facilitator to offer suggestions for opening lines. For example, when role playing "Arthur and Roy," the facilitator might suggest Roy begin by saying, "Oh, there you are again, . . . you think you'll be ready for PE today? Well . . . answer me . . . ." If the players have difficulty or don't stay on task during role playing, stop the action by saying "Freeze" and have the players or substitutes begin again.

Reverse role playing is also helpful in developing both skill and insight.

SCENARIO:
ARTHUR AND ROY

Arthur, a small, somewhat timid-looking young man sat in his counselor's office with his shoulders hunched and his eyes staring at the floor. "Get me out of that gym class. I can't stand being in the locker room with Roy for another day!"

This is what Roy usually sounds like in the PE locker room when the teacher is out of sight:

> "Well, well, if it isn't Arthur, changing into his Discount Store clothes! My, my, did your mamma take you shopping last weekend? Those socks are just sooooo cute. Oh, come on, Arthur, be a sport, tell me where your mama buys your clothes."

Several students gather around, looking amused and ready to watch the action.

How do you think Arthur feels?

_____

How do you think Roy feels?

_____

Why is Roy acting like this?

_____

What do you think Arthur should do?

_____

TEASING (6S-3)

— REASONS FOR TEASING —

anger   revenge   power   attention   feeling important

— WAYS TO HANDLE TEASING —

❐ USE AN "I MESSAGE."

❐ HAVE A READY ANSWER TO RESPOND.

❐ WALK AWAY.

❐ GO SOMEWHERE NEAR FRIENDS OR ADULTS.

❐ DON'T TEASE BACK.

❐ DON'T OVERREACT.

❐ DON'T BE GUILTY OF TEASING.

❐ DON'T JOIN A GROUP IN TEASING.

❐ DON'T BE AFRAID TO HELP SOMEONE WHO IS BEING TEASED.

❐ CHANGE YOUR INNER DIALOGUE:

Switch from thinking "It's terrible to be teased" to "I don't like to be teased, but it's not the end of the world . . . I can just ignore it."

Adapted from materials developed by Eleanor Mandes, Fairfax County Public Schools.

— SESSION FOUR (GROUP A) —

Objectives: Students will practice assertiveness skills.

Students will practice coping skills for dealing with teasing.

Students will develop an awareness of their nonverbal communication.

Activities:

1. Check in: Ask students to share their experiences with dealing with "I statements" and teasing.

2. Ask the group to offer suggestions to students describing difficulties.

3. Ask volunteers to role play a situation in which a student is picking on someone.

4. Ask volunteers to role play ways of dealing with the situation presented. If possible, videotape the role play.

5. Discuss nonverbal responses that make people appear to be likely targets (e.g., head down, avoiding eye contact, slumping, walking away quickly, trembling).

6. Distribute the sheet "Positive Self-talk" (65-4).

7. Discuss how students can talk themselves into looking at something differently.

8. Ask students to practice "positive self-talk."

POSITIVE SELF-TALK (65-4)

It's his problem, not mine . . . what a harmless waste of hot air . . . what do I care what she says? . . . I can ignore him . . . I'm not going to let these words get to me . . . oh, well, at least I don't have to live with that person . . . maybe I can laugh to myself about this silliness . . . what's the worst thing that can happen? . . . I wonder what her problem is? . . . I can ignore it until I calm down, then I'll calmly tell him to stop . . . I can calm down and use an "I statement" . . . in a few minutes I can get out of here . . . .

— SESSION FIVE (GROUP A) —

Objectives: Students will help each other handle difficulties with conflict.

Students will acquire better anger management skills.

Activities:

1.   Check in: Ask students to share how their week went and discuss their experiences with practicing "positive self-talk." Offer them the chance to present problems with which they would like the group to help.

2.   Ask students to offer each other appropriate suggestions.

3.   Distribute a stick of clay to each student and ask students to stretch the clay as if it represents their tempers. Students with short tempers should leave the clay alone, and students who do not get angry as easily can stretch the clay slowly, illustrating their "longer" tempers.

4.   Ask students to describe how quickly they become angry on a scale of 1–10.

5.   Ask students to discuss how they might slow down their anger responses (count to ten, take a deep breath, create appropriate interior dialogue, bite your tongue, etc.).

6.   Demonstrate a knee-jerk reflex and explain that hitting your knee triggers a reflex reaction. Explain that hitting your knee is a trigger.

7.   Discuss what an anger trigger might be. What reactions do they trigger?

8.   Ask students to share some of their anger triggers and reactions in pairs.

9.   Ask students to share their triggers and have the group offer suggestions for appropriate responses to the triggers.

10.   Ask students to share goals for anger management for the next week.

Session Six (Group A)

Objectives: Students will feel affirmed.

Students will evaluate their learning in the group.

Activities:
1. Check in: Ask students to report about "unfinished business."

2. Ask the group to share suggestions for concerns.

3. Model affirmations by affirming yourself for something you learned as a leader and affirming a student for his or her individual contribution.

4. Ask each group member to make two affirmation statements: one praising himself or herself, the other praising another member of the group.

5. Ask each member to share something he or she learned from the group.

6. Distribute evaluation sheets and ask students to complete them.

To the Counselor: As an alternative to the affirmation activity suggested in this plan, students can draw names from a hat and offer affirmation statements, write affirmation letters to other members of the group, describe imaginary gifts for each of the other group members, or say something positive about the person seated to his or her right. Any of these activities will help group members leave feeling more positive about themselves.

66   CONDUCTING GROUP B (DEALING WITH CONFLICT)

Whom to Include (Group B)

All students can benefit from participation in a group dealing with conflict. For maximum gain, invite a diverse group of 8 to 12 students, including at least a few who are good listeners who can relate to all kinds of students. Ideally, all students should be sincerely interested in learning how to deal with conflict and how to help others deal with it. Completely irrational students are not ready for this kind of group and should receive individual counseling.

Activities (Group B)

Like Group A, the group primarily for victims of aggression, activities should match the needs of the group. The first session should begin with introductions and an ice breaking exercise, setting of ground rules, and sharing issues.

For a six-session group, the second through fifth sessions can begin with a "checking in," where students share successes in resolving conflicts and observations and concerns. During the sessions participants can brainstorm solutions to problems presented and the group can help the presenter evaluate the ideas and select ones to try. Facilitators should plan communication exercises and problem-solving activities and organize role playing as appropriate.

The concluding session should include comments about unfinished business, affirmations of group members, and an evaluation. Like all groups, this group should move through three developmental stages: orientation, work, and conclusion.

Many of the activities in Part One of this book are applicable to this kind of group. In addition, the five problem-solving activities included in Sessions One through Five can work well as problem-solving and communication activities for a small group.

Sample Group Plan

The six-session plans for Group B are sample plans. As suggested earlier, activities can vary with the specific needs of the group.

The ice breaker in Session One asks students to indicate an object or toy they resemble when they are in conflict. Responses might include light switches, tape recorders, toy trucks, puzzles, or beach balls. Students' explanations of their choices can reveal much about their conflict management styles.

In the scenario, "The Ugly List" (66-1), Terisita is appropriately angry and demonstrates some good assertive behavior, but she threatens Darryl when she says, "You and your buddies are going to know how nasty it is one day REAL soon," and she puts him down with the comment, "Listen at you; you can't even talk right." The activity enables the group to practice handling anger and practice problem solving through discussion and role playing.

In the scenario "Dancing in PE" (66-2), a teacher-student conflict enables students to see different points of view and practice communication skills. When processing the discussion about this scenario, students can learn how to appropriately handle conflicts with teachers.

In the scenario "Revenge After the Party" (66-3), students need to recognize that this situation should be referred to the police. Although someone might convince the party crashers to pay for the damaged furniture and the neighbor might drop charges, students cannot take the law into their hands. If they proceed to try to punish the party crashers by damaging their car, they are contributing to the problem rather than solving it. Students can understand that the situation in this scenario does incite anger and that there are better ways to handle anger than to seek retaliation. The "Revenge" scenario is an example of a situation that is NOT appropriate for peer mediation.

The handout "What Happened?" (66-4) is a useful tool for encouraging students to explore the consequences of their actions and try different ways of dealing with conflict.

— Session One (Group B) —

Objectives: Students will get acquainted.

Students will understand ground rules.

Students will think about how they handle conflict.

Students will begin to develop problem-solving skills.

Activities:
1. Ask students to introduce themselves with rhyming words (e.g., "I'm Ruth and I have a broken tooth.").

2. Ask students to imagine what kind of object (toy or mechanical device) they resemble when they are in a conflict at home, school, or in an extra-curricular activity.

3. Ask students to volunteer explanations for their choices of objects.

4. Affirm the group for their insight into how people deal with conflict.

5. Agree upon ground rules for the group: maintain confidentiality, no interruptions or putdowns, arrive on time.

6. Confirm the meeting schedule.

7. Ask students to share their expectations for the group.

8. Subdivide the group into pairs and ask students to share what they think most students fight about.

9. Ask a member from each pair to report what the pair discussed.

10. Choose a conflict that students mention and ask students to brainstorm ways to deal with the conflict.

11. Ask students to evaluate the ideas presented and choose acceptable solutions.

— Session Two (Group B) —

Objectives: Students will practice problem-solving skills.

Students will explore ways to deal with anger.

Activities:

1. Check in: Offer students the chance to share concerns about conflicts that arose during the week.

2. Briefly explore ways of resolving one of the conflicts presented if the conflict is relevant and the group is ready to deal with it.

3. Distribute the handout "The Ugly List."

4. Discuss Terisita's handling of Darryl.

5. Discuss what students think Darryl's point of view and motivation might be.

6. Ask students to role play the situation, with Terisita handling Darryl differently.

7. Ask the group to discuss how Darryl might feel about the approaches demonstrated. Would anyone like to speak for Darryl?

8. Ask the group to brainstorm ways to handle the situation.

9. Discuss the probable consequences of the suggestions.

10. Ask the group to choose a method of dealing with the problem.

11. Ask participants how they can apply what they learned.

To the Counselor: The counselor must determine the best use of time. If students bring up conflicts and discuss them productively, problem-solving activities involving their real conflicts can replace the use of the "Ugly List" scenario.

When students role play Terisita, they can practice expressing and diffusing anger. Without really knowing Darryl, it is difficult to know whether he just wants to play an inappropriate joke for attention or whether he is really cruel. When the group discusses what the school should do, one alternative is to ignore the situation rather than call attention to it. Other approaches include referring it to mediation, having an administrator suspend Darryl, and so on. Although different groups will decide how to handle this situation differently, all groups need to consider alternatives and their consequences before deciding.

SCENARIO:
THE UGLY LIST

Terisita:	But it's just not right. No one has the right to send around a list with people's names on it . . . "Central High's Ugliest Girl" . . . "Biggest Nose" . . . "Worst Breath." That's nasty, and you and your buddies are going to know how nasty it is one day REAL soon.
Darryl:	What? Are you threatening me again with your so-called boyfriend and his gang? Look, it's a free country and if we want to write something down and show it to the guys, WE WILL and you and your wussy boyfriend ain't gonna stop us!
Terisita:	How would you like it if WE made our own list? "Biggest mouth" . . . "Ugliest ears?"
Darryl:	I wouldn't care, cuz YOU don't matter.
Terisita:	Yeah, right.
Darryl:	Weez boys . . .
Terisita:	Listen at you . . . you can't even talk right. You . . .
Darryl:	Wait, don't you even . . .

Questions to think about:

What do you like about what Terisita said?

Was there anything she might be better off not saying? If so, what? Why?

If you were Terisita, how would you handle Darryl?

What do you think the purpose of Darryl's behavior is?

If you were a friend of Terisita and Darryl, how could you help out with this conflict?

What should the school do?

— SESSION THREE (GROUP B) —

Objectives: Students will develop skill in seeing someone else's point of view.

Students will practice communication and problem-solving skills.

Students will learn how to more effectively handle conflicts with teachers.

Activities:

1. Briefly check in: Ask students how their week went.

2. Distribute the scenario "Dancing in PE."

3. Ask students to define the problem. What does each party want? What do they need?

4. Ask students if they were Sadia's friend, what would they say to her?

5. How might this conflict be resolved so that everyone saves face?

6. Ask volunteers to offer situations in which they are having conflicts with a teacher. (Omit names of the teacher.)

7. Have students role play the teacher and student in the situation offered, demonstrating how the student might handle the situation with the teacher.

8. Process the role plays.

9. Review the use of "I statements" and clarify the different points of view.

To the Counselor: Most public schools have policies that would solve the problem in this scenario. The teacher should not place the student in the position of dancing when this violates her religion, even if the student has some ambivalence. Unfortunately, all teachers are not sensitive to students' points of view, and all teachers sometimes feel that students take advantage of them. Counselors and administrators often function as mediators, and parent conferences are sometimes appropriate.

When students discuss how to handle their own conflicts with teachers, practicing "I statements" and seeing the teacher's point of view are important.

SCENARIO:
DANCING IN PE

Sadia and Ms. Joynes have been rubbing each other the wrong way all quarter. PE class is over and Ms. Joynes calls Sadia aside.

Ms. Joynes:	Sadia, you know that the physical education department has a policy of requiring final projects each quarter. Since we have been doing aerobics, we are requiring all students in this class to perform an aerobic dance routine for their quarter exam. What seems to be the problem?
Sadia:	Well, you see, my father wouldn't like it.
Ms. Joynes:	What do you mean, "Your father wouldn't like it? . . . what does this have to do with your father?"
Sadia:	Well, we are Moslems, and we are not allowed to dance. You know we wear sweatsuits over gym clothes because we must cover our arms and legs.
Ms. Joynes:	But, Sadia, you have been doing aerobic dances in class all quarter. Why did you pick the class in the first place? Besides, I saw you dancing in the hall with those friends of yours. And your friend Trina is also a Moslem and she will dance.
Sadia:	But those steps in class were exercises, and my friends do folk dances . . . that's different.
Ms. Joynes:	I don't like being taken advantage of. You just don't want to practice the routine, Sadia.
Sadia:	(Head down and lips quivering) But I don't want to dance.
Ms. Joynes:	Well, if your father writes a note that you can't dance, I'll consider assigning a 30-page report on how aerobics affects different muscles.
Sadia:	(Pause) Can I go see my counselor?
Ms. Joynes:	(Muttering) OK, go ahead and whine to her!

— Session Four (Group B) —

Objectives: Students will understand that the police need to handle situations where someone has broken the law.

Students will understand the consequences of acts of revenge.

Students will consider effective ways to handle anger.

Students will develop strategies to deal with people who threaten them.

Activities:

1. Distribute the scenario "Revenge After the Party" and have a student read it aloud.

2. Discuss what will happen if Mike and his friends damage the party crashers' car. (What will this really accomplish?)

3. Make it clear that stealing is an illegal offense and that Mike and his friends have no authority to deal with it.

4. Discuss what students think Mike should do.

5. Ask students, "If you were Mike, how would you handle your anger?"

6. Discuss how Mike might deal with these students. (Include paraphrasing them, ignoring them, and having a humorous remark ready.)

7. Explain that it takes a stronger person to walk away from something than it does to stay and fight.

8. Discuss the consequences of provoking angry people: Suppose the other person is armed? Is a fight worth being in a wheel chair or without an eye for the rest of your life?

9. Ask students to describe similar situations and what people did in the situation that was helpful or detrimental.

SCENARIO:
REVENGE AFTER THE PARTY (66-3)

Mike slips into a chair in the back of the cafeteria to talk with his friend. His whole body seems to reek of a curious combination of tension and exhaustion. After a long hesitation, he starts his story.

Mike:	It shouldn't have happened.
Friend:	What shouldn't have happened?
Mike:	The threats. The stealing. All for nothing. And now this . . .
Friend:	What happened?
Mike:	I threw a party Friday night when school was out . . . for the holidays.

Some skinheads from school came to crash it. Me and some friends managed to keep them out of the house, but they stole some of my neighbor's furniture. Because of the noise, neighbors called and the police came, and the party was over. I wouldn't have known except the first day back at school, they were bragging about the stash they made off of me and my neighbors. They didn't take anything from my house, but they're acting all bad and everything, and it gets to me and my friends. How can they get away with that? They're always causing trouble. Today they wrote something on my book. Skinhead language. Bunch of freaks. I don't know what it means, but me and my friends are sick of their stuff. It's gonna get out of hand. |
| *Friend:* | What do you mean by "out of hand?" |
| *Mike:* | Why should we have to put up with this? I mean, why are they allowed to steal, threaten, break up parties, leave mean notes . . . they should be taught a lesson. They get away with stuff and that's not right.

We look like wusses because we don't do anything. That's why we started threatening back. Wait 'til they see what we'll do to their car!

They need to be threatened. Get a taste of their own medicine. |
| *Friend:* | Exactly what are you going to do? |
| *Mike:* | Beats me! |

SESSION FIVE (GROUP B)

Objectives: Students will understand the importance of exploring consequences of ways they handle anger.

Students will explore different ways of handling anger and conflict.

Activities:
1. Check in: Ask students to evaluate their week on a scale of 1 to 10.

2. Distribute the reproducible "What Happened?"

3. Ask students to take a few minutes to jot notes on the sheet.

4. Ask volunteers to share their experiences.

5. Ask group members to help each other explore different ways to handle their anger in their specific situations.

6. Ask students to volunteer personal goals for conflict resolution and anger management for the next week.

To the Counselor: At this point the group will have developed considerable cohesiveness, and students will support one another. It is hoped that they will be willing to work on trying out new behaviors. The counselor will find activities on anger management and listening in Part One useful as background.

WHAT HAPPENED? (66-4)

To the Student: Think about a recent incident that really bent you out of shape. What started it all? As you replay the experience in your mind, jot notes to answer the questions below.

1. What happened?_____

   _____

   _____

2. What specific behavior set you off?_____

   _____

   _____

3. Do you think this behavior was intentional?_____

4. How do you know?_____

   _____

5. How do you feel about this situation?_____

   _____

6. What will you do about it?_____

   _____

7. What will be the consequences of what you do?_____

   _____

SESSION SIX (GROUP B)

Objectives: Students will evaluate their learning.

Students will feel affirmed.

The group will conclude.

Activities:

1. Check in: Ask students to report about "unfinished business."

2. Ask students to share something they have learned from the group.

3. Offer imaginary gifts symbolizing positive contributions each student has made to the group (e.g., Offer an imaginary light bulb to one student for wonderful ideas, a conch shell to an excellent listener).

4. Ask students to take turns complimenting the others in a round, offering imaginary gifts.

5. Ask students to fill in evaluation sheets.

BLENDING CONFLICTING GROUPS

Much of the violence we observe in schools begins with a remark, a roll of the eyes, an unconscious gesture, or an unintentional bump. Before long, groups take sides and everyone seems to think his or her honor has been attacked. In more than one school the flick of a French fry has caused a near riot.

Officers Carl Taylor and Jim Nida of the Fairfax County police are trained mediators who have volunteered to run groups in schools. Thoroughly trained in multicultural awareness and prejudice reduction, Officers Nida and Taylor meet with opposing groups separately for about six sessions each before combining the groups.

Separate Sessions

In each session they offer group members an opportunity to share experiences and provide support for each other. Like all groups, the groups move through three phases.

First, Officers Taylor and Nida build rapport and trust with the group. They quickly begin to break down stereotyping with their own personal introductions. Officer Taylor, who is an African American, grew up in a white middle-class neighborhood, and Officer Nida, who is white, grew up in a lower-class, predominately black neighborhood. Group members establish ground rules and begin to share personal experiences.

During the work phase of the group, members discuss problems and brainstorm solutions. They frequently express their intention to fight. Officers Nida and Taylor assure students that it's okay to feel a certain way, but that they need to investigate before they act. They encourage students to explore consequences. Gradually, group members set goals to try new behaviors.

In the concluding sessions, Officers Taylor and Nida encourage students to meet with the opposing group. Although there is no quick fix, members eventually will agree.

Combined Group

After assembling the combined groups, Officers Nida and Taylor blend the groups and meet for several new sessions, repeating the phases of orientation, problem solving, and affirmation at the conclusion of the group.

Not surprisingly, some of the students try to sabotage the group. When a sabotaging sniper emerges, the facilitators either remove the sniper or let him have a chance to facilitate the group to meet his needs for attention.

The reproducible "What Happened?" (66-4) is an appropriate tool for use with the combined group during the work stage. Having students jot notes on the form, or at least read it and think about it, helps them focus on what happened and can produce productive discussion.

THE UNWILLING, MISMATCHED GROUP

Group composition is rarely perfect. Sometimes it is not possible to screen members, and sometimes group members have hidden agendas and little commitment to solving problems. What if a group has a number of bullies and a victim, and the bullies want to gang up on the victim during the group?

Consider the following worst case scenario:

It is the second session of a rambunctious group of seventh grade boys whom an administrator placed in a conflict resolution group. Somehow Carl, a typical victim, has joined the group and the other guys are warming up to having a field day.

"Oh, here comes the little nerd. He ruined our retreat. He wanted to go to sleep at midnight and spoil our fun!" chides Milton. "Yeh, yeh! the sissy has to go nighty night," piped up his buddy, Paul.

At this point most of the boys start giggling and pointing at Carl's untied shoelaces. Every time the counselor reminds them that the ground rules include "no putdowns," there is a three-minute reprieve. Then the dirty looks and jokes resume.

The counselor thinks, "Why are these guys doing this? What do they really want?" The counselor supposes they might want revenge for having cold water thrown on their retreat when Carl asked them to be quiet at midnight. Perhaps they want to feel important by picking a target who gets upset. And do they ever love a good fight!

Realizing that he or she must resume control, the counselor stands up and firmly says, "Look, we talked about conflict styles last week. You guys are really competitive and just love a good fight."

(The boys laugh and nod in agreement.)

If the counselor cannot disband the group, he or she needs to consider various strategies to capture the members' interest. These strategies can apply to all groups.

Appeal to Group Members' Need for Attention

Ask the group to choose an appropriate reward for following ground rules. Help them by offering suggestions to consider. Perhaps the group might like to prepare a videotape or a skit and perform for the whole school if they cooperate in planning the performance.

Sometimes removal from the group can be a real threat to someone who relishes the limelight. Calmly but firmly remove a group member who is particularly talkative and tell that student to stand behind the door until he or she is ready to return and listen.

Videotape a group session and replay the tape for the group as a problem-solving activity. Discuss what is happening and how the group might accomplish more.

Add More Structure to the Group Setting

Change the seating arrangement. Arranging chairs in a tight circle can be extremely effective. Try placing the most difficult students next to the facilitator, where a pat on the shoulder or a whisper in the ear is convenient. Place the most cooperative student across from the facilitator to open communication.

Reinforce the Ground Rules

Display a visual chart with the rules. Simply ask students, "What did we agree about putdowns?" Then ask group members to suggest what should be the consequences of breaking the ground rules. Give them concrete choices like receiving points for good behavior toward earning a pizza lunch or being removed from the group.

Use Rounds

In group counseling a round is simply asking students to participate in sequence, going around the circle. The counselor can use rounds to get information, get members focused, and get them involved. Some examples of ways to use a round follow:

❑ Numbers: "On a scale of 1 to 10, tell us how much that bothers you."

❑ Yes or No: "Are you ready to work on . . . ?"

❑ Word or Phrase: "In a word or phrase describe how you think someone who has been put down feels . . ."

❑ Sentence completions: "One way to solve this problem is to . . ."

Use Props

A visit to a novelty store or your attic and a little imagination can yield some wonderful ideas to help focus difficult group members. When using props, make instructions clear, praise appropriate responses, and keep the activity moving quickly. When you have terminated the activity, have a wastepaper basket ready to collect the props so they are not tossed about the room.
Some examples of props and their uses as metaphors follow.

❑ Pipe cleaners: Ask, "How much does . . . bend you out of shape? . . . how can you *straighten out?*"

❑ Buttons: When discussing anger, pass out an old button or a paper button to each student who then shares something that triggers anger, or let students push a buzzer when someone shares to reinforce positive contributions.

❑ Balls: Toss a ball to a student to indicate a turn to speak. Then have that person pass the ball to the person he or she chooses to respond.

❑ Paper bags: Ask students to place imaginary concerns in their bags. Ask volunteers to share their bags with the group.

❑ Pictures: Distribute photographs or magazine clippings and ask students to describe which feelings the pictures convey.

❑ Chairs: Place three chairs in a triangle. Ask a bully to sit in the *speaker chair* and two volunteers in the other seats, one to paraphrase content, the other to paraphrase feeling. (See Lesson 27-1.)

Use Role Playing

Set up a situation similar to the one you would like the group to discuss, but avoid using a person in the group as an example. Without focusing on what members of the room have done, role play the situation and try reverse role playing as well. (See page 227.)

Keep Encouraging Problem Solving

When something doesn't work, ask students, "What is happening?" Focus on the situation, not a person, and brainstorm ways to improve the situation. Remember, the facilitator is trying to teach skills, not humiliate individuals.

Use Videotaping

Videotaping can be a powerful tool. Try videotaping a problem-solving exercise and ask group members to evaluate how they solve problems. Be sure to get group members' permission to tape before using this approach.

Reinforce the Positive

Have students share successes and ask students to affirm each other's improvements. Difficult students are often starving for acceptance, recognition, and praise.

Keep Developing Skill in Working with Groups

Working with groups is a worthwhile, rewarding activity. Co-facilitation is particularly useful because it provides the opportunity for facilitators to give one another feedback. It also provides the kind of flexibility that enables one facilitator to leave with a difficult group member.

Groups usually work smoothly, particularly when members have been screened. Sometimes, however, the reluctant group members have the most to learn. Even when they appear not to be listening, they can gain much.

Group facilitators can also personally benefit from keeping a journal in which the facilitator keeps notes about each session and comments about personal reactions. Through the journal the group counselor can develop even more skill.

Section Ten

CONFLICT RESOLUTION IN THE CLASSROOM
(Background Information)

PREVENTING CONFLICT IN THE CLASSROOM

Teachers deal with conflicts on a daily basis. Conflicts resulting from putdowns, power plays, threats, miscommunication, and unwillingness to share responsibility appear in classrooms everywhere. All teachers face the question of how they might resolve these conflicts. Since the teacher's primary duty is to teach and provide a maximum learning experience, prevention is particularly important.

Ground Rules

Good classroom management rules can prevent an entire range of conflicts before they begin. Establishing clear ground rules can avert many conflicts. These basic procedures work because students frequently cite fairness as their number one concern when dealing with teachers.

Sticking to the ground rules involves consistency and follow-through. The teacher who allows students to walk in late to class on some days and then punishes students for the same action on other days is asking for trouble. In addition to applying to discipline matters such as talking and tardiness, consistency applies to grading. It's difficult to argue about a clearly defined procedure consistently carried out. Follow-up is also important. If a teacher tells a student that he or she will call parents if the student doesn't show up for detention, the teacher must follow through or suffer the consequences.

Positive Relationships

Students read teachers like books. The way a teacher communicates rules and grading systems matter. The teacher who nonverbally looks as if he or she is asking for trouble or cannot handle it will usually get it. Almost innately students have a feeling about teachers and how teachers are going to react toward them as individuals and as a class. These initial thoughts are usually verified with the teacher's first major "dealing" with them. Few students complain if the teacher outlines rules and regulations and sticks to them from day one. Grumble, probably. Resist or become insubordinate? Not usually.

Because students do need security and recognition, kindness is important. It is important not only because kindness should be the way of the world, but because any kindness offered is like money in the bank on those days when the teacher and the student are at odds. In addition, teachers need to remember that in this day and age, their kindnesses to a young person may, unfortunately, be the only act of grace a kid gets—either in school or out.

Awareness of Student Needs

"Reading a student" can be a valuable skill. There's a time to call attention in a positive or negative way to a particular child, and there's a time to postpone any such attention directed toward the young person. What does the student need? How will the student(s) react to praise or discipline?

Consider the following scenario in which students are teasing an overweight student in a gym class.

It was a touchy situation, Ms. Boone thought. They were ganging up on Todd again, but the group was smart. They were teasing him just enough to make him feel badly. Just enough to make her wonder: Should I ignore it or intervene?

But it was hard to ignore Todd's lumbering body cross the basketball court. Personal fouls or foul play? It did seem that he was getting the raw end of each play. And yet . . .

Although the teacher probably could not have prevented this conflict, prior knowledge about the students could help the teacher "read" the students, anticipate reactions, and prevent escalation of a conflict. If the gang is a group of guys who will only up the ante if the teacher disciplines them, then poor Todd will only suffer more. If that is the case, administrative action will be necessary. If this gang includes a bunch of cutups or "wanna be toughs," then the teacher can probably stop the teasing right there in gym class with a firm comment or gesture. Again, close teacher readings are necessary.

Even praise at the wrong moment can illicit an unwanted response from the recipient of the good intentions. The scenario "Travis the Terrible Troublemaker" (Lesson 61) illustrates this point. Praising the student who argues to get attention is really feeding the dispute.

Consider the needs of the entire class. Some things are handled better in public to make a point to the class and to ensure that class members cannot say that someone got away with an action. Students in the gym class need to learn that teasing the overweight student is unacceptable. However, backing a student into a corner can backfire. When a student needs to save face, the teacher needs to remove the student and deal with the behavior privately.

Often the time of day or class composition affects students in ways the teacher cannot control. Difficult students who function poorly at the end of the day do have to attend afternoon classes, and classes with feuding cliques cannot often be separated. In matching discipline to needs, teachers need to remember to pick their battles. Sometimes a teacher must walk a fine line, determining how much horse play to ignore and when to draw the line.

When a teacher can anticipate reactions, he or she can prevent many conflicts.

Setting Up Prevention Plans with Several Steps

Students with limited impulse control need reminders. When struggling with a student who asks for attention on a daily basis, consider meeting with the student after class and working out a preventive plan that has several steps. For example, when the student starts to act out, you might agree to place a stick-on that reads "THINK." If the "THINK" stick-on appears twice in a class period, the student serves detention.

When dealing with a class of attention-getting students, consider establishing a clearly announced procedure. When a student acts out, why not write a portion of his or her name on the board, with the idea that if the whole name goes up, the student has detention? Alternative ideas might include devising simple point systems.

Detention

Detention, that consequence detested by student and teacher alike, does offer constructive opportunities. First, the detention period can offer the teacher the chance to get to know the student better and engage the student in resolving conflict. Detention offers a place for the teacher to mediate between two disputing students who have disrupted class or to explore ways to change disruptive behavior without backing a student into a corner before an audience of classmates. Students need to change behavior, but they also need to save face.

Detention really does not serve its purpose if it becomes a study hall or sleepfest. Why not use the time constructively? Why not consider community service? Students can fill out a sheet of paper that reads: "I WOULD BE DELIGHTED TO WASH YOUR BOARDS AND CLEAN YOUR DESKS." The teacher can require students to obtain ten signatures of teachers whose rooms they will clean. Supply the buckets and materials, and let the students supply the energy. Teachers will like this approach, and students will usually comply with rules to avoid detention.

70 RESOLVING CONFLICTS IN THE CLASSROOM

Unfortunately, there are conflicts that cannot be prevented. Whenever possible, it is advisable for the teacher to deal with the conflicting students outside of the classroom because teaching needs to be uninterrupted. Nevertheless, constant bickering, threats, miscommunication, and unwillingness to share responsibility appear in many classrooms. Teachers do observe conflicts and need to explore ways to resolve them.

What Is the Problem?

In the scenario "Constant Bickering: Looking for Trouble" (70-1), Missy and Tina are constantly picking on each other. The teacher's primary responsibility is to teach the class and he or she cannot stop the class to mediate. The teacher has to quickly figure out what is going on and how much intervention to make. Since these two girls have a history of fighting, threats cannot be taken lightly. On the other hand, if they are possibly showing off for the benefit of the class, it might be better to ignore the bantering if it is brief.

Exploring Possible Short-Term Solutions

What are some interventions that the teacher might use?

- ❏ Separate the students.
- ❏ Remove one of the students from the room.
- ❏ Isolate the students and ask them to write out what happened and what they see as the problem. Then discuss their written comments with them after school.
- ❏ Use humor.
- ❏ Give the students a nonverbal signal to stop.

Evaluating Possibilities

Before choosing an intervention, consider the consequences. If a teacher has good rapport with a student, jokes and nonverbal signals work well. However, if the teacher has not previously used humor, or if the teacher has not been consistently firm and fair, a joke or a hand on the shoulder of the girls will be perceived as patronizing. These well-intentioned actions could even escalate the argument and draw the teacher into the fight.

Exploring Possibilities for Long-Term Solutions

Hopefully, the teacher has some sense of the students' history of disciplinary action. What are the teacher's bargaining chips? What leverage does she have? What do the students really want or need?

- ❏ Are there strong, supportive parents? Would a telephone call or a conference help?
- ❏ Are either one of them on a sports team? Could an influential coach be called on to help?
- ❏ Could the chance to discuss the situation with a counselor help? What about a conference with the student, counselor, and parent together?

❏ Are peer mediators available to help?

❏ How often are these students suspended? How might an administrative referral help?

❏ Would you consider negotiating a behavioral contract with the student, including signatures of enforcing parties?

Choosing a Solution

There are many possible ways to handle these difficult students. After evaluating the possibilities in light of the background of the problem and the teacher's relationship with the students, the teacher can choose a number of good strategies. Perhaps the teacher can request a conference including the student, counselor, and parent to define the problem and generate ways of resolving it. Solutions might include peer mediation, clearly defined consequences at home, or any other strategy the student might choose.

Implementing the Plan

As with all preventative measures, consistency and follow up enable the plan to work. For example, if the teacher agrees to notify Missy and Tina's parents when they bicker again, she must follow through. Similarly, if Missy and Tina's parents agree to use a particular strategy, they must follow through. If Missy and Tina agree to go to mediation and their solution isn't working, they must agree to try again.

SCENARIO:
CONSTANT BICKERING: LOOKING FOR TROUBLE (70-1)

The girls are "at each other" again.

Ms. Hall watched uneasily as the two girls bantered about, upping the stakes as the word "fight" promised to turn into a physical fight later. "Heaven knows they both know how to fight; they've been in enough of them already this year," she thought. Ironically, at the middle school, they had been friends running around in the same basic group, but, as often happens when reaching high school, the girls joined different groups, almost gangs, and tolerance of other groups seemed impossible, even between old friends. And now this, this constant bickering.

Missy:	How embarrisin'.
Tina:	Pick it up, witch.
Missy:	I don't think so.
Tina:	For real? I don't think you heard me. Pick it up.
Missy:	Look, the book dropped out of your hand . . . .
Tina:	When you knocked it out of my hand.
Missy:	And now, *you* pick it up. It's that easy.
Tina:	It'd be easier for me to see you later.
Missy:	I'm around.

The two girls settled in to working on their projects again, content for awhile with just snide remarks under their breaths, with eyes glaring at each other. But the tension was real and palpable, and the other girls waited to see what the "actors" in this play would do.

SCENARIO:
THREATS: BRIDGET, SHAUNA, AND THE BOYFRIEND (70-2)

Since the following scenario occurs at the end of class, it does not threaten to disrupt instruction. However, the teacher needs to deal with the conflict.

> At the end of class Ms. Jones heard Bridget's frightened voice: "I can't leave. What'll I do?"
>
> Bridget's voice sounded even more scared than her face looked as she stared at Dottie, hoping her best friend could tell her what to do.
>
> "Look, you've *got* to leave," advised Dottie. "The bell's going to ring. You can't just stay in seventh period forever. Anyway, Shauna's crazy. She was probably just running her mouth to make a scene."
>
> Bridget muttered, "Yeah, I know how crazy she is, and that's the problem. When we walked past her in the cafeteria, we both heard her say, "I'll get you, you witch." She *had* to be talking to me. I'm the one who's been seeing her boyfriend. Who else could she have meant? And remember what I told you about what happened in fifth period? Those girls warning me about taking the bus home? Did they imagine that? . . . God, I wish I had never gone out with Trevor. He hit on me; I didn't go after him. She's crazy. You saw Shauna fight her own brother in the library that day he argued with her. I'm trapped. Why doesn't she beat up on Trevor? He's the one who started this whole mess. What am I going to do?"

The bell rang, and all the students headed out. All except Dottie and Bridget.

What Is the Problem?

Clearly, Bridget and Dottie feel threatened and need safe passage home. Underlying the problem are the needs for security, control, and recognition. Shauna lost her boyfriend, her security, control, and recognition to Bridget and is responding with a threat. In turn, Bridget's safety, or security, is in jeopardy. Shauna's position is that no one else can date Trevor.

Exploring Solutions

In many cases like this scenario, the threat is an idle threat. The track record of the persons in question becomes important. If there is no immediate information about those making the threats, then the teacher must act to protect Bridget and possibly Dottie too. This action might include calling their parents, arranging rides home for the girls, notifying an administrator of possible trouble on the bus or at bus stops, escorting the students, setting up a conference, and/or setting up a mediation between Bridget and Shauna .

Evaluating Possibilities

The number of options the teacher selects will depend on the availability of resources. If Shauna has a track record indicating she is dangerous, administrative referral is important. Shauna needs to know the consequences of her threats.

Counseling is appropriate for all students to help them more appropriately handle their anger and fear. A counselor can help Bridget explore ways to deal with Shauna and become more assertive toward anyone who might threaten her.

Mediation is a particularly appropriate referral, and the teacher can help if she can convince Bridget and Shauna that mediation will help them find a long-term solution to their problem. Although a ride home with the teacher, the counselor, or one of their parents may protect them for the moment, the girls must find a long-term solution to their conflict.

SCENARIO:
MISCOMMUNICATION: SPIC AND SPAN (70-3)

Some conflicts simply arise out of miscommunication, which often cannot be prevented. In this day and age of schools housing students from many different countries, the chances of miscommunication are even greater. Unfortunately, many of our students coming from other countries know very little English. Consider the following scenario from a basic study skills class.

Manuel and Mercedes were almost touching as they sat in the classroom. In their native language, they began to talk softly to one another.

"Study tools? What are study tools?"

"I don't know," Manuel shrugged.

"But, Manuel, that's the name of this class."

"Maybe it's a construction class. Did you bring your hammer today?"

They laughed together, but then stopped as they noticed that the teacher and everyone else was looking at them. After an interminable and embarrassing moment, the class members got back to work.

"Why does that guy keep looking over here?" Mercedes whispered.

"Ignore him, Mercedes. We're brand new and they're all checking us out. That's all. Besides, you're beautiful!"

They both looked at the guy and laughed. The guy, Brian, felt uneasy. He was sure they were making fun of him. He turned to his buddy, pointed in Mercedes and Manuel's direction, and asked, "Hey, Greg, what'd ya think of the new students? . . . Isn't she pretty?"

Greg shrugged as if to say he could care less. They laughed and the bantering began. Brian and Greg started quietly joking around, occasionally pausing to look at the new students before continuing to talk and share clandestine laughter. Before long, Greg caught himself trapped in a huge laugh that got the whole room's attention.

"Okay, everybody, back to work," the teacher remarked as she walked around the room. As she continued to walk around, Brian caught Manuel's eyes. Eyes talked, and then talked some more. It wasn't a pleasant conversation.

Brian got so caught up in the staring game that he knocked over his coke can. The teacher at once became furious.

"That's it, Brian. You've spilled your last coke in my class. Go get some water and paper towels and clean that up GOOD."

"OK, OK, Ms. Doane, I'll get it up. I'll get it up right now. Don't worry," he said with his charming smile, "This floor will be good as new. Spic and span!"

Manuel didn't know many English words, but he knew "Spic." He'd see Brian later. Correction. Manuel and his friends would see Brian later.

When the bell rang ending the class, Manuel "accidentally" nudged Brian as they passed through the doorway. As if on cue, Brian nudged back and they began to circle each other like Bantam roosters getting ready to fight.

© 1996 by Ruth Perlstein and Gloria Thrall

Ms. Doane came into the hallway saying, "OK, OK, get to class. Brian, hold up."

Pulling him aside, she said, "Manuel's new here. Give him some slack. He doesn't understand . . ."

"Oh, he understands all right. He understands what he WANTS to understand."

Brian left it at that and walked off. As she watched him turn the corner, Ms. Doane felt somewhat relieved that the possible conflict had not occurred, but she also felt uneasy. Was the situation ended, or had a fight just been postponed?

This scenario shows Ms. Doane making some good choices. Since she knows the makeup of the group, she monitors behavior closely by walking around the room and staying involved with what her students are doing. She stays aware.

Second, she stands at the hallway at the changing of classes. Many skirmishes could be avoided if teachers stood at the hallways at class changes. Ms. Doane knows her kids and knows that Brian is a cutup, not a bad kid at all. He is little young for his age, but that's all. There's no history of fighting or suspensions, and she wants to help keep it that way.

Ms. Doane has had enough students to know that Manuel is a gentle person and is also not looking for a problem. In addition, she knows that pride and getting locked into a corner are the pitfalls that could change this miscommunication into something bigger. She has nipped it in the bud, but will continue to monitor them closely. Knowing your kids and really looking at them closely and as individuals are keys to good classroom management. If these students had been two roustabouts or gang members, the situation would be different. But Ms. Doane knows her kids and she watches them continuously. She does a lot to prevent problems.

But suppose Manuel is quick tempered and likely to fight? Suppose Brian is insensitive and a bit arrogant?

What Is the Problem?

The problem may be a simple miscommunication, or a real threat to the students' identity, security, and recognition. Both sets of students thought the others were talking about them. Both suspected prejudice.

Exploring Possible Solutions

Ms. Doane has several options. Among them are the following possibilities:

- ❐ Refer Brian and Manuel to their counselors. A third party can help them understand each other's point of view, deal with their feelings, and explore ways to communicate with each other.
- ❐ Refer Brian and Manuel to mediation. Ms. Doane can help by telling them about mediation, which can help them talk to one another and work out their misunderstanding.
- ❐ Deal with each of them directly, pointing out the other's points of view and feelings.
- ❐ Consult with the ESL teacher for a class activity on cultural differences and work the activity into classroom instruction.
- ❐ As an opening activity, use Lesson 21, "Exploring Cross-cultural Miscommunication."

Choosing a Solution

Ms. Doane would use her knowledge about her students to make an appropriate decision and continue to monitor them during class.

CARRYING WEIGHT ON THE TEAM
ALGEBRA CLASS (70-4)

Collaborative learning has caught on in the high school for good reason. Learning in groups is an effective means of digesting, incorporating, and using information. Collaborative learning is also the way adults work at their jobs in the real world. But oftentimes, or maybe even most of the time, groups for learning are "uneven." One or two students work harder than the rest; they "carry" the group. This situation may not be harmful for the doers, but it doesn't enhance the learning experience of the slackers, and sometimes it can even cause conflict.

A mathematics teacher has asked groups to prepare presentations about different ways to solve a problem. When the groups were working, the teacher overheard the following conversation.

"But YOU were supposed to bring in the problems today. I brought in some solution ideas and the posterboard, but that won't go too far without the problems."

"Geez, I said I was sorry. Don't I always come through in the clutch? You always get so hyper. We'll meet the deadline. Just chill out. You always want to be two weeks ahead of schedule, and it's driving me nuts."

"Oh, yeah? And you're always flying by the seat of your pants. How ANYONE . . ."

The teacher listened on. He'd heard that argument many times before. And not just from Mindy and Janice. These were typical comments made by all of the students as they worked in their groups. It seemed opposites always attracted whenever groups formed. Typical were Mindy, the creative one, and Janice, the born organizer.

While Mr. Berger genuinely believed in collaborative projects, there was always the problem of how to get along and get the job done. He was open for any and all suggestions.

Exploring Possible Solutions

❏ Have checkpoints or checklists that divide a big project into workable chunks.

❏ Consider if students should or should not pick their own groups.

❏ Give both a group grade and an individual grade to encourage the unorganized genius, but not penalize the organized plugger.

❏ Give students the opportunity to report on their input and to evaluate what they have learned.

DEALING WITH UNDERCURRENTS OF DISSENSION

Every year teachers seem to experience one class in particular that appears to thrive on putdowns. Students feed on each other and consider the day complete only if they've made someone feel badly or if they've managed to put someone down in some form or fashion.

Bad chemistry can make a classroom almost intolerable, breaking down the spirit of both the teacher and the students as individuals and as members of a group. Forget learning because survival becomes the name of this game, the objective of both teacher and classmates alike. Although the following activity is not a quick solution, it could help in many of these situations.

Provisions for the lesson include a small paper bag for each group. Each bag should contain five stick-on labels with each of the following words: IGNORE ME, DISTRACT ME, TEASE ME, PRAISE ME, AGREE WITH ME, and ARGUE WITH ME.

Objective: Students will become more aware of how their words and actions affect others.

Activities:
1. Divide the class into groups of six.

2. Explain that when you distribute bags to each group, students are to follow these directions:

   Each of you will reach in the bag and pull out a stick-on label. Without looking at it, you will place it on your forehead. NO ONE is to tell you what it says, but each of you will follow the instructions on each other's stick-on label. The topic of discussion will be: "Why students should be able to leave campus for lunch."

3. Distribute a bag to each group and instruct students to draw their labels, place them on their foreheads, and begin discussing their topic.

4. Lead a discussion about how it feels to be treated a certain way during a discussion.

5. Assign a writing on how this activity relates to personal behavior and a commitment to improve.

To the Teacher: Beware of a field day with putdowns. This activity requires equal time for reflection and the establishment of clear consequences for putdowns.

72   TEACHER-STUDENT CONFLICTS

Teachers are human too. When a student provokes a teacher, intentionally or otherwise, it is easy to overreact and figuratively push the student into a corner. Sometimes the defiant student will refuse to back down, and the teacher can become involved in a power play in which the war for control becomes destructive. Since the balance of power is not and should not be equal in the student-teacher relationship, win-wins are difficult.

Consider the following scenario.

SCENARIO:
YOLANDA STUCK IN HER SEAT (72-1)

Yolanda was at it again. There she was in the back of the room snickering and goofing off. That was bad enough, but she was suckering Mike and Kathleen in, and now they were having trouble getting their work done. Was there any end to Yolanda's path of destruction?

"Yolanda," the teacher called. "Please get back to work."

"Back to work?" Yolanda retorted. "I never started!" Laughter abounded as Yolanda basked in the positive feedback she was getting from her classmates.

"Yolanda."

"Yeeeees?"

"Get to work."

Yolanda shrugged, and for the briefest of moments the teacher labored under the delusion that all was well.

"WHOA!"

It had to be Yolanda.

"Yolanda!"

"No, it's not my fault this time. Mike pushed me and that's why I fell out of my chair. I . . ."

"Yolanda, move to the seat by my desk."

"Why should *I?* Mike's the one who . . ."

"Yolanda . . ."

"No, I want you to tell me why *I* have to move and Mike doesn't?"

"Because you have been causing problems all period long and Mike hasn't."

Yolanda's eyes glared and she muttered, "You can't make me move."

Consider the Needs of Both Teacher and Student

Although the teacher's need for control is really nonnegotiable, it is important to respect the student's need to save face. If the teacher can ultimately gain Yolanda's cooperation and Yolanda can save face, this difficult situation can be turned into a win-win.

Consider Alternative Approaches

What approaches might the teacher take to prevent a shouting match or the need to remove the student from the class?

What if the teacher were to try the following approaches?

❒ Offer Yolanda a choice within clear limits.

"Okay, Yolanda, I'm not going to argue with you. You have two choices. You can move to another part of the room or you can plan to spend some time in the In School Suspension Room next week. Take your choice."

❒ Try to negotiate a truce.

"Okay, Yolanda. Maybe I am jumping the gun. Tell you what, let's do this. If you can manage to sit there without there being any more problems, then that'll work just fine. But if there's another problem, then you have to move. Agreed?"

❒ Temporarily remove Yolanda's audience.

"Mike and Kathleen, you don't seem to be able to work next to Yolanda. Please move over near the windows." (Meet with Yolanda later.)

❒ Focus on the important issue.

"Look, the seat's not really the important issue. We need to be quiet to complete this lesson."

It would be helpful to meet outside of class at a later time without an audience. In the one-to-one conversation between teacher and student, it is possible to temporarily neutralize the power struggle between them. Once they remove the power issue, the disputants can really negotiate. They can more easily find a way to prevent this scenario from recurring. Sometimes a third party, a counselor or administrator, can help.

Position Versus Interest

Understanding the difference between position and interest can help resolve conflicts between teachers and students. For example, teachers often maintain the position that students receive grades based on homework handed in. Yet their interest is really that students learn content, concepts, or skills, which might be measured in many different ways. Students and teachers certainly share an interest in success, and the student and teacher might negotiate alternative ways to give the student credit. On the other hand, the teacher's position might be nonnegotiable. If so, they will have to find the next best alternative and find an acceptable way to earn credit.

Communicating with Angry Students

Teachers sometimes encounter angry students who perceive themselves as having been dealt with unfairly. It is really frustrating to have a student's eyes glare at a teacher when hours have been spent devising assignments and grading papers. The following tips might be helpful.

❐ Don't get defensive.

❐ Acknowledge the anger and offer a time and place to listen to the student outside of class.

❐ When privately discussing the situation,
  - Let the student vent.
  - Paraphrase the student's feelings.
  - Clarify limits.
  - Offer to work together to solve the problem.
  - Explore possible solutions.
  - Agree on a solution.
  - Meet with a counselor acting as a third party.

Dealing with an Angry Perfectionist

Student-teacher conflicts involve all kinds of students. The following scenario involves an excellent student who does not write particularly well. In addition, Cloe has relatively weak analytical skills and sometimes has difficulty following instructions.

SCENARIO:
CLOE CLAMORING FOR GRADES (72-2)

Cloe is a serious student, who values excellence and strives for perfection in all of her work. She works so hard that sometimes she can barely see straight.

Last week she handed in a 12-page research paper on the English Romantic poets for her honors English class. She had worked on the paper for weeks and stayed up all night before the paper was due to make sure that the paper had no errors.

Cloe knew that some other students simply slapped their work together at the last minute and didn't bother to revise their work. But Cloe didn't care, as long as she received credit for producing the best work. Cloe was really proud of this English paper and knew that she would earn one of the very few A's in this difficult class.

This morning Miss Price, her English teacher, returned the papers. Cloe received a B+. To make matters worse, she saw that Ed Hanley, who threw things together at the last minute, received an A. Why Ed couldn't have spent more than two hours on that paper! She *knew* her work was the best and Miss Price simply wasn't fair. Cloe was absolutely furious. She scowled at the teacher.

Cloe approached Miss Price's desk, taut with tension. "Why did I get a B+ when I deserved an A?" demanded Cloe.

Miss Price quietly invited Cloe to come in after school to review the paper. As Cloe left class, Miss Price overheard Cloe muttering comments about how much she hates this English class. No doubt Cloe will be badmouthing Miss Price until the last bell rings.

After school Cloe stumbles into Miss Price's room with a huge chip on her shoulder and proceeds to tell Miss Price just how she feels.

Avoiding the Defensive Trap

While Miss Price lets Cloe vent, she silently talks to herself, saying, "Don't let her get to you . . . she has a problem . . . don't take her dumping personally . . . you'll be okay." Then she paraphrases, "You really worked hard on this paper and you are really upset about this grade."

Position Versus Interest

Miss Price and Cloe's positions are at odds: Miss Price thinks the paper is worth a B+, and Cloe thinks it is worth an A. It also appears that their interests differ. Miss Price wants Cloe to learn to write better, and Cloe wants to get A's more than she wants to learn. Cloe's values will not be changed quickly, and the conflict begs a solution in the present. Where is the shared interest? Both Miss Price and Cloe would like Cloe to end up with an A at the end of the quarter. It is also in both of their interests to have the criteria for grading clarified. The grade results from an evaluation of the product and not the time the process takes.

Problem Solving

Miss Price continues, "Can we talk about how we might work things out?"

Cloe snaps, "There's nothing to work out . . . I deserve the A."

Miss Price calmly comments, "Cloe, you're upset, but you are a bright, reasonable person . . . could we talk about what makes an A paper an A paper? . . . grades are really important to you . . . could we discuss how you might earn an A?"

Cloe reluctantly agrees and Miss Price explains that she bases her grading on expectations for a particular assignment and not on the time it takes to produce the product. Unfortunately, some excellent students sometimes get stuck, spin their wheels, and take a long time to produce results. Miss Price reexplains the criteria she looks for in an A paper, and she offers some specific constructive comments about how Cloe's paper might have been improved. Then she offers some suggestions for helping Cloe raise her grade to an A.

She asks:

❏ What if you revised this paper?

❐ What if you were to show me a draft of your next paper and let me suggest improvements for revision before you hand it in?

❐ What if I agreed to change your grade if you worked on improving your writing in the writing lab?

❐ What if you submitted a plan to produce papers that met the criteria for an A?

Although Miss Price in this scenario is an appropriate model, different teachers might generate different possible solutions.

TEACHING THE CONCEPTS IN ACADEMIC CLASSES

Practice makes perfect. Application of a principle allows the student to incorporate a lesson into his or her own world. The connections between "book learning" and real-world experiences can enhance students' understanding of conflict resolution. Since conflict is a part of human nature and therefore a part of all literature and history, there are an inexhaustible number of lessons to be taught. The concepts can be taught across the curriculum.

Social Studies Classes

Conflict is an essential concept in history and current affairs. In a way history is the study of the confrontations between different groups and how their approaches to conflict shaped the world. The lesson "Yugoslavia" (Lesson 74) offers students a chance to apply problem-solving skills to current affairs. As with conflicts between individuals, conflicts between countries are based on unmet needs. Disputes about territory are based on the need for security, identity, and control. The lesson plan "Taiwan and China" (Lesson 75) illustrates the importance of shared interest in problem solving. A common interest enables groups to more easily find a win-win solution. Unfortunately, it is extremely difficult to mediate some conflicts because disputants become stuck in different positions or because disputing parties are not committed to conflict resolution.

Social studies teachers can easily devise lesson plans to help students understand different points of view. For example, students can write letters from the point of view of the Native American, the Northerner or Southerner during the American Civil War, the American colonists and the English during the American colonial period, or the English- or French-speaking Quebecers.

The perusal of the first part of this book can give social studies teachers ideas about how to adapt lessons to help students understand the concepts of conflict resolution.

Foreign Language Classes

Many of the lesson plans and concepts in this book can be used in foreign language classes. Students can write about and role play simple conflicts and analyze them in any language. Students can even practice mediation in different languages. Why not have two student mediators practice mediating a conflict about sharing a locker, car, or textbook in German, French, Spanish, or Russian?

Science and Mathematics Classes

"The Physics Olympics" (Lesson 80) is applicable to all classes in which teachers use collaborative learning. In this lesson Phillip does not want to work with his team. Although Phillip is not interested in a relationship with his team members, he shares an interest in winning. Because he cannot do all the work required in the physics class competition by himself in the required amount of time, he needs the help of the other team members. It is in Phillip's best interest to tutor them in physics so that they can do a good job of helping him. Phillip's team can review their course work in a variety of ways. Brainstorming ways to divide up tasks and work together can also be an extremely useful activity in many academic areas.

English Classes

All fiction is based on conflict. Plots move through attempts at resolution and consequences result. Characters have needs, points of view, and they communicate. The study of character and communication comprise much of the content of English curricula.

In this section the lessons based on *I Know Why the Caged Bird Sings* (Lesson 76) and *The Adventures of Huckleberry Finn* (Lesson 77) offer students the chance to practice understanding different points of view. The lesson on Huck Finn also addresses different kinds of conflict.

This section also includes two lessons based on *King Lear* (Lessons 78 and 79). The first helps students practice defining problems, looking at how the characters deal with problems, and practicing collaborative problem solving. The second lesson helps students clarify different points of view and practice communication skills.

Literature also communicates ideas. Studying works of writers like Thoreau, Ghandi, and Martin Luther King, who advocated nonviolence, can teach students to respect peaceful conflict resolution. The Center for Teaching Peace in Washington, D.C., has developed a 16-week course about alternatives to violence based on peace literature.

The following activities are only a smattering of the many possible lesson plans that combine the real world with the world of books.

YUGOSLAVIA

To the Teacher: This lesson plan assumes that students have studied or researched the Serbian/Bosnian/Croatian conflict. The background information sheet "The Former Yugoslavia" (74-1) provides a brief summary of the situation.

Objectives: Students will analyze the conflicts in the former Yugoslavia.

Students will understand the different points of view represented in the conflict.

Students will attempt to apply collaborative problem-solving techniques to the Serbian/Bosnian/Croatian conflict.

Activities:

1. Divide the class into small groups and distribute the background information sheet (74-1) along with relevant magazine articles.

2. Ask students to review the conflict in the former Yugoslavia and answer the following questions:

   ❏ What is the problem? . . . What are the needs of each group?
   ❏ Explain the point of view of each of the warring factions.
   ❏ What are some ways that the warring factions can arrive at a peace agreement?

3. Explain that mediation is a process where the mediators help disputants arrive at a resolution of their conflict and distribute a sample Mediation Menu (47-1).

4. Ask groups to plan a mock mediation. Two students will choose the role of co-mediators, and three students will represent Serbia, Bosnia, and Croatia, respectively.

5. Ask one group to volunteer to act out their mock mediation.

6. Discuss the factors that make mediation difficult in the former Yugoslavia.

7. As an assignment ask students to research another conflict and write a paper defining the conflict (e.g., India and Pakistan, Irish Protestants and Catholics, or the Arabs and Israelis).

BACKGROUND SHEET:
THE FORMER YUGOSLAVIA (74-1)

During the summer of 1991, deep-seated ethnic hatreds erupted into a brutal and widespread war. The roots of conflict in Yugoslavia began more than 1,500 years ago. Religious and ethic differences combined with a history of oppression to create enemies for generations.

Yugoslavia became a separate country after World War I. The majority of its people are Slavs, who have historically split into antagonistic factions. Most Serbians belong to the Orthodox Church, which separated from the Roman Catholic Church. The majority of the Croatians are Roman Catholics. Most Bosnians are Slavic Muslims.

After World War II, Communist Marshal Tito led a federation of Serbia, Montenegro, Croatia, Slovenia, Bosnia-Herzegovinia, and Macedonia. Tito was strong enough to unify Yugoslavia, but the federation began to collapse after his death.

President Tito's death in 1980 created great instability in the Yugoslavian government. Representatives from each of the republics rotated as heads of the Yugoslavian state. However, unless a president had Serbian support, he had very little power.

By the late 1980s, the inflation rate rose to 80 percent and each republic decided to operate its own affairs. Many Serbians in Bosnia and Croatia decided that only Serbians should govern Serbians.

In 1990, Slovenia and Croatia declared their independence. Macedonia and Bosnia followed. Serbia, the most powerful of the republics, and Montenegro were all that remained of Yugoslavia, and the Serbians took control of the federal government. Clashes of troops began to erupt.

Outside nations tried to encourage truce talks, but they also began to side with the breakaway states. The Croatians had thought that the European Community would help them against the Serbians. The Serbians had also thought that the EC would help them, and they planned to gain as much land as they could before the European intervention, which never came.

Despite many peacemaking attempts, the war continues. Both sides have accused the other of atrocities beyond description. One atrocity leads to another as the hatred and need for revenge continues and the fighting escalates.

Some analysts argue that although they are enemies, the Croatians and the Serbians are equally antagonistic toward the Bosnians. Both the Croatians and the Serbians have taken over most of what used to be Bosnia.

TAIWAN AND CHINA

Objectives: Students will understand the difference between position and interest in international conflicts.

Students will understand the importance of common interests in conflict resolution.

Activities:

1. Explain how Communist China and Taiwan arrived at a peaceful agreement:

   The Nationalist Chinese refused to be governed by the Communist Government and set up an independent government on Taiwan, which the Communist Chinese government refused to recognize. The Communist government threatened to declare war on Taiwan. The United States intervened militarily to keep the two disputing parties apart. When the Chinese Communist government adopted a more open policy toward the outside world, the United States stated that it would not trade with mainland China if it declared war on Taiwan. The Communist and Nationalist Chinese then agreed not to fight, even though the Communist Government would still like to control Taiwan.

2. Discuss the following questions:

   ❑ What was the position of the mainland Chinese?
   ❑ What was the position of the Taiwanese?
   ❑ What interests did the Chinese and the Taiwanese share?
   ❑ How did they achieve a peaceful agreement?

3. Discuss why the Chinese were more able to reach a peaceful agreement than the republics of the former Yugoslavia.

4. Discuss alternatives to violence that different countries might consider. What common interests might they be encouraged to focus upon?

76   *I KNOW WHY THE CAGED BIRD SINGS*

To the Teacher: Maya Angelou's *I Know Why the Caged Bird Sings* is a novel rich in lessons about human behavior, family dynamics, and the indomitable human spirit. Two scenes are particularly abundant in anecdotes that help us to begin to understand Maya and how she views the world and her place in it. The first scene finds Maya upset with her grandmother. This grandmother has raised Maya and her brother, serving as both their mother and mentor. Maya is angry with her because the grandmother allows some "po white trash" to taunt and tease her. The second reading comes later in the book when Maya's father has a girlfriend and she and Maya do not get along at all. The following exercises give students an opportunity to practice looking at situations through someone else's eyes.

This lesson can be used with the dialogue journal activity described in Lesson 25.

Objective: Students will practice looking at situations and people from a different point of view.

Activities: 1. Ask students to read the "po white trash" scene. At the end of this scene the grandmother and Maya say little about the differing views they have about how grandmother handled the situation.

2. Ask students to work in pairs and create a dialogue about what Maya and her grandmother would have said if they had had an extended conversation about the event.

3. Have volunteers present their dialogues to the class and discuss the different ways Maya and her grandmother view what happened and how the event should have been handled.

4. Ask students to read the section of the book in which the father's girlfriend first appears and the problems between Maya and her begin.

5. Distribute the reproducible "Letter About Maya" (76-1) and ask students to write letters, pretending to be the girlfriend.

Name _____ Date _____ (76-1)

LETTER ABOUT MAYA
(from the girlfriend)

To the Student: Assuming that you are Maya's father's girlfriend, write a letter to one of your friends or a family member.

In this letter explain how you see Maya and how you feel about Maya and your relationship with her.

HUCKLEBERRY FINN

Objectives: Students will understand the different points of view of the characters in *The Adventures of Huckleberry Finn.*

Students will understand the different kinds of conflict (intrapersonal, interpersonal, intergroup).

Activities:

1. Ask by a show of hands how many students think they need to be "civilized."

2. Subdivide the class into small groups and ask them to discuss how they think the following characters would define "civilized."

    ❏ Miss Watson
    ❏ Huck Finn
    ❏ Widow Douglas
    ❏ Jim

3. Ask spokespersons from each group to report the definitions.

4. Record the definitions on the board and discuss them.

5. Ask four volunteers to role play each of the characters (Miss Watson, Huck Finn, Widow Douglas, and Jim) following these directions:

    Imagine sitting at a conference table together and sharing your understanding of everyone else's point of view to be about "being civilized." Use paraphrasing to show that you really understand. For example, Jim might begin saying to Widow Douglas, "You really want Huck to have better manners."

6. Discuss the scenario that the role players have created.

7. Discuss how Huck, Jim, Tom, Widow Douglas, Miss Watson, Pap, Aunt Sally, and Uncle Silas might complete the following sentences: "I believe . . . I resent . . . I am hurt by . . . I want . . . I realize . . . I hope . . . I need . . . I expect . . .".

8. Discuss examples of the kinds of conflict found in the book: intrapersonal conflict (e.g., Huck: whether to protect Jim), interpersonal conflict (e.g., Huck and his father), and intergroup (e.g., Huck and Joe versus the community).

KING LEAR'S PROBLEMS

To the Teacher: The teacher may want to use the reproducible "Conflict Problem Characteristics" (1-1) at the beginning of this book. The major conflicts in *King Lear* result from both Lear and the Earl of Gloucester listening to the wrong people. The tragedy might have been averted if Lear had listened to Kent and if the Earl had not believed Edmund's story about Edgar.

Objectives: Students will practice defining conflicts, observing conflict resolution styles, and using collaborative problem solving.

Activities:

1. Explain that conflicts are based on problems. Common problems underlying conflict are unmet psychological needs: identity, security, recognition, control, and fairness.

2. Ask the class what the underlying problem is between Lear and each one of his daughters.

3. Ask what the underlying problem is between the Earl of Gloucester and his sons.

4. Discuss specific examples of other problems that lie at the root of conflicts in *King Lear:*
   - ❒ incomplete communication
   - ❒ inaccurate information
   - ❒ different viewpoints

5. What do each of the characters want? . . . need?

6. Explain that people deal with conflict differently and ask the class to cite textual examples of the following approaches to dealing with conflict: denial, confrontation, and problem solving.

7. Discuss several examples of times that the tragedies might have been averted.

8. Subdivide the class into groups and ask them to create a different ending to the play that more satisfactorily meets all of the character's needs.

9. Distribute the Assignment Sheet (78-1) and plan a follow-up discussion.

KING LEAR'S PROBLEMS
ASSIGNMENT SHEET

Think of a conflict you have experienced or observed recently.

_____

_____

_____

Describe how one of the leading characters in *King Lear* handled a conflict.

_____

_____

_____

Compare and contrast the handling of the recent conflict with the one in the play.

_____

_____

_____

_____

_____

_____

_____

_____

_____

79   **MORE ABOUT KING LEAR'S CHARACTERS**

Objectives: Students will understand the points of view of the main characters in *King Lear*.

Students will practice "I messages."

Activities:
1. Subdivide the class into small groups.

2. Ask each group to plan a presentation in which students role play the characters of Cordelia, Regan, and Goneril, explaining their points of view.

3. Ask the groups to present their role plays and discuss them.

4. Explain how to formulate "I messages" (Lesson 33).

5. Ask students to complete the reproducible "I Messages for *King Lear*" (79-1), composing appropriate "I messages" for characters in the play.

6. Ask volunteers to share the "I messages."

7. Discuss how "I messages" can help people deal with anger.

8. Assign a "Dear Diary" in which one of the characters gives a chronological overview of the plot of *King Lear* from his or her point of view.

"I MESSAGES" FOR KING LEAR

To the Student: An "I message" or an "I statement" is an effective way to get someone else to hear how you feel and why. The format for an "I message" follows:

I feel_____when you_____

because_____(and I need_____).

Choose two characters in *King Lear* who might have used an "I message" appropriately in the play. Formulate the "I messages" and cite the scenes in which the characters could have used them effectively to avoid problems.

Character A:_____

Scene/Situation:_____

"I message":_____

Character B:_____

Scene/Situation:_____

"I message":_____

THE PHYSICS OLYMPICS

Objectives: Students will be motivated to study for their final exam.

Students will recognize the value of collaborative problem solving.

Students will understand how mediation can help resolve conflicts.

Activities:

1. Explain that the class will form teams to compete in a classroom competition, The Physics Olympics, composed of a series of events: Heat, Light, Sound, Electricity, Velocity, and so on.

2. Explain that each winning team member will receive a Gold Medal, worth an "A" on the physics final exam. Silver medal winners will receive an additional 20 points on their exam grade, and bronze medal winners will receive an additional 10 points.

3. Announce the names of the six team captains, the students with the highest numerical averages to date in the physics class, and call them up to the front of the room.

4. Ask the team captains to take turns drawing names of class members out of a hat to form teams.

5. Tell the teams they will have two weeks to practice for the event.

6. Distribute the scenario "Phillip's Fighting Physics Team" (80-1) and ask students to read it.

7. Discuss how the conflict between Phillip and his team members might be resolved.

8. Discuss how a third party might help provide a win-win solution for Phillip's team.

9. Explain that mediation is a process that can help students resolve various conflicts by encouraging collaborative problem solving. Inform students about mediation procedures in your school.

10. Wish the teams luck as they collaborate in their practicing physics problem skills on various topics or "events."

To the Teacher: Since The Physics Olympics is too long for Phillip to complete on his own, he cannot win without the help of the others on the team.

SCENARIO:
PHILLIP'S FIGHTING PHYSICS TEAM

When Phillip heard about The Physics Olympics, he was really annoyed. His "A" in physics class was secure. He might have to review a few old tests before taking the exam, but he could probably ace the exam cold. He looked over his team members, folded his hands in front of him, sighed, and rolled his eyes.

Phillip thought, "Why do I have to spend my valuable time making that stupid Jamie learn how to do a physics problem? Jamie couldn't distinguish mass from velocity if he were the ball rolling on an incline!"

Even though Jamie was the worst physics student in the group, he was willing to work, and he really did understand those sound problems. "It's good to have a brain like Phillip on the team, but why is he such an arrogant snob? Everyone hates him . . . he's such an impossible nerd!"

Joe and Mary, the other team members, really like Jamie and respect his willingness to work. They are average physics students who would like a higher grade. After all, a good grade in physics would improve their college applications. Phillip could help them, but working with Phillip will be such a pain. Who wants to ask him anything? Will they be able to stand his condescending tone?

The group plans to meet for practice at 4 P.M. at the stadium bleachers. Phillip is late, and Joe and Mary begin plotting a way to show Phillip what they think. Maybe they'll TP his house this evening. Jamie quietly hopes Phillip gets his whole house trashed. He says nothing because he realizes it's silly to get involved.

When Phillip shows up, the tension could be measured in pounds per square inch.

What do you think Phillip wants? . . . needs?

What do the other team members want? . . . need?

What common interests might they have?

What are some ways they might resolve their conflict?

What strategies might they use to work as a team?

What would be the consequences of some of these ideas?

Section Eleven

EXTRACURRICULAR ACTIVITIES
(Background Information)

EXTRACURRICULAR ACTIVITIES
(Background Information)

In an ideal world, activities proceed with the mellow harmony of a finely tuned orchestra. In reality, what extracurricular activity sponsor or coach doesn't see harmony threatened by various conflicts? In all activities from the pep squad to the chess club, control, fairness, and recognition become important issues. Even in honor societies students want the glory of membership, but argue over requirements for community service. Band members vie for positions, drama club actors and stage hands sometimes bicker backstage, students argue about which band to hire for the prom, and athletic teams fume about who gets top billing in the school newspaper. Everywhere students and sponsors complain that others don't carry their weight.

Prevention

As in the classroom, setting ground rules or clearly presented guidelines for activities can prevent a host of problems. Carefully developed constitutions can go a long way in preventing arguments in clubs. Similarly, when sponsors and students develop behavioral guidelines and spell out consequences for breaking rules at a retreat, fewer conflicts occur. Although teams often do work together smoothly at most activities, many conflicts naturally arise during activities.

Mediation Can Help

The mediation process can really help club sponsors. When a conflict arises that does not clearly require disciplinary action, mediation can work wonders. The sponsor can either act as a mediator, refer the conflict to peer mediation, or choose an impartial mediator such as a counselor. In "My Fair Lady," (81) a scenario in this section, the sponsor calls in a parent trained in mediation to deal with a rather large group. Because the sponsor is perceived as being biased, he is really not an appropriate mediator. The sponsor wisely calls in a neutral party whom everyone finds acceptable.

Practicing Collaborative Problem Solving

To resolve conflicts, sponsors and students need to practice their collaborative problem-solving skills. In the scenarios "The Dunking Booth" (82-1) "The Lead Story" (82-2), and "The Key Club" (82-3), the sponsor offers students the chance to brainstorm solutions to their problems. In each of these scenarios, the sponsors can help students when they get stuck by proposing "what if" questions. These questions serve as trial balloons for students to think about. They can become jumping boards for other ideas. By focusing on the problem, helping students generate possible solutions, and asking them to consider consequences, the sponsor is acting as a mediator.

Focusing on the Future

In many disputes students get stuck in their pursuit of fairness and truth when truth cannot easily be determined. For example, in the scenario "The Dunking Booth," students may never find out whether or not the student government officers have a "deal" with the company that rents the dunking booth. Spending much time arguing this point may be a waste of time. Problem solving and mediation is future oriented. Students need to look ahead and find ways to prevent anger about the dunking booth in the future.

Dealing with Anger

Sponsors can also help students learn to handle anger. Anger is a natural emotion. When channeled into goal setting and competitive activities, it can become a positive force. When anger threatens to escalate and become destructive, sponsors and coaches can help students express their anger and cope with the anger of others more effectively. In addition, sponsors need to closely examine their own anger management skills as they work with difficult people themselves.

Encouraging Nonviolence

Preventing fights is difficult. Students all too often perceive walking away from a fight as a sign of weakness. A sponsor or coach is in an excellent position to encourage students to see fighting as an inadequate way of resolving conflict. Athletic coaches have both the status and capability to encourage peaceful conflict resolution. Through role modeling and discussion an athletic coach can help athletes see avoiding a fight as appropriate. Coaches can use the handout "Questions for Role Models" (85-2) to encourage athletes and student leaders to think about how they might reduce violence. The scenario "I'm Going to Beat Him Up" (85-1) provides a tool for discussing ways to prevent fighting.

A Program for Sponsors

This section concludes with an appropriate activity for a faculty meeting or a brief training session for sponsors. There is nothing like practicing collaboration to convince sponsors that it works.

In addition to the approaches this section describes, sponsors will find the activities in Part One useful for helping students resolve conflicts.

81 USING MEDIATION TO RESOLVE A CONFLICT: "MY FAIR LADY"

Mediation can help sponsors resolve conflicts. Consider the following scenario:

The fall drama production is "My Fair Lady," and opening night is only a week away.

As usual, the cast is tense, and nothing seems ready. However, this week is much worse than usual. The cast members look as if they are about to declare war. They are rude to each other, and the stage hands are all ready to quit.

The chorus is a particularly angry group. They think the leads are so uppity that members of the chorus are considering dropping out of the performance. One of the chorus members grumbles, "We can't even get into a real dressing room. They dumped us into that dingy *other room* with half mirrors. Snooty Eliza Doolittle needs a 12-foot mirror all for her highness self. La-de-da!"

The drama coach, Mr. Anders, is really worried that the production will fall apart. Since he fears that students might say he plays favorites, Mr. Anders selects an impartial counselor or parent to meet with the cast.

The impartial counselor or parent, Mr. Falls, functions as a mediator, and practices the standard five steps.

Introduction

Mr. Falls begins by saying,

"I understand that you have all worked hard on this production and that you are having some difficulty. I am here to help you work things out so that "My Fair Lady" can continue. I promise to be impartial . . . I am not here to judge you, but I will help you work things out.

"Before we begin, we need to agree on some ground rules. First, all of you will have a chance to speak, but only one person can talk at a time. In other words, there can be no interruptions.

"Second, can you agree not to put other people down?

"Last, can we keep this meeting confidential? In other words, let's not talk about what is said outside of this room?

"Do we need any other rules? Are these agreeable? Is it okay for me to be your mediator?"

The group members shuffle, mumble a bit, but agree and settle down and sit in a large semicircle on the floor of the stage.

Defining the Problem

Mr. Falls continues, "Who would like to begin?"

A timid-looking sophomore, a soprano in the chorus, raises her hand and comments, "Those leads just try to walk all over us. Who do they think we are . . . they won't even let us in the dressing rooms . . . we're just dirt around here."

Mr. Falls paraphrases, "You don't feel valued as a cast member."

The student playing Professor Higgins speaks out: "We need that chorus . . . that scene where the chorus sings will look stupid without them, and they'll sound awful without the soprano . . . she's the singer with a strong voice!"

Mr. Falls paraphrases, "You *do* need that soprano."

A number of students voice their various complaints of being ignored, snubbed, talked about, told to pick up after others. Group members also complain that the coach takes sides, always defending his favorites.

Mr. Falls listens and paraphrases and carefully seeks a common interest. Mentally, he groups the concerns and says, "Looks like there are two problems here: lack of communication and respect . . . do I understand that right?"

The cast nods, almost in unison.

Mr. Falls focuses on a common interest and says, "But you all really would like to see this production be good."

The cast nods affirmatively again.

Problem Solving

Mr. Falls separates the problems before exploring solutions. "Let's begin with communication, and we can talk about respect after we tackle the first problem . . . is this okay?

"What are some of things we might do to solve the communication problem?"

Various cast members offer suggestions. Students propose assigning someone the task of posting daily notes, agreeing not to gossip, organizing daily feedback sessions, simply telling others when they feel left out (see the "I Statements" in Lesson 33), remembering that the show needs everyone's participation, sharing dressing rooms, and trying to see the other person's point of view.

Choosing Solutions

Mr. Falls explores each idea with questions like "How might you go about sharing dressing rooms? . . . How will this improve communication?" After the group selects a strategy, he asks, "How might you ensure that you can follow through on this idea?"

Eventually the group chooses several solutions and returns to the topic of respect. Again, the group listens to different points of view, brainstorms ideas, and chooses some approaches.

Concluding

Mr. Falls summarizes the progress the group has made and rephrases the solutions. When he asks what role the coach might play in helping the group follow through, the group agrees that Mr. Andrews might help monitor their progress.

Suggestions to Keep in Mind

In this situation or a similar one, several ideas the drama coach might keep in mind follow:

❏ Try to focus on issues and separate them from people. In this way students are less likely to gang up on someone.

❏ Try to focus on the data: What happened?

❏ Deal with real out of field behavior individually.

❏ Focus on interest. It is in all cast members' interest to have a successful production.

❏ Deal with students' anger with you: acknowledge the anger, don't get defensive, and offer to discuss possible solutions.

❏ Clarify areas of responsibility.

❏ Establish clear consequences for not meeting specific responsibilities.

USING COLLABORATION TO RESOLVE ACTIVITY DISPUTES

Knowing about mediation can really help a sponsor out. Sponsors can help students sort out their difficulties and explore ways to resolve their disputes.

Consider the situation in the following scenario.

SCENARIO: THE DUNKING BOOTH (82-1)

The Mayfest was a highly anticipated happening at Haywood High School. In addition to making money for all the participating clubs, it signaled the time of good weather, spring break, and the end of school. It was no wonder that all the clubs looked forward to it, spent long hours preparing for it, and wanted the dunking booth for their main event. What could be better than seeing old man Higgins being dunked? Or to see what Ms. Franklin's hair really looked like without all that hair spray? Would Ms. Bitters's tons of mascara run? Did Mr. Withers wear a rug? These were burning questions that could only be answered by a dunk in the booth.

But there was a problem. The Student Government Association had had the dunking booth for the past two years. Somehow they had a "deal" with the company that rented it out, and no matter how far in advance the French Club and the Drama Club called to reserve it, it was always "already taken." The clubs were calling "foul play" and wondered why the "rich" SGA needed anymore money or attention at this all-important event. It was beginning to turn a school unity event into an exercise of division and hard feelings. What to do?

Defining the Problem

Defining what seems to be an obvious problem can become complicated. What is the problem? What do the students want? What do they need? Fairness seems to be a major issue, but what do the arguing parties perceive as fair? Is not Student Government Association an umbrella organization? If so, why should other clubs have equivalent status?

What about the basic needs for security, recognition, and control? Do the students in the French Club really feel slighted and need to be recognized as an important group in the school? Do they see getting a chance to sponsor the dunking booth as their only chance to enhance their status?

Is the issue money? After all, the dunking booth is a good fund raiser, and the clubs really need money. What does SGA spend its money on anyway?

On a different note, is the real problem procedural? How much hard feeling has resulted from the elusive reservation system that always has SGA in charge of the dunking booth?

Brainstorming Possible Solutions

After the sponsor helps students define their problem, he or she can ask students to brainstorm possible solutions. If the group agrees that there are a combination of problems, then the sponsor might separate the issues and deal with them one at a time or in groups.

Focusing on the Future: A Win-Win Solution

Mediation is not an investigative process. Whether the SGA had a "deal" with the company that rents it out or not is less important than agreeing to establish clear rules for reserving the booth in the future. Time would be better spent if the sponsor focused on fairness in the future. The sponsor might simply ask, "In the future, how might sponsorship of the dunking booth be handled more fairly?"

Brainstorming Possible Solutions

Although students are often creative about brainstorming, they occasionally get stuck. If they get stuck, the sponsor can offer a few suggestions in the form of "what if" questions or sharing ideas that "others have found helpful." This procedure may encourage students to take ownership for some of the ideas. If they feel the ideas came from their group, they are more likely to accept them.

In "The Dunking Booth" scenario the sponsor might offer the following suggestions if students do not think of them:

- ❑ Have club representatives bid for preferred calendar dates at a summer leadership retreat.
- ❑ Assign the dunking booth by a lottery.
- ❑ Understand that SGA is an umbrella organization and devise a system to share manpower shifts and profits.
- ❑ Rotate the sponsorship of booths.
- ❑ Explore other attractive events that different groups might sponsor. How might sponsorship be distributed?
- ❑ Be creative; think of more ideas for good booths.

Choosing a Solution

After the group brainstorms a number of possibilities, the sponsor can ask students to evaluate each idea in terms of whether it offers all students what they want. Then the group can choose a solution.

Continuing to Practice Problem Solving

The need for recognition and control also appears in the scenario "The Lead Story" (82-2), where a club sponsor overhears a discussion between two students on the school's winning wrestling team. The sponsor fears that Stephan, the wrestler who is upset, might start a fight with some of the guys on the newspaper staff. How might he help Stephan explore alternative ways of responding to the slight?

In "The Lead Story" scenario the club sponsor can paraphrase Stephan's anger: "Stephan, this newspaper article really has you upset . . . you really feel the wrestlers get a raw deal."

Then the sponsor might encourage Stephan to explore ways of changing the situation. The following are some suggestions that might come up during the discussion.

- ❐ Talk to the newspaper sponsor: Tell the sponsor how you feel and ask how this might be prevented in the future.
- ❐ Talk to the coaches.
- ❐ Talk with the new administrator who always attends the wrestling meets.
- ❐ Meet with the athletic director or the principal.

"The Key Club" scenario (82-3) is another example of a conflict with the potential to escalate. The sponsor can help the group resolve the conflict by asking the group to collaboratively problem solve.

Before helping the group resolve the conflict in the scenario "The Key Club," the sponsor needs to make sure the Key Club members understand the different points of view of the disputing parties.

Again they need to explore what the parties want and what they need. After some discussion the Key Club members will probably agree that parents have a common interest: a need to know that their children are safely and appropriately entertained. Sometimes a situation like this one can get out of hand because the different groups might feel their identities threatened. Certainly a conflict can be avoided by brainstorming ways to achieve the win-win. The dispute is over what is appropriate. Might there be another way?

SCENARIO:
THE LEAD STORY (82-2)

"Well, they did it again," Stephan muttered as he looked at the school newspaper.

"Did what?"

"Put our winning the districts on the bottom of page two, while the basketball's latest fiasco, fifth loss in a row, is plastered on the front page. That's incredible!"

"Well, what'd you expect? You know basketball rules around here."

"Yeah, I know that. I just don't know why. We work our butts off for this school, just as hard, if not harder, than the basketball players. And this. It's just not right, I tell you."

"No, it isn't, but what are you going to do? What can you do?"

"You'll see!"

SCENARIO:
THE KEY CLUB (82-3)

The Key Club at Crew High School sponsors community service projects each year. This year a group of four Key Club members decided to act as big brothers to a group of neighborhood second graders and take them bowling Thursday evenings.

The car pool came early, and the second graders usually had to wait for 20 minutes before they could have their bowling alley. Since the children often became impatient, one of the Key Club members, who is a popular Sunday School teacher at a nearby Fundamentalist church, decided to organize a Bible class to occupy the children while they were waiting. They reasoned that this class would be a constructive activity to keep the children from being restless.

Most of the children's parents thought the Bible class was a wonderful idea, but one of the children was Jewish and his mother did not want him to take a Bible class taught by a Fundamentalist Christian. This child really enjoyed bowling and was upset about the possibility of his mother removing him from the league.

Community members had differing positions and were getting hostile.

83   DEALING WITH A DIFFICULT COLLEAGUE

Occasionally, power plays occur between the sponsors themselves. In the scenario "Wrestling Mats" (83-1), the sponsor needs to deal with her own anger. Some assertiveness is also in order because the cheerleading coach has every right to feel angry.

When the coach considers what to do with the cheerleaders, she needs to quickly explore the consequences of her decision. What are her interests? She wants the wrestling coach to share the mats, but she is not interested in creating more bad feeling between the cheerleaders and the wrestling coach.

Once the cheerleading coach decides to approach the wrestling coach, she should try the following approach:

❒ Begin by saying something positive (e.g., she might compliment a wrestler for winning a match.).

❒ Tell the coach exactly how she feels and why, using an "I statement" (e.g., "When you forget to let the cheerleaders have the mats for their practice, I really get angry because they have a right to use them too.").

❒ Ask how this situation can be avoided in the future (e.g., "What can we do to prevent this from happening again?" "What do you suggest I do if you forget again?" "How can we work this out?").

❒ Discuss ways for the cheerleaders to get the mats in advance of the practice.

SCENARIO:
WRESTLING MATS (83-1)

The cheerleading coach was furious. As the cheerleaders stood around, doing nothing, time was running out for this practice session. This was their day to use the wrestling mats, and the mats were all gone. And she knew where. The only question was: Should she go down to the wrestling room and create a hassle, or should she have the girls work on something else besides their building? It wasn't so much that the girls didn't have other skills to work on; it was the fact that the mats had been "missing" twice before. The wrestling coach said he "forgot," but she wondered. He didn't sound remorseful. Was this just one more putdown for her and her girls? One more putdown for their sport? What should she do?

84   HELPING STUDENTS DEAL WITH ANGER

Sponsors can prevent many conflicts from escalating by helping students to deal with angry people. When one group provokes another, there is nothing to be gained by the revenge tactic or screaming back. It is difficult not to want to lash back in anger, but sponsors can help students find alternative ways to deal with anger.

In the "The Football Dump" scenario (84-1), the cheerleading coach is preparing to follow the athletic bus to their away game.

Exploring Solutions

First, Ms. Collins listens, trying to figure out what happened. After awhile the girls agree that they need to solve some problems. First, they need to find a way to get to the game. Second, they need to find a way for Amanda, Julie, and Lisa to feel they can depend on Tina, Shannon, and Collette to show up at the bus on time and cooperate. And the three girls also need to save face. Third, the cheerleaders need to plan what to say to the football coach.

With the sponsor's guidance, the cheerleaders can probably resolve the first two problems fairly quickly. But dealing with the football coach is tough. Ms. Collins might suggest the girls make an appointment to talk with the football coach and the football captains. Before the meeting Ms. Collins might ask the girls to describe how they think the football players feel. She might suggest the following strategies for the meeting:

❒ Let the football coach or captains vent.

❒ Paraphrase them (e.g., "We see that being on time and remaining quiet on the bus are really important to you.").

❒ Let the football players know how you feel and why.

❒ Offer to work out a way to prevent this situation from occurring again.

If possible, the coach might help the girls out by quietly discussing their need to save face with the football coach.

SCENARIO:
THE FOOTBALL DUMP (84-1)

As Ms. Collins, the cheerleading coach, assembles her equipment, she hears the girls coming before she sees them. She suddenly remembers that the cheerleaders are supposed to be on the bus with the football players on their way to the game. As they approach her room, she distinguishes voices, words, and anger.

"The nerve. He is the most pig-headed person I've yet to meet. How are we supposed to get to the game now?" Amanda, the cheerleading captain, steamed.

"We weren't even late, Ms. Collins. In fact, we were a couple of minutes early, and the bus was gone. We thought maybe the bus was parked somewhere else, but Lisa checked. How can they do this?"

"The football coach is still mad about last time when we were late," Julie answered. "This is payback time."

"Yeah, we were late," Tina chimed in, "but now we miss the biggest game. All because we were late for one game."

"Not 'we,' Tina. You, Shannon, and Collette were late. The rest of us were on time. Then you three sealed it by not abiding by their 'no talking on the way over' rule," answered Julie. "C'mon you know how seriously the players and coach take their game."

"And we don't? What's a football game without cheerleaders?" Amanda asked.

"It's not that," Ms. Collins replied, "it's just with the budget cuts you are sort of their guests on that bus, and guests . . . ."

"Should be treated with respect," Julie retorted, "not with punishment. Didn't we decorate all of their lockers and give them candy this past week, even though we usually only do that at the Homecoming game? We tried to make up to them."

"Well, apparently that wasn't enough," Amanda said. The group sat around wondering: "What was enough?"

85 **ENCOURAGING NONVIOLENCE**

Students who tend to fight frequently believe that fighting is the only way to resolve a conflict. "Right is might" is part of some students' value system. It's difficult to convince the aggressive young person that it takes a stronger person to walk away from a fight than it does to attack someone. More than most adults, sponsors are in a position to influence students to explore alternatives to fighting. They often hear students like the following one in the scenario which is reproduced in (85-1) on page 300 as a handout for staff development discussion.

SCENARIO: I'M GOING TO BEAT HIM UP

"That nerd really bugs me! He keeps walking up to me at practice and saying, 'You took my baseball glove.' He sounds like a parrot: 'you took . . . you took . . . you took . . . you took.' I'm not going to put up with his stuff anymore.

"I'm going to get him . . . I am. Not during practice, of course. I'm not dumb enough to punch him in school, but just wait til me and them guys get to the parking lot. [Eyes narrow and nostrils enlarge.] I'm going to beat him up."

What can the activity sponsor who heard this young person do?

Listen

First, the sponsor can let the person vent and acknowledge his or her right to be angry. Paraphrasing helps. For example, the sponsor might say, "Sounds as if his accusations really get on your nerves."

Explore Consequences

The sponsor might ask, "What will happen if you beat him up?" The student will probably shrug his or her shoulders and mumble, "Nothing." The sponsor might ask some of the following questions:

- ❐ Suppose he has a weapon? Is beating him up worth getting injured . . . maybe getting stuck in a wheelchair?
- ❐ Do you really think people admire students with short fuses?
- ❐ Do you really think that is the right thing to do?
- ❐ Do you really want to stoop so low as to assault him?

Consider Using Humor

The sponsor who has excellent rapport with this student and a record of successfully using humor might try a riskier paraphrase to break the tension. For example, he or she might say, "Oh, no . . . you're going to start a WAR OF THE GLOVES, are you? I can just see the headlines now . . . I can also see the suspension list . . . oh no!"

Suggest Alternatives

The sponsor can suggest a variety of alternatives by posing "what if" questions. Some examples follow.

- ❐ What if I were to get the two of you together and help you talk this out?
- ❐ What if you were to tell him exactly how you feel and why?
- ❐ What if one of us were to let the coach know about this?
- ❐ What if you were to at least investigate before you act?

Other Alternatives

The sponsor can certainly talk with the other student and try to get him to change his behavior or refer the situation to a counselor or administrator. In addition, the sponsor might arrange for an adult to be near the bus stop after school.

Referral to Mediation

If the sponsor suspects that the conflict masks another conflict that the two students might need to resolve, mediation might be appropriate. However, if either of the students is really irrational or uninterested in solving the problem, mediation is not appropriate.

Student Role Models

One of the sponsor's most effective tools for encouraging nonviolence is the ability to empower athletes and student leaders to be role models.

Many schools have formal mentorship programs in which athletes and leaders mentor younger high-risk students. This pairing offers recognition to the mentor and a superb opportunity to encourage high-risk students to avoid violence. When dealing with leaders and athletes, sponsors can encourage them to spread the word that it takes a stronger person to walk away from a fight than it does to fight.

Sponsors can meet with student role models to discuss concerns and ways to avoid violence. Peer mediation training and discussion of the scenarios in this section can help. In addition, the reproducible "Questions for Role Models" (85-2) can provide the coach with a useful discussion tool. After filling in the questionnaire, coaches can ask mentors to discuss their responses and share ideas for encouraging younger students to consider alternatives to fighting.

Since athletes and student leaders interact with a wide variety of students, it is an excellent idea to train them to become peer mediators.

SCENARIO:
I'M GOING TO BEAT HIM UP (85-1)

"That nerd really bugs me! He keeps walking up to me at practice and saying, 'You took my base-ball glove.' He sounds like a parrot: 'you took . . . you took . . . you took . . . you took.' I'm not going to put up with his stuff anymore.

"I'm going to get him . . . I am. Not during practice, of course. I'm not dumb enough to punch him in school, but just wait til me and them guys get to the parking lot. [Eyes narrow and nostrils enlarge.] I'm going to beat him up."

Name _____ Date _____ (85-2)

QUESTIONS FOR ROLE MODELS

1. Try to recall a time you got into a fight but should have handled your problem better.

   What happened?_____

   _____

   What do you think you should have done?_____

   _____

   Why?_____

2. Try to recall a time you wanted to fight but didn't.

   What happened?_____

   _____

   What did you gain?_____

3. Think of a person you really admire._____

   How does that person handle conflict?_____

   _____

4. If you were a mentor to a younger student, which of the above experiences would you share with that student?_____

   _____

5. What advice would you give the younger student about fighting?_____

   _____

   _____

   Why?_____

   _____

86 A FACULTY ACTIVITY: COLLABORATION

The following activity is appropriate for a faculty meeting or a training session for sponsors.

Objective: Sponsors will hone conflict resolution skills.

Sponsors will share ideas for how to encourage conflict resolution in activities.

Activities:

1. Divide the group into small groups.

2. Distribute a scenario from this section to each group. Choose from "The Dunking Booth" (82-1), "The Lead Story" (82-2), "The Key Club" (82-3), "Wrestling Mats" (83-1), or "The Football Dump" (84-1).

3. Ask each group to discuss how group members might deal with the situation described in the scenario.

4. Ask a spokesperson from each group to share a summary of the group discussion.

5. Discuss the consequences of various strategies mentioned by participants.

6. Show the reproducible "Dealing with Anger" (86-1) on an overhead projector, giving examples of interior dialogue (see "Avoiding the Defensive Trap," 39-2). Ask participants to comment and add suggestions.

7. Show the reproducible "I Statements" (86-2) on an overhead projector and explain that these statements are a way to express how you feel and why.

8. Project the reproducible "Problem Solving" (86-3) and explain and discuss it.

9. Discuss how sponsors might use the strategies in this presentation.

To the Facilitator: You may choose either to give each group the same scenario or to distribute different scenarios to each group.

DEALING WITH ANGER (86-1)

WHEN YOU ARE ANGRY,

- ❏ SAY SOMETHING POSITIVE IF POSSIBLE.

- ❏ USE APPROPRIATE INTERNAL DIALOGUE.

- ❏ EXPRESS HOW YOU FEEL AND WHY.

- ❏ ASK TO DISCUSS HOW TO SOLVE THE PROBLEM.

WHEN YOU ARE DEALING WITH AN ANGRY PERSON,

- ❏ LISTEN: LET THE ANGRY PERSON VENT.

- ❏ RELAX: DON'T GET DEFENSIVE.

- ❏ PARAPHRASE: MAKE SURE THE PERSON KNOWS YOU UNDERSTAND.

- ❏ PROBLEM SOLVE: WHAT CAN BE DONE TO MAKE THINGS BETTER?

I STATEMENTS (86-2)

I FEEL_____

WHEN YOU_____

BECAUSE_____

(AND I WANT)

I GET IRRITATED WHEN THE MATS ARE NOT IN THE WRESTLING ROOM BECAUSE I NEED THEM FOR PRACTICE.

WHEN YOU DON'T SHOW UP FOR REHEARSAL ON TIME, I FEEL UPSET BECAUSE WE CAN'T REHEARSE WITH PEOPLE WANDERING IN LATE, AND I NEED YOUR HELP TO GET THIS PRODUCTION POLISHED.

PROBLEM SOLVING (86-3)

DEFINE THE PROBLEM:

What is the problem?

How complex is the problem?

- ❑ Can it be subdivided?
- ❑ Can it be combined with other problems?

What basic needs are involved?

- ❑ What do the disputants want?
- ❑ What do they need?

GENERATE A "HOW TO" STATEMENT:

- ❑ Rephrase the problem and ask, "How might we . . . ?"

BRAINSTORM POSSIBLE SOLUTIONS.

CHOOSE AN ALTERNATIVE.

DEVELOP A FOLLOW-UP PLAN.

Part Three

IMPLEMENTING A PEER MEDIATION PROGRAM

Section Twelve

SETTING UP A PEER MEDIATION PROGRAM
(Background Information)

ORGANIZING A PEER MEDIATION TEAM MODEL

When organizing a peer mediation program, communication and collaboration are crucial. People who are involved in the actual design of a program are more likely to buy into the concept of peer mediation than bystanders. If administrators, teachers, counselors, parents, and students understand the value of a peer mediation program, it will succeed.

Setting Up a Committee to Explore Mediation

Think about which are the important constituencies in the school community. Who would represent them well? Ideally an administrator or a faculty member with administrative support should begin by inviting key representatives from different groups to meet with someone knowledgeable about mediation.

Invite different experts to meet with the group at different sessions to field questions about mediation—what it is, and how it might help reduce conflict. At planning meetings teachers, administrators, counselors, social workers, psychologists, parents, police officers, and students can discuss conflict in the school and learn how mediation might reduce it.

When group members commit themselves to establishing a peer mediation program, they must address the following questions:

- ❏ How will student mediators be selected?
- ❏ How will faculty members be involved?
- ❏ Who will coordinate the program?
- ❏ Who will train the mediators?
- ❏ How will mediations be set up?
- ❏ When and where will mediations take place?
- ❏ What kinds of records will be maintained? Where will they be kept and by whom?
- ❏ What kind of monitoring process is necessary?
- ❏ How will the program be publicized?
- ❏ How will the program be evaluated?

A Sample Model Program

The chart "Mediation Model" (87-1) is a flow diagram of a sample peer mediation program implementation plan. It begins with a faculty presentation which introduces the program and requests volunteers and student nominations.

Faculty Introduction. Faculty knowledge about and support of the program is extremely important. Either the program manager or committee can present a brief overview of a plan at a faculty meeting.

Like all effective presentations, the faculty introduction should begin with a hook. For example, consider asking the faculty what kinds of conflicts present problems at school. Then discuss typical disciplinary actions and their limitations, and point out the need for additional, creative options.

As an alternative to simply asking about conflict, begin by sharing an anecdote. For example, consider the following opening comments made by a counselor:

> The other day an angry student appeared in my office, all in a huff. She said, "I heard that Jodie called me a wh____. And I *know* she did it because Mike told it to Peter, and Peter told it to Juan, and Juan told it to Maureen, and Maureen *always* tells the truth! And I'm going to beat her up but good!!!"

How many of you have heard something like this?

After the faculty acknowledges the existence of frustrating conflicts, present the following information:

❑ Suspension as a consequence to fights and verbal assaults has limitations.

❑ A need for additional, creative options to reducing conflict exists.

❑ Mediation is a process in which the disputants find solutions that meet their respective needs.

❑ Research indicates that mediation reduces the number of suspensions in schools across the land.

Explain how the program will work, using the charts "Mediation Model" (87-1) and "Mediation Referral Procedures" (87-2) to clarify the implementation and referral procedures.

A mediation role play, preferably by students, can be an excellent addition to the faculty presentation.

After informing the faculty about peer mediation, ask them to nominate possible peer mediators whom they think will be good listeners and relate to all kinds of students.

In addition, ask faculty members to volunteer to become involved in the program.

Recruiting Participants. The committee should screen both the faculty volunteers and student nominees, assembling a group of both faculty members and students who are good listeners and can relate to all kinds of students. It is particularly important to find students who represent different student groups, different socioeconomic and ethnic groups, and different grade levels. Thirty students and eight or ten faculty members would be an ideal group with which to begin training.

Mediation coordinators can also set up assembly programs for students to attract volunteers or nominees for mediation.

The Mediation Conferences. This model uses a two-day "Mediation Conference." Two eight-hour training sessions off school grounds are ideal. If offering two full-day sessions is not feasible, the activities offered in the advanced mediation training can be offered during shorter update training sessions.

If faculty members function as trainers, they should be trained during several meetings prior to the "Mediation Conference." Professional mediation trainers are extremely useful for either training the faculty members or actually facilitating the training of students at the conference. Should faculty members wish to organize a training program, sample agendas appear in this section.

The Mediation Team. After the conference, most students will become committed to the mediation process. The most talented mediators will emerge and later become student leaders in the program.

Once mediators appear competent in using the process, they can become part of a "Mediation Team," a pool of students available to mediate conflicts. Actual practice in mediating becomes the most effective way to acquire skill. All mediators will belong to an "extended team," where they will meet regularly to discuss problems and continue to learn skills.

Mediations. Once a small group of students are trained, the program can begin. With this model, the program works in the following manner:

When a conflict occurs or appears likely to occur, a teacher reports it to the designated administrator, who assigns the case to a "mediation manager," one of the faculty members involved in the program. The mediation manager schedules the mediation and provides feedback to the administrator, who keeps the records. The flow chart of instructions "Mediation Referral Procedure" (87-2) illustrates the referral process in greater detail.

The Case Manager. Faculty members chosen to participate in the program become case managers, who set up the mediations. They play an important role for three reasons. First, case managers have their ears tuned to potential conflict and tend to refer students to mediation. Second, they share the logistical work with other staff members, making the total work load more manageable. Unless a school can afford to hire someone to manage the mediation program, the management tasks need to be shared. Third, involvement in managing mediations helps the case managers hone their own mediation skills so that they can more effectively manage conflict in classrooms, activities, and in the hallways.

Although the case manager does not sit in the room with the mediators, he or see is available so that if mediators experience difficulty, they can get help. Occasionally, students need to stop a mediation because disputants will not comply with ground rules. At other times, mediators need to call a caucus. In these situations having a case manager nearby can be quite helpful to the mediators.

The chart "Case Manager's 'To Do' List" (87-3) explains what the case manager does: interviews the disputants, sets up the mediation, processes the mediation with the mediators, and files the report form.

The initial interviewing process is important because it enables the case manager to smooth the way for the mediation. The case manager has the chance to promote mediation to the disputants and help them understand that it is a voluntary process that can really help them. In addition, the case manager can screen out disputants who are irrational and not ready for mediation.

Choosing the Mediators. The case manager chooses the mediators, attempting to match them to disputants with respect to sex and ethnic background if possible. As they become familiar with the mediators, case managers can intuitively place them appropriately. It is generally desirable to pair an inexperienced mediator with a highly skilled one. Occasionally, a trainee might sit in as an observer.

Scheduling Mediations. Mediations can be scheduled in a designated mediation room convenient for the case manager. Although some schools may hold mediations at a specific time, (for example, lunch periods), disputants often need to go to mediation quickly, before their anger escalates. In this model case managers can schedule mediations at any time they are available. For example, if a conflict is about to erupt before school, a teacher with the third period open can schedule a mediation during the third period on that day. The group can meet in the teacher's classroom, and the case manager can grade papers nearby in the hallway.

Schools need to work on specific scheduling details. Sometimes counselors can act as case managers for disputes that need immediate attention.

Filing Forms. Forms need to be filed in a central location. The person designated to maintain the files needs to keep track of disputants and mediators and maintain data for program evaluation. For example, he or she needs to be able to keep track of the number of mediations held and outcome success so that the school administration can learn what the effect of the program really is.

Arranging for Follow-up. Case managers discuss the follow-up procedure with the mediators. Do they think he or she should schedule a follow-up session? If so, when? If not, who will check with the disputants to make sure that they follow their plan? Students can often monitor the follow-up, but the case manager needs to coordinate the process and add notes to the referral form as needed.

MEDIATION MODEL (87-1)

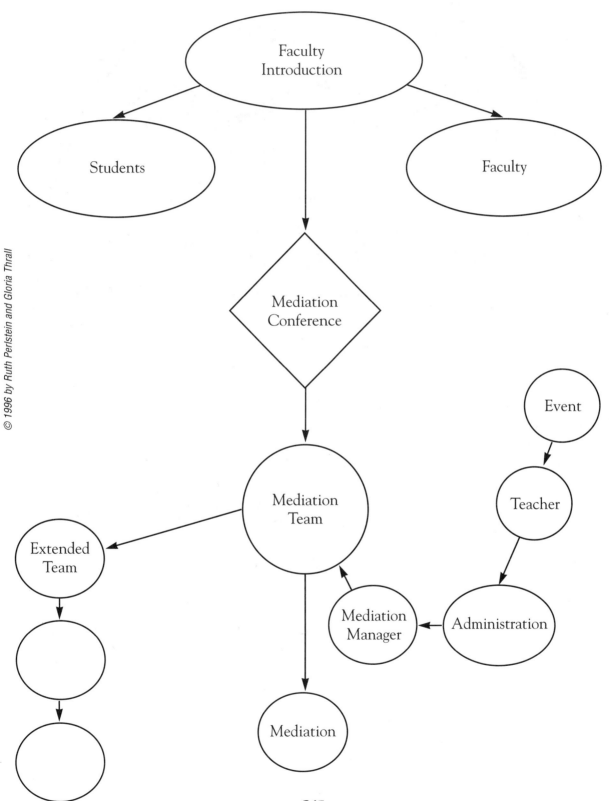

MEDIATION REFERRAL PROCEDURE (87-2)

SEEKING SOLUTIONS ...

CENTRAL H. S. PEER MEDIATION

Mediation Process

Student/Incident

Counselor/Teacher ————————————————→ Administrator

Case Manager

Pool of Mediators

Mediation

Case Manager Debriefing

CASE MANAGER'S "TO DO" LIST (87-3)

CHOOSE MEDIATORS FROM THE LIST IN MR./MS. X'S OFFICE.

↓

PHOTOCOPY CLASS LOCATORS OF DISPUTANTS.

↓

SEND FOR DISPUTANTS:

↓

MEET WITH DISPUTANTS:
Explain how mediation can help them find solutions;
determine several convenient times to meet.

↓

MEET WITH MEDIATORS:
Share referral forms;
arrange time and place for the mediation;
review the mediation process;
explain where you will be;
remind students that if parties do not observe rules, the mediation will end;
give mediators passes to the mediation room.

↓

MANAGE MEDIATION:
Send passes to disputants;
be available near mediation site;
review mediation with mediators following the mediation;
file the referral form in Mr./Ms. X's office.

↓

ARRANGE FOR FOLLOW-UP.

SAMPLE PEER MEDIATION REFERRAL FORM (87-4)

Date_____ Case Manager_____

Disputants: Grade: Availability:

_____   _____   _____

_____   _____   _____

Referral source:_____

_____

Situation:_____

_____

_____

_____

_____

_____

_____

Mediation date, time, place_____

_____

Mediation results:

_____Satisfactory   _____Unsatisfactory

Comments:_____

_____

_____

_____

Review recommendations by (date)_____

TRAINING MEDIATORS

Appropriate training programs are experiential programs in which students practice paraphrasing, problem solving, and mediating. Simply explained, mediating teaches mediation.

Although professional mediation trainers are usually preferable to trainers with limited experience, the first part of this book offers appropriate material for use in training mediators.

A Sample Model: The Mediation Conference

In the model presented in this section, a training coordinator organizes the training program. Pairs of faculty members can co-facilitate the activities in small groups in different rooms, and the large group can convene for sharing. Prior to the mediation conference, the co-facilitators need to experience the same training that they will offer students, but their activities may be condensed. If time does not allow for this procedure, teachers can act as observers while trainers adapt the activities to a larger group. Faculty involvement is particularly valuable when several groups of students are role playing mediations.

The conference in this model is a two-day conference. The agendas in this section assume that there is a time lapse between the two days. Agenda A is appropriate for beginners; Agenda B is the advanced, or follow-up, training program.

Inviting the Students. No conference can succeed without attenders. With the conflicting demands of student time, it is important that the students feel it is an honor to attend the program. We have included a sample invitation (88-1) and permission slip for parents (88-2). To motivate students, we suggest hand delivering the invitations to the students and mailing the permission slips to the parents. We also recommend an attractive setting for the conference.

Although this invitation procedure does take time, it is well worth pursuing because of the resulting commitment it helps create in the participants.

The Mediation Agendas. Two sample agendas illustrate how the mediation training activities can be organized.

Ongoing training must continue as the group of mediators comes together on a regular basis. During the meetings, students can discuss problems, and facilitators can introduce various activities to hone their skills. They should continue role playing at regular meetings.

SAMPLE STUDENT INVITATION (88-1)

Dear_____,

You are invited to attend a conference on conflict management. We have selected you because you have demonstrated strong communication skills, and we think you would make an excellent mediator at Central High School.

The conference will be held at_____ on_____ from 8 A.M. to 3:00 P.M.

This conference should provide you with a wonderful opportunity to sharpen your communication and problem-solving skills. You will also begin to learn about mediation as an extremely effective way to help others solve conflict. Not only will you have the chance to make a real difference at Central High, but you will learn skills that will help you in many settings throughout life.

Please return the attached permission slip as soon as possible before the deadline on_____.

We look forward to an enjoyable, exciting day.

Sincerely,

Principal

I will be able to attend the conflict mediation conference on_____.

_____
Student Signature

I give my son/daughter permission to attend the conflict mediation conference on_____.

_____
Parent Signature

SAMPLE PARENT PERMISSION FORM (88-2)

Dear_____,

Your son/daughter has been selected to attend a conference on conflict management. We have chosen this student because the student has demonstrated good communication skills, and we think the student would make an excellent mediator at Central High School.

The conference will be held at_____ on_____ from 8 A.M. to 3 P.M. The conference should provide a wonderful opportunity to learn effective communication and problem-solving skills. Students will also begin to learn about mediation as an extremely effective way to help others solve conflict. Not only will students have the chance to make a real difference at Central High School, but they will learn skills that will be helpful in many settings throughout life.

Please remind your son/daughter to return the response card (copy attached) as soon as possible before the deadline on_____.

We look forward to an enjoyable, exciting conference.

Sincerely,

Principal

I will be able to attend the conflict mediation conference on _____.

_____
Student Signature

I give my son/daughter permission to attend the mediation conference.

_____
Parent Signature

TRAINING AGENDA A (88-3)

DATE
8:00-8:30   Arrive at destination (refreshments)

1. Getting acquainted (approximately 20 minutes)

   Students place one shoe in the center of the room.

   Students find partners by matching a shoe they choose.

   Students interview partners.

   Students introduce partners to the group.

2. Defining conflict (approximately 30 minutes)

   The trainer defines conflict as a clash or disagreement (Section I: Background Information).

   Students interview new partners about types of conflicts they observe at school.

   Students paraphrase their partners, and the trainer records the types of conflicts mentioned.

   Group members review the list of conflicts and discuss what each of the problems really is (1-1).

3. Identifying conflict management styles (30 minutes)

   Students take the styles inventory (8-1).

   The trainer explains the styles (Section III: Background Information).

   Group members discuss how using a different style might have resolved a conflict on the list.

4. Understanding different points of view (30 minutes)

   The group discusses optical illusions on an overhead projector (16-1).

   The group explores other points of view with "Glasses" (Lesson 17) or "Exploring Cross-Cultural Miscommunication" (Lesson 21).

BREAK

5. Communicating (30 minutes)

Students practice a paraphrasing activity (Lesson 27, 29, or 30).

6. Solving problems

Trainer explains the model (42-1).

Groups practice problem solving (42 and 43).

LUNCH

7. Mediating (approximately two hours with a break after an hour)

The trainer explains the model (48-1).

Volunteers role play a simple mediation (48-3 or 48-4).

Groups of students role play mediations.

Students role play and critique introductions (Lesson 52).

Students discuss ways of finding solutions (Lesson 51).

Groups of students role play mediations on videotape.

Students critique the videotape.

8. Concluding

Students share learning from the conference.

ADVANCED TRAINING AGENDA (88-4)

— I. REVIEWING BASIC CONCEPTS —

Students share ways they have used what they learned in triads.

Spokespersons from each triad reports learning.

— II. ROLE PLAYING A MEDIATION —

Volunteers role play a mediation for the group or show a videotape from a practice session. Group members critique the mediation, using either the general observation sheets (55-4) or the "Colored Paper" activity (Lesson 56).

— III. PARAPHRASING —

Students practice paraphrasing (Lessons 29 and 30).

— IV. PRACTICING MEDIATION —

Students role play mediations.

Observers offer feedback.

Students report experiences to the large group.

— V. APPLYING SKILLS —

Students discuss what can or cannot be mediated.
(Review Section VII: Background Information.)

Students discuss referral procedures (87-2).

Students discuss concerns.

89 MEDIATING THROUGH A CLASS

Training peer mediators through an elective class is an excellent way to establish a mediation program and keep it going. Mediation training can be appropriately incorporated in several classes routinely offered in secondary schools. Among these are peer counseling, relationship courses, leadership, and social studies electives.

In addition to incorporating mediation training into a related course, there is sufficient material available to create a worthwhile full-year course in mediation. The curriculum can include intensive training activities, peace research, community projects, journal writings, critiques of mediation experiences, and extensive writing about conflict. A number of school systems offer courses in mediation and peace studies.

Having trained mediators in the classroom at a given time with an available supervisor is one of the most obvious advantages of a mediation course. Since scheduling and follow-up activities can be simplified by offering mediation through a class, it is probably the best way to keep the mediation program going. The class can also provide an in-depth learning experience about handling conflict.

Many good potential mediators cannot find time in their schedules to sign up for a class in mediation. These students can provide additional help through the extracurricular team. There is nothing mutually exclusive about having more than one group of mediators available to prevent, diffuse, and resolve conflict.

90 **ONGOING TRAINING**

The ongoing training of mediators is extremely important. Since mediators are usually busy students, consider scheduling the meetings during lunch. Provide food if you can. Regularly scheduled meetings with mediators will help them hone their skills and keep the program going. As the group continues to meet, the group will become cohesive, and members will motivate one other to promote the program and use it informally as well.

At each meeting students can share their difficulties and successes without mentioning the names of disputants or the details of their mediations. As students share what they have learned and express their concerns, mediators can learn more about the mediation process. When students experience difficulty, the others can help them explore different ways to deal with problems. Brainstorming and journal writing, described in Lesson 58 in Section VII, is particularly helpful and can also provide an avenue for personal growth.

Experienced mediators can become mentors and help in training sessions. It is really exciting to see mediators teach others by demonstrating their role-playing skills.

TRAINING ADMINISTRATORS AND COUNSELORS

The administrative and counseling staffs are the lifeblood of a mediation program. Strong administrative support for the program is vital. Without it the program will be weakened.

Administrators and counselors work on the front lines, observing conflict on a daily basis. Because they spend so much time putting out fires, a strong mediation program is really in their best interest. Mediators can become an extra pair of hands, preventing and resolving conflict and saving them time.

It is curious that many administrators and counselors do not think of using mediators to help them deal with conflict. Much of their lack of interest comes from lack of familiarity. One cannot assume that administrators and counselors understand what mediation is and what it can do for them.

Brief orientation programs for administrators and counselors can help gain support. A presentation should include the following topics:

- ❐ Definition of mediation
- ❐ Prerequisites for mediation
- ❐ Types of conflict appropriate for mediation
- ❐ Voluntary nature of the program
- ❐ Explanation of the referral process

Section Thirteen

PUBLICIZING PEER MEDIATION
(Background Information)

USING A VIDEOTAPE

There is nothing like a live demonstration or a videotape to illustrate quickly what mediation is all about. Mediation makes sense to people when they actually see it.

When students learn about mediation in a course, they can create a videotape as a project. Producing a videotape of professional quality takes time and good facilities, but it is worth the effort. Students become engaged when they see their peers on the television screen. Their familiarity with the setting and people makes the presentation appear relevant, and a professional-looking presentation will be taken seriously.

Setting the Stage

Before showing the videotape, student leaders can visit classes to explore student concerns. Inevitably, students will express a concern about some kind of conflict. Although the dialogue between student leaders and their constituencies can produce many positive results, one outcome can be setting the stage for openness to mediation.

Students can also discuss conflict resolution during homeroom periods, in targeted classes like all ninth and tenth grade English classes or world geography classes, or at school assemblies.

Producing a Videotape

Although it is easier to produce a videotape through a course, where students meet regularly, students committed to mediation can write scripts and produce videotapes on their own, with the help of professional staff members.

The "Sample Videotape Script" (92-1) is suitable for promoting mediation in the secondary school. In this script the student government president introduces the tape. The sample script assumes that school leaders have visited physical education classes to listen to student concerns prior to producing the tape.

After the introduction in the mock mediation, the roles of the two mediators are not distinguished from one another. In an actual taping, the mediators will naturally share the mediation role, each pitching in where the other left off.

When producing the tape, student mediators will normally improvise, and the mediators should paraphrase and focus on the general mediation outline accordingly.

Follow-up Discussion

When students create a videotape to demonstrate mediation, they can take it on the road to classrooms, club meetings, and community gatherings. The videotape can be presented in a variety of ways. For example, the participants might present it in targeted classes or televise it to all classes on closed circuit television.

After viewing a videotape, either the teacher or students presenting the tape should engage students in a discussion. We have provided two different lesson plans which can be used to generate discussion about mediation. The first has the broad purpose of teaching students that there are alternatives to fighting as well as introducing mediation. The second focuses only on the peer mediation program. Both end with a clear explanation of the referral process. Both are suitable for orientating groups.

SAMPLE VIDEOTAPE SCRIPT (92-1)

Student Government President:	We really appreciate your sharing your concerns when we visited PE classes. Thank you for your input.

When we discussed concerns, a number of students mentioned fighting. We asked them what sorts of things students fight about. They mentioned a variety of issues, but almost all of them mentioned rumors, the "he said/she said stuff."

We have been discussing these problems and we have been learning a little about mediation.

Peer mediation is a process where student mediators help disputants, or students who have a conflict, solve their problems. We'd like you to watch a portion of mediation role play.

It looks something like this. . .

Mediator A:	Hello, my name is Marie, and this is Tanya. We are your mediators. We are not judges, but we will listen, and we can help you resolve your conflict.
Mediator B:	It's great that you are here to try to resolve your difficulties. We have found that ground rules are really helpful. Before we begin, we would like to establish some ground rules.
Mediator A:	Most people agree to try to understand and solve the problem, not to put the other person down, not to interrupt. . . let the other person finish, and keep what is said in this room confidential. . . that is, in this room. Are these rules acceptable?
Disputants:	Uh huh. . . I guess
Mediator A:	Are there any other rules you would like included?
Mediator B:	Are we acceptable as your mediators?
Disputants:	. . . Okay.
Mediator:	Tell us what happened.
Sherry:	I heard that Serita came over to our lunch table and started flirting with Ted, my new boyfriend. I want to go to the prom with Ted, and I don't want him to get any ideas.
Serita:	I don't have a problem, but I heard that Sherry was getting a group of her friends to beat me up after school, and I don't know why, but I have friends too.
Mediators: (paraphrasing)	Sherry, you're upset about Serita joining Ted at the lunch table. . . Serita, you heard that Sherry's friends plan to fight with you?
Mediator:	What do you think the problem is?
Sherry:	Serita was deliberately trying to steal Ted, and I'm going to get her.
Mediators: (paraphrasing)	You think Serita wants your boyfriend and that makes you angry.
Serita: (angrily snapping)	I could care less about Ted. What makes you think I would want to go out with someone who would go out with you? I've got better taste!

Mediators: (paraphrasing)	You don't want Ted, but you're really insulted that Sherry thinks you do.
Mediators:	What do you think the problem really is?
Sherry:	Serita needs to keep her hands to herself and get a life of her own.
Serita:	Who told you that I'm interested in Ted? Where did you hear that garbage?
Sherry:	You know who told me. They wouldn't say so if it wasn't the truth.
Serita:	Your so-called friends tell you a whole lot of trash.
Mediators: (cooling disputants down and reminding them of rules)	We agreed that no one would interrupt. What do you think the problem really is?
Serita:	Sherry just believes anything she hears.
Mediators: (paraphrasing)	Rumors really bother you.
Mediator: (to Sherry)	What is the real problem?
Sherry:	Serita needs to get her own boyfriend and a life of her own.
Serita:	Sherry needs to tell her friends to butt out.
Student Government President:	We all have needs, based on who we are. Conflict is a clash based on our unmet needs: identity (who we are), security (we all need to feel safe), recognition (we all want to feel important), control, and fairness. We often see people get angry and jump on the escalator of anger to scream or punch instead of slowing down on a lower step to stop and talk.
	As the mediation continues, Sherry and Serita will define their problem and find ways for them to both get what they want and need. They can both win. In mediation they must come up with solutions and agree upon them.
	What are some ways they might resolve their conflict?

STUDENT LESSON PLAN A (92-2)

Objectives: Students will understand that there are other and better ways to solve problems than fighting.

Students will become aware of the peer mediation program and understand how to use it.

Activities: 1.   Discuss the following questions.

❑   What do each of these girls (Sherry and Serita) need?. . . want?

❑   How else might they get what they want/need other than fighting?

❑   What does Sherry need to do? What does Serita need to do?

❑   What are the long-range consequences of fighting? other options?

❑   Is it possible for both to get what they want and need and win? How?

❑   What kinds of conflicts do you observe at school?

❑   Where do we get messages that fighting can solve problems?

❑   How can you solve problems without fighting?

❑   What is it that prevents people from talking directly about their conflicts?

❑   What can we do to slow down the process of escalating conflicts to fights?

❑   How might mediation help?

❑   How can we help people to talk about their problems before they get out of hand?

2.   Explain how to arrange for a mediation (e.g., see your counselor or drop a note in the mediation boxes in the front office or attendance office).

STUDENT LESSON PLAN B (92-3)

Objective: Students will become aware of the peer mediation program and how to use it.

Activities: 1. Brainstorm types of conflicts students observe in school.

2. Show the videotape.

3. Discuss how mediation can be helpful.

4. Explain the referral process.

5. Answer questions.

93 **USING THE ART DEPARTMENT**

The art department makes a superb addition to the team promoting conflict resolution. Flyers, posters, and tee-shirts are wonderful vehicles of communication that can provide constant reminders that there are ways to resolve conflict and that mediation works.

By becoming involved in publicizing peer mediation, art students will automatically become aware of the program and support the project as well as publicize it.

Creating a Logo

An effective way to involve young artists in the mediation program is to hold a logo design contest. Perhaps a graphics design teacher can assign the logo design to teams of students and have them compete for the winning design. Perhaps all art students can submit designs as an assignment. Better yet, the art department can sponsor a schoolwide contest for a logo.

Program managers can be creative about the logo selection process as well. Why not have a schoolwide contest to choose the logo?

Once mediators select a logo, it can be reproduced for many uses. Among them are the following:

❐ Give student mediators a mediation tee-shirt after they complete their training.

❐ Use the logo for stationery when the coordinator sends memos and invitations.

❐ Use the logo on handouts for training and orientation.

❐ Use the logo as a header on a videotape.

❐ Use the logo for posters and flyers to advertise the program.

❐ Create an exhibit of all logo designs.

A sample student-produced logo follows.

SPREADING THE WORD

Getting a peer mediation program up and running is only a beginning. To really affect school climate, peer mediation requires a publicity plan that will keep peer mediation visible. Everyone in the school should know how to refer disputants to mediation. Everyone should know that peer mediation really works.

Publicizing Success While Maintaining Confidentiality

Although it is imperative that peer mediators and faculty members spread the word about mediation's success, mediators and faculty members must avoid discussing specific mediations or identifying names of disputants. When enthusiastically sharing success, it is tempting to refer to specific cases. However, identifying names and situations leads to gossip that can irreparably damage the program. Disputants do need to trust mediators to maintain their confidentiality.

Sharing success and maintaining confidentiality is like walking on a tightrope. Maintaining balance is crucial. Consider the following suggestions:

- ❏ Set the tone and model discussion about the success of the mediation program.
- ❏ Have peer mediators role play ways to share success without violating confidentiality.
- ❏ Discuss types of mediation handled (rumors, sharing property, putdowns, girl/boy misunderstandings, etc.).
- ❏ Publicize statistics: How many successful mediations have occurred this month?
- ❏ Remind faculty case managers about the importance of publicizing success while maintaining confidentiality.

Keeping Peer Mediation Visible

Explore sources of communication, including daily announcements, posters, bulletin boards, faculty memos, newspaper articles, and classroom visits. Many types of publicity can appropriately promote mediation. A carefully planned approach to publicity will maintain public awareness of the program.

After brainstorming possible ways to advertise the peer mediation program, build a publicity plan on a calendar so that a peer mediation group can publicize mediation in some way every month of the school year. As opportunities arise, like an inquiry from a local newspaper, the program will receive additional support.

Remembering the Big Picture

Keeping a large general plan usually helps. Begin with a needs assessment and continue with the careful establishment of a program to meet needs and provide the ongoing training, monitoring, and publicizing of a program. The appeal of a new idea energizes people, and implementing a program is exciting. Although it takes almost as much energy to maintain a program as it does to establish it, conflict resolution is worth every hour of the work.

Helping Other Schools Establish a Program

After a school has experience with a successful mediation program, a team of faculty members and students can take their program to other schools to encourage the creation of mediation programs. By building a network of conflict resolution programs, the efforts of a group can affect an entire community.

Appendix

 CROSSWORD PUZZLE

 EXAM

 RESOURCES

CROSSWORD PUZZLE

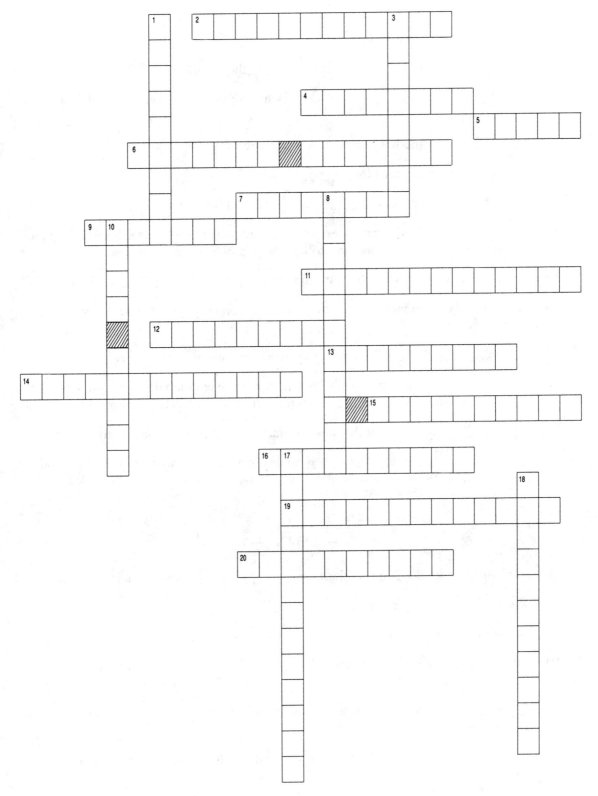

— ACROSS —

2. When a listener repeats what he has heard in his own words, this technique is called _ _ _ _ _ _ _ _ _ _ _ _.

4. One of our basic needs is the need for _ _ _ _ _ _ _ _.

5. One way of dealing with conflict is to _ _ _ _ _ the situation.

6. _ _ _ _ _ _ _ _ _ _ _ _ _ _ skills can help people in their personal and professional relationships.

7. _ _ _ _ _ _ _ _ is another basic need we all share.

9. We also have a basic need for _ _ _ _ _ _ _.

11. In conflict management, _ _ _ _ _ _ _ _ _ _ _ _ _ is the key.

12. _ _ _ _ _ _ _ _ _ _ _ _ is a process where a third party helps disputants solve their problems by guiding them through the collaborative problem-solving process.

13. One basic rule in mediation is that disputants cannot _ _ _ _ _ _ _ _ _ each other.

14. In the collaborative problem-solving process, the process used to generate possible solutions is called _ _ _ _ _ _ _ _ _ _ _ _ _ _.

15. _ _ _ _ _ _ _ _ _ _ _ are effective ways to express anger.

16. _ _ _ _ _ _ _ _ _ _ _ language helps tone down the emotional intensity of a word and helps diffuse the anger and hostility often experienced between the disputants.

19. _ _ _ _ _ _ _ _ _ _ produces the most satisfactory long-term resolutions to conflict.

20. _ _ _ _ _ _ _ _ _ _ is an effective way to deal with conflict when time is short and the way of finding a solution is clear.

— DOWN —

1. A mediator helps disputants understand _ _ _ _ _ _ _ _ _ points of view.

3. We all share the basic need for _ _ _ _ _ _ _ _.

8. We all have a basic need for _ _ _ _ _ _ _ _ _ _ _.

10. "What's happening?" is an example of an _ _ _ _ _ _ _ _ _ question that encourages the speaker to keep on talking.

17. _ _ _ _ _ _ _ _ _ _ _ _ is an effective way to deal with conflict when one person's needs are greater than the other person's.

18. _ _ _ _ _ _ _ _ _ _ may be the best way to deal with conflict when there is an emergency.

CROSSWORD PUZZLE ANSWER KEY

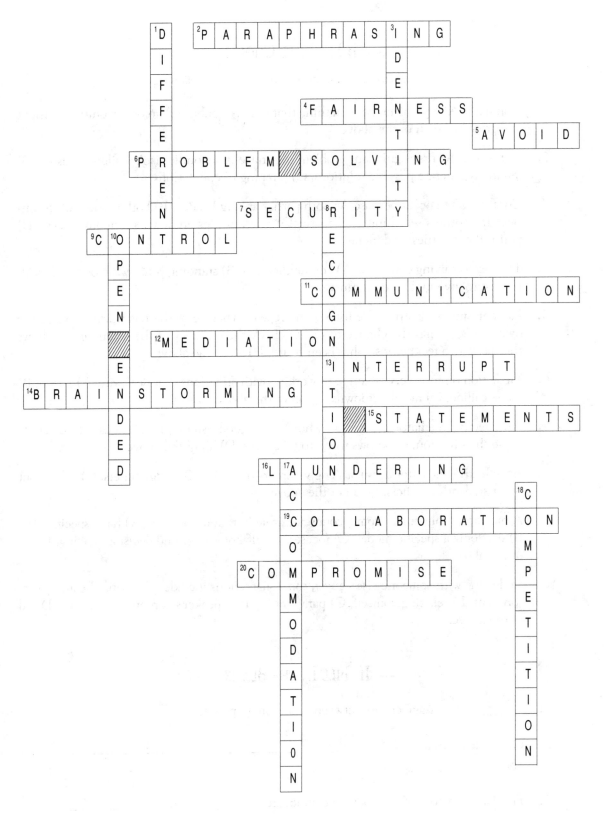

EXAM

— I: Multiple Choice —

Please select the best answer for each of the following.

1. Conflict is A) a problem, B) something that signals trouble, C) an opportunity for insight and growth, D) all of the above.

2. Generally, the first significant problem to surface in a conflict is A) failure to listen, B) failure to generate possible solutions, C) jumping to conclusions.

3. Conflicts often occur because A) both parties are pig-headed, B) both parties fail to consider that others see things differently, C) relationships are always tenuous at best, D) political correctness is difficult.

4. The key to solving conflict is A) communication, B) standing your own ground, C) willingness to give in, D) commitment.

5. Paraphrasing means that the listener A) repeats what he or she has heard in his or her own words, B) has the chance to reality check the accuracy of the listening, C) allows the speaker to feel he or she has been heard, D) all of the above.

6. Mediation often is very effective in working with situations that deal with A) gossip, B) name calling, C) racial putdowns, D) all of the above.

7. An effective mediator is a person who A) is a good listener, B) takes care to carefully judge the situation, C) knows when to take sides, D) all of the above.

8. An effective mediator *does not* A) give orders or advice, B) judge others, C) talk about other student's conflicts, D) all of the above.

9. A mediator's role differs from a counselor's role in that a counselor A) has a specific role, B) uses only a specific model, C) focuses on self-knowledge and decision making, D) all of the above.

10. In dealing with someone else's anger, some suggestions include A) letting the angry person vent, B) relaxing yourself, C) paraphrasing the speaker's content and feeling, D) all of the above.

— II: Fill In the Blanks —

1. _____ is a disagreement between two or more parties.

2. Our basic needs are _____, _____, _____, _____, and _____.

3. Five basic methods of dealing with conflict are _____, _____, _____, _____, and _____.

4. An example of an open-ended question would be _____
_____.

5. An example of a closed question would be _____
_____.

6. An example of laundering language would be _____
_____.

7. There are four steps to take in diffusing anger. _____,
_____, _____, and
_____.

8. Mediation is defined as _____.

9. A shift from position to interest means _____
_____.

— III: Matching —

Place the letter corresponding to the definition on the right next to the appropriate spaces on the left. Letters may be used more than once.

_____ Identity

_____ Eye contact

_____ Security

_____ Competition

_____ One eyebrow raised

_____ Walk away

_____ Recognition

_____ Fairness

_____ Avoidance

_____ Have a ready response

_____ Hands clenched

_____ Control

_____ Caucus

_____ Accommodation

_____ Compromise

_____ Collaboration

_____ Shrugged shoulders

A. Nonverbal communication

B. Conflict management style

C. Method of handling teasing

D. Basic human need

E. Time-out period during mediation in which mediators speak individually with the disputants

F. Winning and being right are everything

G. Produces the most satisfactory long-term result

— IV: CLOSURE —

Complete the following sentences in the blanks provided.

1. There are several characteristics that are generally present in a conflict situation. Often there is incomplete communication, which means _____ _____.

2. Also, there may be inaccurate information, which implies that _____ _____.

3. In addition, there may be stress overload, defined as _____ _____.

4. Different viewpoints may cause problems. This means that _____ _____.

5. Also, there are different types of conflicts. Intrapersonal conflicts are those that _____ _____.

6. Interpersonal conflicts involve _____ _____.

— V: SEQUENCE —

Fill in the blanks.

1. The steps in collaborative problem solving are

_____

_____

_____

_____

_____

_____

2. Using either the five- or seven-step model, list the stages in the mediation session.

_____

_____

_____

_____

_____

_____

— VI. Essay —

A good way to generate an appropriate essay question as well as create more role plays for future practice is to have each student create a conflict, real or imagined, that needs to be resolved. Then use one of these conflicts for the essay question that follows.

Using ideas you learned from this course, explain how you would help someone deal with the conflict in this role play.

EXAM KEY

— MULTIPLE CHOICE —

1-D; 2-A; 3-B; 4-A; 5-D; 6-D; 7-A; 8-D; 9-C; 10-D

— FILL IN THE BLANKS —

1—conflict; 2—identity, security, recognition, fairness, control; 3—competition, avoidance, cooperation, accommodation, compromise; 4—"What do you want your friend to do?"; 5—"Do you want your friend to talk to you?"; 6—She's really a miserable witch," changed to "She's really hard to get along with"; 7—let the person vent, relax and don't get defensive, paraphrase content and feeling, problem solve; 8—a process where a third party helps disputants solve their problems by guiding them through the collaborative problem-solving process; 9—helping disputants find common ground on which they can solve their problems.

— MATCHING —

D, A, D, F/B, A, C(B), D, D, B, C, A, D, E, B, B, B/G, A

— CLOSURE —

1—either one or both parties do not have adequate information

2—either one or both parties are using incorrect information

3—a situation in which one or both parties are so strained that they cannot deal with solving a problem

4—disputants perceive the conflict differently

5—exist within one's self

6—two or more people

— SEQUENCE —

1. Define the problem, generate a "how to" statement, brainstorm possible solutions, choose an alternative, develop a plan

2. Five steps: introduction, listening, problem solving, choosing a solution, implementing plans (Section VII).

   Seven steps: introduction, listening (or finding out what happened), defining the problem, finding common interests, exploring solutions, choosing a solution, concluding (or implementing plans) (Section VIII).

The sequence and basic concepts are the same in both models. (see Lesson 59).

SUGGESTED RESOURCES

Beer, Jennifer, Adams, Sandi, Avery, Chel, Stief, Eileen, and Walker, Charles. *Peacemaking in Your Neighborhood, Mediator's Handbook*. Philadelphia: Friends Suburban Project of the Philadelphia Yearly Meeting, 1990.

Burton, John W. *Resolving Deep Rooted Conflict, A Handbook*. Lanham: Maryland University Press, 1987.

Cheatham, Annie. *Annotated Bibliography for Teaching Conflict Resolution in Schools*. Amherst: University of Massachusetts, 1989.

Cohn, Benjamin, and Osborne, W. Larry. *Group Counseling, A Practical Self-Concept Approach for the Helping Professional*. Chappaqua, NY: LS Communications, 1992.

Fairfield, Kathryn Stoltzfus, Hart, Barry, Hess, Susan A., Hoover, Larry, Mast, Ervin J., and Sider, Nancy Good. *Mediation and Conflict Resolution*. Harrisonburg, VA: Community Mediation Center, 1989.

Gladding, Samuel T. *Effective Group Counseling*. Greensboro: University of North Carolina, 1994.

Moore, Christopher W. *The Mediation Process, Practical Strategies for Resolving Conflict*. San Francisco: Jossey-Bass, 1986.

"Peace Studies for High School," a teaching manual. Center for Teaching Peace, 4501 Van Ness Street, NW, Washington, D.C. 20016.

Sadalla, Gail, Henriquez, Manti, and Holmberg, Meg. *Conflict Resolution: A Secondary School Curriculum*. San Francisco: The Community Board Program, 1987.

Schafer, Charles, Johnson, Lynette, and Wherry, Jeffrey N. *Group Therapies for Children and Youth*. San Francisco: Jossey-Bass Publishers, 1988.

Sorenson, Don. L. *Conflict Resolution and Mediation for Peer Helpers*. Minneapolis, MN: Educational Media Corporation, 1992.

Wampler, Faye W. *Mediation Role Plays*. Harrisonburg, VA: Community Mediation Center, 1993.

Wampler, Faye W., and Hess, Susan. *Conflict Mediation for a New Generation*. Harrisonburg, VA: Community Mediation Center, 1992.

Weeks, Dudley. *The Eight Essential Steps to Conflict Resolution*. Los Angeles: Jeremy B. Tarcher, 1992.

Yalom, Irvin D. *The Theory and Practice of Group Psychotherapy*. New York: Basic Books, 1970.